Lecture Notes in Computer Sc

Edited by G. Goos, J. Hartmanis and J. va

T0230200

Springer
Berlin
Heidelberg
New York
Barcelona
Hong Kong
London
Milan
Paris
Singapore
Tokyo

Philippe Palanque   Fabio Paternò (Eds.)

Interactive Systems

Design, Specification, and Verification

7th International Workshop, DSV-IS 2000
Limerick, Ireland, June 5-6, 2000
Revised Papers

 Springer

Series Editors

Gerhard Goos, Karlsruhe University, Germany
Juris Hartmanis, Cornell University, NY, USA
Jan van Leeuwen, Utrecht University, The Netherlands

Volume Editors

Philippe Palanque
LIHS University Toulouse 1
Place Anatole France, 31042 Toulouse Cedex, France
E-mail: palanque@univ-tlse1.fr
Fabio Paternò
Consiglio Nazionale delle Ricerche, Istituto CNUCE
Via V. Alfieri 1, 56010 Ghezzano-Pisa, Italia
E-mail: F.Paterno@cnuce.cnr.it

Cataloging-in-Publication Data applied for

Die Deutsche Bibliothek - CIP-Einheitsaufnahme

Interactive systems : design, specification, and verification ;
7th international workshop ; revised papers / DSV-IS 2000,
Limerick, Ireland, June 5 - 6, 2000. Philippe Palanque ; Fabio Paternò
(ed.). - Berlin ; Heidelberg ; New York ; Barcelona ; Hong Kong ; London ;
Milan ; Paris ; Singapore ; Tokyo : Springer, 2001
　　(Lecture notes in computer science ; Vol. 1946)
　　ISBN 3-540-41663-3

CR Subject Classification (1998): H.5.2, H.5, I.3, D.2, F.3

ISSN 0302-9743
ISBN 3-540-41663-3 Springer-Verlag Berlin Heidelberg New York

Springer-Verlag Berlin Heidelberg New York
a member of BertelsmannSpringer Science+Business Media GmbH
© Springer-Verlag Berlin Heidelberg 2001
Printed in Germany

Typesetting: Camera-ready by author, data conversion by PTP-Berlin, Stefan Sossna
Printed on acid-free paper　　　SPIN: 10780903　　　06/3142　　　5 4 3 2 1 0

Preface

The wait for the year 2000 was marked by the fear of possible bugs that might have arisen at its beginning. One additional fear we had during this wait was whether organising this event would have generated a boon or another bug.

The reasons for this fear originated in the awareness that the design of interactive systems is a fast moving area. The type of research work presented at this unique event has received limited support from funding agencies and industries making it more difficult to keep up with the rapid technological changes occurring in interaction technology.

However, despite our fear, the workshop was successful because of the high-quality level of participation and discussion.

Before discussing such results, let us step back and look at the evolution of DSV-IS (Design, Specification and Verification of Interactive Systems), an international workshop that has been organised every year since 1994.

The first books that addressed this issue in a complete and thorough manner were the collection of contributions edited by Harrison and Thimbleby and the book written by Alan Dix, which focused on abstractions useful to highlight important concepts in the design of interactive systems. Since then, this area has attracted the interest of a wider number of research groups, and some workshops on related topics started to be organised. DSV-IS had its origins in this spreading and growing interest. The first workshop was held in a monastery located in the hills above Bocca di Magra (Italy). The event has been held in Italy, France, Belgium, Spain, U.K, Portugal and Ireland, under the auspices of Eurographics, with proceedings regularly published by Springer-Verlag.

After 10 years of research some considerable results have been achieved: we have built a community working on these topics; several projects (European, National, Industrial) have been carried out; various books, journal publications and other related events have been produced; and first industrial products, automatic tools and applications are also appearing based on such approaches.

However, we must admit that interest is growing less quickly than in other areas (Web, mobile communication, usability, ...). The number of new groups working in this area is increasing gradually. One reason is that time-to-market is a crucial factor in industry (and academia!), and consequently more elaborated approaches are less attractive.

To further promote the event and the related topics, we decided to hold it as an ICSE workshop. ICSE is the major international software engineering conference, and we aimed at expounding the topic to this community in order to facilitate interaction and stimulate multidisciplinary approaches and to reach a wider audience. Our proposal was accepted by the ICSE organising committee.

We received 30 submissions from 13 countries. Each paper was reviewed by at least three members of the Programme Committee, and the final selection was made at a meeting held at CHI'2000. Refined versions of less than half of these submissions were selected for inclusion in this book.

The workshop provided a forum for the exchange of ideas on diverse approaches to the design and implementation of interactive systems. The particular focus of this year's event was on models (e.g., for devices, users, tasks, contexts, architectures, etc.) and their role in supporting the design and development of interactive systems.

As in previous years, we still devoted considerable attention to the use of formal representations and their role in supporting the design, specification, verification, validation and evaluation of interactive systems. Contributions pertaining to less formal representations of interactive system designs and model-based design approaches were also encouraged.

During the workshop discussion and presentations were grouped according to a set of major topics: Designing Interactive Distributed Systems, Designing User Interfaces, Tools for User Interfaces, Formal Methods for HCI and Model-Based Design of Interactive Systems.

At the end of the sessions participants were split into discussion groups. One aspect that attracted the attention of the participants was the book "What is in the future of software engineering" that was distributed to all ICSE participants: we noticed the complete lack of a chapter addressing human-computer interaction. Thus, we feel that these proceedings also have an additional role: to provide the background information for the missing chapter, that on software engineering for human-computer interaction. This lack underscores how the academic community has not yet completely understood the importance of this subject and the importance of the research area aiming at identifying ergonomic properties and improving the design process so that such ergonomic properties are guaranteed in the software systems produced.

If we consider the HCI map proposed in the HCI curriculum produced by ACM SIGCHI we notice that each component (user, computer, development process, use and context) is evolving very rapidly.

It becomes crucial to identify a design space indicating the requirements, modelling techniques, tools, metrics, architectures, representations and evaluation methods characterising this area.

In addition, the research agenda for this field is dense: it includes extending models to deal with dynamicity (mobile users, ...), develop analysis techniques for making use of the models, more tools for usability evaluation, multi * approaches (multimedia, multi users, multi modal, ...) and end user programming.

We think that the reader will find the material presented in this book useful in understanding these issues, and we sincerely hope it will also prove to be useful in stimulating further studies and improving current practise.

September 2000   Philippe Palanque and Fabio Paternò

Programme Committee

Ann Blandford	University of Middlesex, U.K.
Alan Dix	University of Huddersfield and aQtive Ltd.
David Duce	Oxford Brookes University, U.K.
David Duke	University of Bath, U.K.
Giorgio Faconti	CNUCE-C.N.R., Italy
Miguel Gea	University of Granada, Spain
Nicholas Graham	Queen's University, Canada
Michael Harrison	University of York, U.K.
Robert Jacob	Tufts University, U.S.A.
Chris Johnson	University of Glasgow, U.K.
Peter Johnson	University of Bath, U.K.
Fernando Mario Martins	University of Minho, Portugal
Panos Markopoulos	IPO, University of Eindhoven, The Netherlands
Philippe Palanque (Co-chair)	LIHS, Université Toulouse I, France
Fabio Paternò (Co-chair)	CNUCE-CNR, Italy
Angel Puerta	Stanford University and Red Whale, U.S.A.
Jean Vanderdonckt	Université Catholique de Louvain, Belgium

Sponsoring Organisations

Eurographics
The European Association for Computer Graphics

ICSE 2000

The 22nd International Conference on Software Engineering

Limerick, Ireland

Contents

Formal Methods for Human-Computer Interaction

Model-Based Design of Interactive Systems

Indexes

Specifying Temporal Behaviour in Software Architectures for Groupware Systems

Timothy N. Wright[1], T.C. Nicholas Graham[2], and Tore Urnes[3]

[1] University of Canterbury, Private Bag 4800, Christchurch, New Zealand
tnw13@cosc.canterbury.ac.nz
[2] Queen's University, Kingston, Ontario, Canada K7L 3N6
graham@cs.queensu.ca
[3] Telenor Research and Development, P.O. Box 83, N-2007 Kjeller, Norway
tore.urnes@telenor.com

Abstract. This paper presents an example of how software architectures can encode temporal properties as well as the traditional structural ones. In the context of expressing concurrency control in groupware systems, the paper shows how a specification of temporal properties of the semi-replicated groupware architecture can be refined to three different implementations, each with different performance tradeoffs. This refinement approach helps in understanding the temporal properties of groupware applications, and increases confidence in the correctness of their implementation.

1 Introduction

Software architectures traditionally decompose systems into *components* responsible for implementing part of the system, and *connectors* enabling communication between these components. Components implement some part of the system's functionality, while connectors specify the form of intercomponent communication, for example, through method calls or events [28]. We refer to these as structural properties of the architecture.

In synchronous groupware applications, it is not only important to capture *how* components may communicate, but *when*. For example, in a multiuser video annotation system, it is important that all participants see and annotate the same frame [14]. In a shared drawing application, it is important that the drawing operations of participants do not conflict, for example with one person deleting a drawing object that another is moving. As the paper will show, such requirements on sequencing of updates and synchronization of shared state can be expressed as restrictions on when messages can be passed between components involved in an interaction.

This paper investigates how software architectures can specify temporal properties of an application as well as structural ones. From these temporal specifications, a variety of implementations can be derived, embodying different execution properties. This allows an approach where software architectures specify high level temporal properties of implementations, allowing architecture implementers to plug-replace any implementation meeting these properties.

P. Palanque and F. Paternò (Eds.): DSV-IS 2000, LNCS 1946, pp. 1–17, 2001.
© Springer-Verlag Berlin Heidelberg 2001

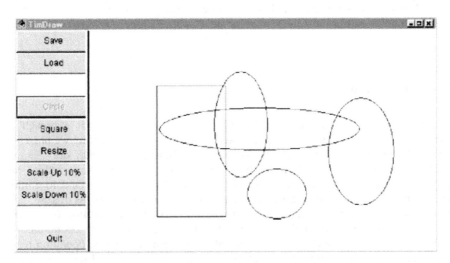

Fig. 1. A Groupware Drawing Program. This program was implemented in Java using the *TeleComputing Developer Toolkit* (TCD) [1].

As will be shown in the paper, the benefits of this approach are:

— Difficult temporal properties of groupware applications can be treated orthogonally to the application's functionality by embedding these properties in the software architecture;
— Premature commitment to algorithms implementing temporal properties can be avoided, as early design of the system focuses on desired behaviour rather than on algorithms implementing that behaviour;
— The process of specifying properties and refining implementations increases confidence in the correctness of the implementations and provides a clearer understanding of the temporal properties of the application.

In order to demonstrate this approach, we take the example of the implementation of concurrency control in a semi-replicated groupware architecture. We show how concurrency control properties can be encoded in the definition of the semi-replicated architecture itself. Specifically, we treat the problem of ensuring that transactions performed on shared data state are serializable, guaranteeing that operations performed by users do not conflict.

As we shall see in the paper, concurrency control algorithms are complex, and embody trade-offs of degree of consistency versus response time. It is therefore beneficial to separate the specification of the desired concurrency properties of an application from the concurrency control algorithm actually implementing it. To demonstrate this assertion, the paper is organized as follows. Section 2 describes the concurrency control problem in groupware, and introduces a simple groupware drawing tool as an example application. Section 3 introduces the widely used semi-replicated implementation architecture for groupware, and shows how it can be described to possess temporal properties ensuring correct concurrent behaviour. In order to show the flexibility of such a specification, sections 4 through 6 introduce the locking, Eager and adaptive concurrency control algorithms as implementations refined from the semi-replicated architecture.   These algorithms have all been implemented as part of the *TeleComputing Developer* (TCD) groupware development toolkit [1].

2   Motivation

To introduce the concurrency control problem and to motivate our approach of encoding temporal properties of applications in the software architecture, we present a simple groupware drawing program. As shown in figure 1, users may draw simple objects such as squares and circles on a shared canvas.   Each user's actions are reflected in the canvases of other users in real time. In addition to standard editing operations, users may scale the entire diagram up or down, in increments of 10%.

In the implementation of the drawing program, a shared data structure (or *shared context*) contains the set of drawing objects. Figure 2 shows how operations for resizing and scaling objects are implemented. For example, a resize operation reads the object to be resized from the shared context, changes its size, and saves the object back to the shared context. Similarly, the scale operation scales each of the drawing objects in the shared context.

Figure 2 shows how concurrency problems can arise if two users simultaneously perform a resize and a scale operation. Here, the resize operation is performed while the scale is taking place, partially undoing the effect of the scale. This leaves the diagram in an inconsistent state, where the scale has been applied to all elements except the first. When two user actions lead to an inconsistent result, those actions are said to *conflict*. Concurrency control algorithms are designed to prevent the negative effects of conflicting actions.

2.1   Concurrency Control Styles

Concurrency control algorithms can be roughly divided into two classes – pessimistic and optimistic. Pessimistic schemes guarantee that when a participant in a groupware session attempts to modify the shared artifact, his/her actions will not conflict with the actions of other participants.   This guarantee leads to intuitive user interface behaviour, but at the cost of responsiveness. Optimistic approaches, on the other hand, assume that actions will not conflict, and must detect and repair conflicts when they occur.

Resize object "1" to newSize	Scale entire diagram by k%
	`n=getNumberObjects()`
	`o1=getObjectAt("1")`
`s=getObjectAt("1")`	
`s.setSize(newSize)`	`o1.scale(k)`
	`setObjectAt("1",o1)`
`setObjectAt("1",s)`	`o2=getObjectAt("2")`
	...

Fig. 2. A resize operation conflicting with a scale operation.

Under pessimistic algorithms, update transactions resulting from user actions never fail. One way of achieving this property is to require clients to obtain a lock on the shared context before attempting to process a new user action [22]. This locking may reduce the potential for concurrent execution of clients and introduces networking overhead to obtain locks.

Under optimistic algorithms, update transactions may fail, potentially requiring work to be undone [16]. Optimistic algorithms improve performance by allowing client machines to process user actions in parallel.

Neither pessimistic nor optimistic approaches are suitable for every application. While optimistic approaches may provide better response times for short transactions that are inexpensive to undo [3,29], pessimistic algorithms are preferable in the following three cases:

- *Undo unacceptable:* In some applications, it is impossible to roll back user actions that are retroactively found to conflict with other actions. Examples of such actions include deleting a file or sending an email message.
- *Pessimistic faster:* To be effective, optimistic schemes rely on conflicts being rare, and the cost of undoing operations being inexpensive. Consider the scale operation of figure 2. This operation performs one read and write to the shared context for every drawing object. In a complex drawing with potentially tens or hundreds of objects, the scale operation is likely to conflict with an operation performed by some other user.
- *Optimistic unfair:* In a wide area network, some users may suffer longer latencies than others when accessing parts of the shared context. The actions of these users may be more likely to conflict than the actions of users with lower latency. Fairness may require that users with poor network connections use pessimistic concurrency control.

Concurrency control algorithms therefore embody tradeoffs in the desired behaviour of systems, but all provide the basic property of guaranteeing serializability of transactions carried out by participants in the groupware session. That is, the algorithm should never permit operations to conflict as in the example of figure 2. Our approach is therefore to encode this temporal property of transaction serializability as part of the definition of the software architecture. We then show how these temporal properties can be implemented by both pessimistic and optimistic algorithms, and by a novel algorithm combining the two. This approach allows us to specify the desired temporal behaviour of the architecture (i.e., transaction serializability) separately from the algorithm used, avoiding premature commitment to a particular concurrency control algorithm.

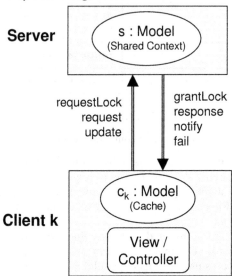

Fig. 3. The semi-replicated implementation architecture for groupware: A shared context is represented on a server machine. Clients contain a cache, a read-only replica of the shared context. Local context does not require concurrency control, and therefore is not represented. Writable replicas of the shared context are assumed to have no concurrency control, and therefore are also not represented.

All of these algorithms have been realized using the Dragonfly [1] implementation of the semi-replicated groupware architecture, in the TCD toolkit. In TCD, we exploit the separation of specification of temporal behaviour from its implementation, allowing concurrency control algorithms to be plug-replaced after the application has been developed.

3   The Semi-Replicated Architecture for Groupware

We model groupware systems using a semi-replicated architecture [15]. Semi-replicated systems are hybrid centralized/replicated systems, where all shared state is represented on a centralized component, some shared state is replicated to the clients, and private state is represented on the clients. Some shared state is replicated in the form of a read-only *client cache*.

Semi-replication is based on the *Model-View-Controller* (MVC) architecture for groupware development [20,15]. In MVC, the shared state underlying each participant's view is located in a *model*, a *controller* is responsible for mapping user actions onto updates to the model, and a *view* is responsible for updating the display in response to changes in the model. MVC (and related architecture styles such as PAC* [5]) underlies a wide range of groupware development tools. Despite earlier suspicion that semi-replication is inherently inefficient [21], performance evaluation has shown this architecture to provide excellent response times, even over very wide area networks [29].

Figure 3 shows the elements of this model that are necessary to illustrate how concurrency control properties can be encoded within a software architecture connector. The figure further shows the set of messages allowing the client and server components to communicate. These messages are described in detail in section 3.2.

We assume that no concurrency control is applied to private state represented on clients (since there is no concurrent access to this state), and therefore omit local context from the model. We assume that the client cache is not writable by the client, and therefore can only be updated by the server. We further assume that any replicated state that is writable by the client has no concurrency control associated with it, and therefore need not be included in the model. Despite what may appear to be restrictive assumptions, this model describes the implementation architecture of a wide range of existing groupware development tools. (The following discussion is based on Phillips' survey of groupware development tools and their implementation architectures [24]).

Semi-replicated tools directly implementing this model (or subsets of the model) include Clock [29], TCD [1], Weasel [13], Suite [9], and Promondia [12]. GroupKit [25] is described by the model, as GroupKit environments implement shared state, and GroupKit provides no concurrency control for replicated shared data. Figure 3 also describes systems with replicated state under centralized coordination such as Habanero [6], Prospero [10], Ensemble [23] and COAST [27]. In these systems, a central component is responsible for concurrency control decisions, allowing the shared context to be modeled via a virtual server. Finally, the model describes fully centralized systems such as RendezVous [17], as the trivial case in which there is no replicated data at all.

Systems not described by the model include fully replicated systems using concurrency control algorithms based on roll-backs [8] or operation transforms [11]. Such fully replicated systems include DECAF [23], DreamTeam [26], Mushroom [19] and Villa [4].

Therefore, while this simplified treatment of the semi-replicated architecture does not cover every possible implementation of groupware, it describes a sufficiently large subset of current development tools to be interesting.

3.1 Encoding Concurrency Control in the Semi-replicated Architecture

In order to show how software architectures can encode temporal properties, we first formalize our simplified version of the semi-replicated architecture, and then define its concurrency control properties as restrictions over the treatment of messages.

As shown in figure 3, a groupware system consists of a set of client machines, each containing a cache, and a server machine containing shared state. Clients communicate with the server by issuing *requests* for information and *updates* that modify information. Parameters to requests and updates and responses to requests are all considered to be *values*.

Client and Server Components

We let $Client \subset \mathbb{N}$ represent a set of client machines. We define *Update*, *Request* and *Value* to be disjoint sets representing updates and requests made by the view/controller, and values returned by the model as the results of requests. We let $Time == \mathbb{N}$ represent time.

Model

A *Model* stores data. Models are queried via requests. The values of these requests may change over time.

$$Model == Time \times Request \rightarrow Value$$

If *m:Model* we write $m(t)$ to represent $\lambda r \bullet m(t,r)$, the snapshot of the model at time t.

As shown in figure 3, we let *s:Model* represent the shared context, and the family of functions c_k :*Model* represent a cache for each client $k \in Client$. When making requests, clients first consult their cache. If the response has not been cached (i.e., the request is not in the domain of the cache), the shared context is consulted. If used efficiently, a cache can considerably reduce the overhead of network communication [15]. We define a request function rq_k for each client $k \in Client$:

$$rq_k : Time \rightarrow Request \rightarrow Value$$
$$rq_k (t,r) ==$$

if $r \in$ dom $(c_k (t))$ then
$\qquad c_k (t,r)$
else
$\qquad s (t,r)$

View/Controller

The purpose of an MVC controller is to map user inputs onto updates to the model. In computing an update, the controller makes a set of requests to the model. We formalize the activity of the controller through an *update function*, which computes an update using values obtained from the model:

$$UpdateFn == seq\ Value \rightarrow Update$$

An update *transaction* represents the application of an update function to values obtained through a sequence of requests executed at given times. Transactions originate from some client.

$$Transaction ==$$
$$Client \times UpdateFn \times seq\ (Time \times Request)$$

The view/controller of each client can be thought of as executing a sequence of transactions. When a user performs an action, an update to the shared state is computed, based on values in the cache and shared context. When a client receives notification that the shared context has changed, it computes an update to the display.

Conflicts

The temporal property of interest in this architecture is that transactions do not conflict with each other. Intuitively, two transactions conflict if the modifications to the shared context performed by one transaction cause inconsistencies in the state being used by another transaction. For example, in figure 2, the resize and scale transactions conflict because the resize transaction changes values being used by the scale transaction, with the result that only some of the diagram elements are scaled. More precisely, a transaction conflicts if the update value that would be obtained from executing the transaction at the time the transaction is to be applied differs from the value of the transaction as computed. That is:

$$conflict : Transaction \times Time \rightarrow Bool$$

is defined as:

$$conflict ((k, u, <(t_1, r_1), ..., (t_n, r_n) >), t)$$
$$== u (<rq_k (t_1, r_1),..., rq_k (t_n, r_n)>)$$
$$\neq u (<s (t, r_1),..., s (t, r_n)>)$$

Within the semi-replicated architecture, we define that no conflicting transaction is committed; that is, that no conflicting transaction is permitted to modify the shared context. We encode this simply as the property that if $tr{:}Transaction$ is committed at time $t{:}Time$, then:

$$\neg conflict (tr, t)$$

Implementations of the semi-replicated architecture must therefore ensure that no conflicting transaction is committed. To achieve this, a *pessimistic* concurrency controller ensures that transactions are computed only at times they will not conflict, while an *optimistic* concurrency controller detects when a transaction conflicts, and rolls it back instead of committing it.

It should be noted that this definition of *conflict* ensures that all committed transactions are serializable [22]. For some applications where unintuitive behaviour resulting from conflicts may be tolerable, this definition may in fact be too restrictive [16,22].

3.2   Implementation of Semi-replication

As shown in figure 3, client and server machines communicate via a set of messages. In sections 4 and 5, we describe how these messages are used to implement the concurrency control requirement of this architecture. These implementations all require the architecture's specification, while providing different performance tradeoffs. First, we informally specify the meaning of the messages themselves:

− The network separating the server and clients is assumed to be lossless and fifo. That is, messages are assumed to arrive at their destination, and if two messages are sent to the same destination, they arrive in the order in which they are sent. Clients are assumed to process messages atomically and in sequence.

- If the server receives the message `requestLock`, it eventually replies with the message `grantLock`.
- If the server receives the message *request* (r) at time $t \in Time$, where $r \in Request$, then the server responds with `response` (r, s (t,r)).
- If the server receives and commits an update `update` (u, tr), where $u \in Update$ and $tr \in Transaction$, then the shared context is modified. Committing an update is the only action that modifies the shared context; therefore if the server commits no updates between times t_1 and t_2, then $\forall t_a, t_b : t_1 .. t_2 \bullet s(t_a) = s(t_b)$.
- If the server receives the update `update` (u, tr), it may issue the message `fail` to indicate that the update has not been committed, and must be recomputed.
- If the server sends the message `notify` at time t_1 and the client receives the message at time t_2, then the client cache may be updated to values provided by the notification message: $\forall r \in dom(c_k (t_2)) \bullet c_k (t_2, r) = s(t_1, r)$
- If client k receives the message `response` (r, s(t_1, r)) at time t_2, where $t_2 \in Time$ and $r \in Request$, then the cache is updated so that $c_k (t_2, r) = s(t_1, r)$
- No other messages modify the client cache. That is, if k receives no messages between times t_1 and t_2, then $\forall t_a, t_b : t_1 .. t_2 \bullet c_k (t_a) = c_k (t_b)$.

The last section showed how the temporal property that transactions not conflict can be encoded as part of the definition of the semi-replicated architecture. In the following sections, we show how this property can be refined to a wide range of implementations. This allows developers using the semi-replicated architecture to reason about the temporal properties of their application without having to make early commitment to a particular concurrency control algorithm.

4   Locking

One standard approach to implementing pessimistic concurrency control is to require clients to obtain a lock before computing a transaction [16]. We first formally define locking, and then specify how locking is implemented. We then show that the locking algorithm satisfies the temporal properties required by the semi-replicated architecture.

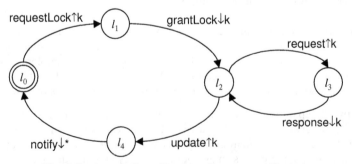

Fig. 4. Implementation of Locking Concurrency Control.

For each client $k \in Client$, we define a *lock* function that specifies whether the client holds a lock between times t_1 and t_2.

$$lock_k : Time \times Time \rightarrow Bool$$

If client k holds a lock over a time interval, the cache is synchronized with the shared context, and the model does not change during the interval:

$$lock_k (t_1, t_2)$$
$$\Rightarrow (\forall t : t_1 .. t_2 \bullet rq_k (t) = s (t))$$
$$\wedge (\forall t_a, t_b : t_1 .. t_2 \bullet s(t_a) = s(t_b))$$

If a lock is held while a transaction is carried out and applied, the transaction will not conflict. Theorem 1 therefore guarantees that locking implements the temporal requirements of the semi-replicated architecture.

Theorem 1. If $k \in Client$, $tr=(k, u, <(t_1, r_1), ..., (t_n, r_n)>) \in Transaction$, $t_a=\min (<t_1, ..., t_n>)$ and $t_b=\max (<t_1, ..., t_n>)$, then

$$lock_k (t_a, t_b) \Rightarrow \neg conflict (tr, t_b)$$

Proof. Follows directly from the definitions of *lock* and *conflict*.

4.1   Implementation of Locking

Figure 4 shows the implementation of locking from the point of view of a server. The implementation is expressed as a finite state machine, starting in state l_0. The notation $m{\uparrow}k$ specifies that client k sends message m to the server; $m{\downarrow}k$ indicates that the server sends m to client k, and $m{\downarrow}*$ specifies that the server multicasts m to all clients.

To carry out a transaction using locking concurrency control, the client sends a requestLock message to the server requesting a lock. If no other client holds a lock, the server responds with a grantLock message; otherwise, the lock request is queued.   The client may issue any number of request messages, receiving corresponding response messages. Request/response pairs may be entered in the client cache. The client ends the transaction by sending an update message. The update is performed on the server.

A notify message is sent to all clients, instructing them to resynchronize their caches. Notification may take many forms. Simple notification simply invalidates all cache entries. More targeted notification (such as the *presend* caching scheme [15]) specifies exactly which cache entries have been invalidated by the update.

The update message implicitly releases the lock.

This implementation of locking guarantees that a client holds a lock from the time the grantLock message is received by the client until the time the update message is committed by the server.

Theorem 2. If client k receives the message grantLock${\downarrow}k$ at time t_1, and the server receives the message update${\uparrow}k$ at time t_2, and the server has in the meantime passed only through states l_2 and l_3, then $lock_k (t_1, t_2)$.

Proof. We must show that between t_1 and t_2, *(i)* the shared context does not change, and *(ii)* the cache remains synchronized with the shared context. *(i)* Between t_1 and t_2, the server remains in states l_2 and l_3. In these states, the value of the shared context does not change. Therefore $\forall t_a, t_b : t_1 .. t_2 \bullet s(t_a) = s(t_b)$. *(ii)* At t_1, either the client has just received a `notify` message from the server, or is in its initial state. Therefore $rq_k (t_1) = s (t_1)$. In states l_2 and l_3, the server issues only `response` messages. Assume the server issues `response` $(r, s(t_a, r))$ at time $t_a \in t_1 .. t_2$, and the message is received by k at time $t_b \in t_1 .. t_2$. Then k may update the cache so that $c_k (t_b, r) = s(t_a, r)$, with the result that $rq_k (t_b, r) = s (t_a, r)$. However, from *(i)* we know that $s(t_b) = s(t_a) \Rightarrow s(t_b, r) = s(t_a, r)$, so the cache has remained synchronized. Therefore, $\forall t : t_1 .. t_2 \bullet rq_k (t) = s (t)$.

5   Eager

The locking approach of the last section provided a direct implementation of the temporal properties specified in the semi-replicated architecture.   Locking is interesting in cases where transactions are long (and therefore likely to generate conflicts), or cases where unrolling conflicting transactions is expensive (or impossible).

Our second approach is to compute the update transaction and apply it only if it is determined not to conflict. This form of concurrency control is optimistic in the sense that updates are computed in the hope that they will not conflict. However, updates are not committed until they are known not to conflict. This differs from purely optimistic algorithms (such as rollback approaches [3,19]), in which updates may also be optimistically committed.

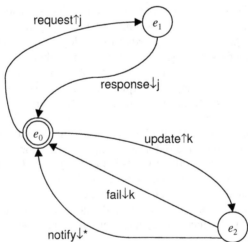

Fig. 5. Implementation of Eager Concurrency Control.

We call this approach *Eager*, an algorithm implementing optimistic update computation with pessimistic update application. Section 5.2 explains how Eager can be implemented efficiently, while providing automatic, fine-grained conflict detection. Eager concurrency control can provide significantly better performance than locking for transactions typically found in groupware applications, and is particularly appropriate to use over wide area networks [29].

The Eager algorithm (and its optimization) are sufficiently complex that its temporal properties are not obvious from reading the algorithm itself. The architectural specification, however, shows clearly what properties the algorithm has. Additionally, our approach of refining the algorithm from this specification lends confidence to the correctness of Eager's implementation.

A sufficient condition to determine whether a transaction conflicts is to examine the current values of the requests which were used to compute the update. If the requests have not changed value, the update does not conflict. The *fail* function determines whether a transaction may conflict at time t:

$fail : Transaction \times Time \rightarrow Bool$

Letting $tr=(k, u, <(t_1, r_1), ..., (t_n, r_n) >) \in Transaction$, we define

$fail\ (tr, t) == \exists\ i{:}1..n \bullet rq_k\ (t_i, r_i) \neq s(t, r_i)$

This condition is conservative, in that some non-conflicting transactions may fail.

Theorem 3 demonstrates that Eager concurrency control satisfies the temporal properties of the semi-replicated architecture:

Theorem 3. Let t:*Time* and tr:*Transaction*. Then

$\neg fail\ (tr,t) \Rightarrow \neg conflict\ (tr,t)$

Proof: Let $tr=(k, u, <(t_1, r_1), ..., (t_n, r_n) >) \in Transaction$. Then

$\neg fail\ (tr,t)$

$\Rightarrow \forall\ i{:}1..n \bullet rq_k\ (t_i, r_i) = s(t, r_i)$

$\Rightarrow u\ (rq_k\ (t_1, r_1),..., rq_k\ (t_n, r_n)$

$\qquad = u\ (s(t_1, r_1),...,s(t_n, r_n))$

$\Rightarrow \neg\ conflict\ (tr,t)$

5.1   Implementation of Eager Concurrency Control

Figure 5 shows how Eager concurrency control is implemented at the server. From a start state of e_0, the server can handle requests from any client j, and responds with the appropriate response message.

If the server receives the message update (u, tr) at time t, for $tr \in Transaction$ and $u \in Update$, then from state e_2, the server must determine whether to commit the update. If *fail* (tr, t), the server issues the fail message. Otherwise, the server commits the update and issues a notify to all clients.

Theorem 4. If the server receives the message update(u,tr) at time t, where $tr \in$ *Transaction* and $u \in Update$, then if *conflict*(tr,t), the server does not commit the update.

Proof. State e_2 only commits u if $\neg fail\ (tr,t)$. By theorem 3, $\neg fail\ (tr,t) \Rightarrow \neg conflict\ (tr,t)$.

5.2   Optimization

Directly computing the *fail* function is expensive, as complete information on the transaction is required. Passing the transaction information over a network can be expensive in bandwidth, and in marshalling and unmarshalling. Computing whether the values of requests have changed places load on the server machine. Eager concurrency control can be optimized, making it substantially faster than locking concurrency control in a wide area context.

Our approach of refining implementations from architectural specifications allows us to demonstrate that this optimized algorithm still satisfies the temporal properties of the semi-replicated architecture.

First, we assign integer id's to cache entries. Let *CacheId* == $\mathbb{N}$. Then assume the existence of a function

$$h : Request \times Value \rightarrow CacheId$$

with the property that $\forall r_1, r_2 \in Request$, $v_1, v_2 \in Value \bullet h(r_1, v_1) = h(r_2, v_2) \Rightarrow r_1 = r_2 \wedge v_1 = v_2$. We then define a new version of the *fail* function that operates over cache id's. If $tr=(k, u, <(t_1, r_1), \ldots, (t_n, r_n) >) \in Transaction$, $t \in Time$, then

$$fail'(tr,t) == \exists i{:}1..n \bullet h(r_i, rq_k (t_i, r_i)) \neq h(r_i, s(t, r_i))$$

h can be implemented efficiently on the clients by having the cache assign an integer id to each of its entries. A server cache [15] can perform the same function on the server. The update message can then simply pass integer cache id's rather than the values of the requests themselves. Computing *fail'* involves integer comparisons over the cache id's, rather than recomputing and comparing request values.

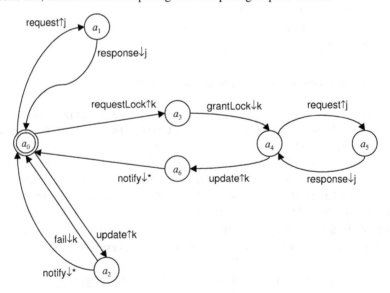

Fig. 6. Implementation of Adaptive Concurrency Control.

Theorem 5. Let *t:Time* and *tr:Transaction*. Then

$$fail'(tr,t) \Rightarrow fail\ (tr,t)$$

Proof. Follows directly from the definitions of *fail*, *fail'* and *h*.

The implementation of Eager concurrency control can therefore be optimized by substituting the computation of *fail* in e_2 with *fail'*. This implementation is used in the Clock [29] and TCD [1] groupware development toolkits.

6   Adaptive Concurrency Control

As discussed in section 2.1, neither pessimistic nor optimistic concurrency control is appropriate for all applications, and in fact a single application should be able to combine both forms of concurrency control. This section describes how locking and Eager concurrency control can be combined to a single adaptive algorithm. This algorithm has the following properties:

- Clients can decide on a per-transaction basis whether to use locking or Eager concurrency control.
- The concurrency controller is associated with the model, and automatically adapts to the concurrency control scheme being used by the clients.
- Multiple transactions can be processed in parallel, where some are locking and some Eager.
- Adaptive concurrency control places no overheads on either the locking or Eager algorithms. Eager transactions may be computed even if another client holds a lock on the model (but may not commit while the lock is in place.)

This example shows that the approach of specifying temporal properties in architectures not only permits the specification of existing, well-understood algorithms, but also supports the development of new algorithms.

The remainder of this section describes the implementation of adaptive concurrency control.

6.1   Implementation of Adaptive Concurrency Control

The server implementation of adaptive concurrency control is shown in figure 6. This implementation simply combines the finite state machines of figures 4 and 5. From start state a_0, if a client requests a lock, locking concurrency control is used for that client's transaction. Otherwise, requests and updates are processed using the Eager method. The one change in the locking algorithm is that from state a_4, any client can make a request, not just the client holding the lock. This does not affect the client holding the lock, as requests do not change the value of the shared context. This change allows Eager transactions to be computed concurrently with locking transactions; however, updates resulting from Eager transactions may not be committed until after the lock is released.

Adaptive concurrency control ensures that no conflicting transaction is committed:

Theorem 6. Assume that clients compute update transactions either using a locking pattern (where the client makes no requests until a `grantLock` message is received) or an Eager pattern (where the client does not request a lock). Then adaptive concurrency control ensures that if the server receives the message update (u,tr) at time t, where $u \in Update$ and $tr \in Transaction$, then if $conflict(tr,t)$, the server does not commit the update.

Proof. Apply the same argument as used in theorems 2 and 4.

From this example, we therefore see it is possible to refine the implementation of a novel concurrency control algorithm permitting both pessimistic and optimistic transactions to be executed in parallel.

7   Conclusion

This paper has introduced the concept that software architectures can encode temporal properties of software systems as well as the traditional structural properties. We have shown an example of such properties in the context of specifying concurrent behaviour of clients and server in the semi-replicated groupware architecture. We have shown that both pessimistic and optimistic concurrency control algorithms can be refined from the required temporal behaviour, as well as a novel adaptive scheme permitting both optimistic and pessimistic transactions to execute in parallel.

This approach allows us to treat architectures as specifications both of the structural and temporal properties of interactive systems. The architecture specifies high level properties of the system's behaviour, while a developer is free to implement such behaviour in any way he/she chooses. This represents a departure from the common approach in groupware, where rather than the specifying the behavioural properties of an application, developers commit early to a particular concurrency control algorithm.

The main weakness of our approach in its current form is that our model of the semi-replicated architecture is simplified, permitting no concurrency control over the replicated data. This does not allow us to treat the operation transform class of concurrency control algorithms such as dOpt [11], CCU [7] and ORESTE [18]. Interesting future work will be to extend our description of semi-replication to address this shortcoming. Additionally, we are currently extending this architectural approach to areas other than concurrency control. This involves the development of a full range of architectural primitives embodying temporal properties accounting for the non-zero latency of real networks, and accounting for architectural evolution over time resulting from session management.

Acknowledgments. This research was carried out by the authors at the Software Technology Laboratory of Queen's University, and was partially supported by the Natural Science and Engineering Research Council (NSERC). The work greatly benefited from the work of Gary Anderson in the TeleComputing Developer toolkit, and from numerous discussions with Greg Phillips.

8   References

1. G.E. Anderson, T.C.N. Graham, and T.N. Wright. Dragonfly: Linking conceptual and implementation architectures of multiuser interactive systems. In *Proc. ICSE 2000*, 2000.
2. R.M. Baecker, editor. *Readings in Groupware and Computer-Supported Cooperative Work: Assisting Human-Human Collaboration*. Morgan Kaufmann Publishers, 1993.
3. G. Banavar, K. Miller, and M. Ward. Adaptive views: Adapting to changing network conditions in optimistic groupware. In *Proc. Euro-PDS '98*, 1998.
4. S. Bhola, B. Mukherjee, S. Doddapaneni, and M. Ahamad. Flexible batching and consistency mechanisms for building interactive groupware applications. In *18th International Conference on Distributed Computing Systems (ICDCS)*, 1998.
5. G. Calvary, J. Coutaz, and L. Nigay. From single-user architectural design to PAC*: A generic software architecture model for CSCW. In *Proc. CHI '97*, pages 242-249. ACM Press, 1997.
6. Chabert, E. Grossman, L. Jackson, S. Pietrowicz, and C. Seguin. *Java object sharing in Habanero*. CACM, 41(6):69-76, June 1998.
7. G.V. Cormack. *A calculus for concurrent update*. Research report CS-95-06, University of Waterloo, 1995. Available from ftp://cs-archive.uwaterloo.ca.
8. G. Coulouris, J. Dollimore, and T. Kindberg. *Distributed Systems: Concepts and Design*. Addison-Wesley, second edition, 1994.
9. P. Dewan and R. Choudhary. A high-level and flexible framework for implementing multiuser user interfaces. *ACM TOIS*, 10(4):345-380, October 1992.
10. P. Dourish. Consistency guarantees: Exploiting application semantics for consistency management in a collaboration toolkit. In *Proc. ACM CSCW '96*. ACM Press, 1996.
11. C.A. Ellis and S.J. Gibbs. Concurrency control in groupware systems. In *Proc. SIGMOD '89*, pages 399-407. ACM Press, 1989.
12. U. Gall and F.J. Hauck. Promondia: A Java-based framework for real-time group communication on the Web. In *Proceedings of the 6th World Wide Web Conference*, Santa Clara, CA. April 7--11. Published as Computers, Networks and ISDN 29(8/13). Elsevier Science Publishers B. V. (North-Holland), 1997.
13. T.C.N. Graham and T. Urnes. Relational views as a model for automatic distributed implementation of multi-user applications. In *Proc. ACM CSCW '92*, pages 59-66. ACM Press, 1992.
14. T.C.N. Graham and T. Urnes. Integrating Support for Temporal Media into an Architecture for Graphical User Interfaces. In *Proc. ICSE 19*, pages 172-182. ACM Press, 1997.
15. T.C.N. Graham, T. Urnes, and R. Nejabi. Efficient distributed implementation of semi-replicated synchronous groupware. In *Proc. ACM UIST '96*, pages 1-10. ACM Press, 1996.
16. S. Greenberg and D. Marwood. Real time groupware as a distributed system: Concurrency control and its effect on the interface. In *Proc. ACM CSCW '94*, pages 207-217. ACM Press, 1994.
17. R.D. Hill, T. Brinck, S.L. Rohall, J.F. Patterson, and W. Wilner. The Rendezvous language and architecture for constructing multi-user applications. *ACM TOCHI*, 1(2):81-125, June 1994.
18. Karsenty and M. Beaudouin-Lafon. An algorithm for distributed groupware applications. In Proc. 13th International Conference on Distributed Computing Systems (ICDCS), pages 195--202, 1993.
19. T. Kindberg, G. Coulouris, J. Dollimore, and J. Heikkinen. Sharing objects over the Internet: The Mushroom approach. In *Proceedings of IEEE Global Internet '96* (Mini-conference at GLOBECOM '96, London, England, Nov. 20-21). IEEE ComSoc, 1996.

20. G.E. Krasner and S.T. Pope. A cookbook for using the Model-View-Controller user interface paradigm in Smalltalk-80. *JOOP*, 1(3):26-49, August/September 1988.

21. J.C. Lauwers and K.A. Lantz. Collaboration awareness in support of collaboration transparency: Requirements for the next generation of shared window systems. In *Proc. CHI '90*, (also in [2]), pages 303-311. ACM Press, 1990.

22. J.P. Munson and P. Dewan. A concurrency control framework for collaborative systems. In *Proc. ACM CSCW '96*, pages 278-287. ACM Press, 1996.

23. R.E. Newman-Wolfe, M.L. Webb, and M. Montes. Implicit locking in the Ensemble concurrent object-oriented graphics editor. In J. Turner and R. Kraut, editors, *Proc. ACM CSCW '92*, pages 265-272. ACM Press, 1992.

24. W.G. Phillips. *Architectures for synchronous groupware*. Technical Report 1999-425, Department of Computing and Information Science, Queen's University, May 1999.

25. M. Roseman and S. Greenberg. Building real time groupware with GroupKit, a groupware toolkit. ACM TOCHI, 3(1):66-106, March 1996.

26. J. Roth and C. Unger. Dreamteam - a platform for synchronous collaborative applications. In Th. Herrmann and K. Just-Hahn, editors, *Groupware und organisatorische Innovation (D-CSCW'98)*, pages 153-165. B.G. Teubner Stuttgart, Leipzig, 1998.

27. Schuckmann, L. Kirchner, J. Schummer, and J.M. Haake. Designing object-oriented synchronous groupware with COAST. In *Proc. ACM CSCW '96*. ACM Press, 1996.

28. M. Shaw and D. Garlan. *Software Architecture: Perspectives on an Emerging Discipline*. Prentice Hall, 1996.

29. T. Urnes and T.C.N. Graham. Flexibly mapping synchronous groupware architectures to distributed implementations. In *Proc. DSVIS'99*, pages 133-148, 1999.

Questioning the Foundations of Utility for Quality of Service in Interface Development

Chris Johnson

University of Glasgow
Department of Computing Science, University of Glasgow, Scotland, G12 8QQ
johnson@dcs.gla.ac.uk
http://www.dsc.gla.ac.uk/~johnson

Abstract. A number of research groups have exploited utility curves to model interaction with distributed systems. For example, they have been used to construct the models of subjective value that support "intelligent" advice giving systems. They have been integrated into ATM architectures to ensure that users' Quality of Service requirements are met by underlying network protocols. They have also been used to represent and reason about the risk aversion and risk preference that users exhibit when retrieving resources from remote servers over unreliable networks. However, much of this previous work has rested upon implicit assumptions about properties of the preference relation that underpins modern consumer theory. This paper examines the mathematical basis of the preference relation. The analysis helps to identify the implications that preference axioms have for the application of consumer theory to interface development.

1   Introduction

This paper builds on the notion that models of utility, or value, can be extended from microeconomics and consumer theory to model interaction with distributed systems. Utility can be thought of as a measure of desire or the capacity of a good or service to satisfy a need [1] The value of remote information can, therefore, be thought of in terms of its capacity to satisfy the demands that particular tasks impose upon users. A number of different approaches can be exploited to represent the utility that users associate with items of information. For instance, March and Simon's satisficing techniques identify the subjective desire for a good or service by iteratively refining the constraining equations that characterize preferences between tasks and services [2]. Unfortunately, the difficulty of accurately identifying an individual's preferences has been a common theme of recent research in economics and consumer theory [3]. A number of research groups have, however, applied elements of utility models to support the development of interactive systems. For example, Horvitz and Rutledge have applied decision theoretic concepts to model users' actions under uncertainty [4]. McAuley's group at Microsoft Research in Cambridge is applying utility curves to model quality of service issues in ATM networks. Similarly, we have used consumer theory to model aspects of human computer interaction with distributed systems ranging from web-based education services [5] to safety-critical interfaces [1].

P. Palanque and F. Paternò (Eds.): DSV-IS 2000, LNCS 1946, pp. 19–33, 2001.

1.1   Assumptions about Utility

This previous work rests upon a number of implicit assumptions about the nature of utility. These assumptions have been directly inherited from the axioms that are used to characterise utility in the field of microeconomics [6]. No previous work has been conducted to examine whether or not these assumptions are valid within the specific context of human computer interaction. This paper, therefore, focuses in much greater detail on the mathematical foundations of consumer theory. In particular, we argue that the preference axioms of microeconomics make strong assumptions about patterns of interaction with mobile, distributed systems.

1.1   A Wireless LAN Case Study

Our analysis is illustrated by the problems of supporting interaction over a wireless local area network. This work is part of an on-going study into the use of personal digital assistants by Anaesthetists in the UK National Health Service. The particular architecture that we are using is based around Lucent's WaveLAN technology. This exploits a cellular architecture and spread-spectrum transmissions. It supports transparent migration between cells that are effective up to two hundred metres from a base station. This case study is appropriate because it typifies the sorts of distributed interactive systems in which users must sacrifice finite resources, both of time and battery power, to access the information that they need.

1.2   Structure of the Paper

This section has introduced the argument that is presented in this paper. Section 2 builds on this analysis by briefly presenting a number of utility curves that have been developed to characterise interaction with our wireless system. In particular, it is argued that appropriate feedback must be provided if relatively high levels of utility are to be sustained in the face of high network latencies [8]. Having illustrated the manner in which utility curves can be applied to represent and reason about interaction with mobile networks, Section 3 goes on to examine the preference relation that provides the formal basis of most utility curves. In particular, we examine the way in which mathematical properties of this relation that have been introduced from consumer theory may not be appropriate for models of human computer interaction. Section 4 builds on this analysis and uses a number of simple topologies to introduce the further axioms. These are necessary in order to move from the simple preference relation of Section 3 to the more familiar models of utility curves that have previously been used to model user preferences during human computer interaction. Later sections then argue that many of these axioms of rationality and taste cannot easily be applied to model interaction with distribued systems such as our WaveLAN case study. Section 5 presents the conclusions that can be drawn from this work and identifies areas for further research.

2   Using Models of Utility for Interface Development

Before exploring the formal model that supports consumer theory in microeconomics, it is first important to provide a brief overview of how this technique can be used to represent and reason about human computer interaction with distributed systems.

2.1   Indications of Cost in Mobile Networks

Figure 1 shows how utility curves can be used to analyse the delays that occur when many independent users share the same mobile infrastructure. Increases in network loading help to increase the costs, in terms of the users' time, that must be met in order to retrieve a remote resource. Initially, the user has some anticipated or predicted minimum for the amount of time that it will take to complete any transfer. Up to this point, the utility of any information retrieved will be relatively high. Documents received before the minimum predicted period could be seen as a bonus from the user's perspective. We show this as a plateau. However, it may be modeled as an extension of the "convex to the origin" curve if relatively small delays affect the utility that the user associates with the resource. After the minimum predicted time, the anticipated value of the information will decline. There are many reasons for this. The time taken to retrieve a document may exceed the total time that is available for any associated tasks. Eventually, there will come a point when users simply run out of time. At this stage, the marginal utility of any remote information will be very low because the user simply cannot afford to wait for the data to be retrieved [7].

It is possible to reduce the problems created by network delays by extending the period of high utility that is associated with the interval before the minimum expected retrieval period. However, the delay that is predicted by the user can be very different from the actual delay. This will be effected by transient conditions, such as the loading of any intermediate networks, and by local conditions associated with the users' position in relation to their nearest transceiver. Figure 2 presents a utility curve that shows how the minimum predicted time can be extended by a transformation along the X-axis. In practical terms, this can be done by providing users with an indication of the capacity of their communications channels, by the size of the resource being transferred and also be the contents of their cache [5]. Ebling argues that this form of translucence is necessary if users are to maximise the allocation of their finite resources during interaction with mobile systems, such as our WaveLAN case study [8]. If the available network capacity is relatively low and the resource is relatively large then users will expect a considerable delay before the information is available.

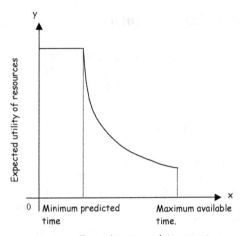

Fig. 1. Expected Utility in Distributed Systems

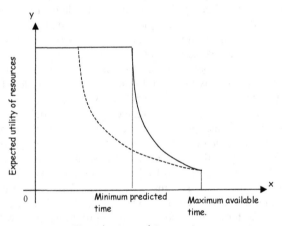

Fig. 2. Indications of Cost Extend Minimum Predictions

Under these circumstances, the minimum expected time will be extended and high levels of utility will be associated with any request that completes before this interval has finished. All of this depends upon the user receiving appropriate feedback both about the size of the requested resources and about network latencies. One of the simplest means of providing this feedback using our mobile architecture is to support one of the commercial web browsers that provides information about the progress of retrieval requests. Unfortunately, these browsers typically exploit multi-threaded Java implementation techniques. These easily defeat attempts to provide accurate assessments of download latencies in the general case. Further problems arise because it can be difficult to make a priori predictions about available bandwidth in mobile systems. For instance, communications shadows and multipath transmissions can introduce delays while error correction routines call for the retransmission of corrupted or missing data.

2.2   Indications of Value

Instead of increasing the minimum expected download latency, it is possible to sustain high levels of subjective satisfaction in the face of wireless communications delays by providing users with information about the quality of a remote resource. An earlier paper explains how this technique can be applied to support the presentation of video material over distributed networks [9]. Significantly more requests are abandoned if hypertext tags are used to represent remote resources rather than thumbnail images. Figure 3 presents a utility curve that can be used to explain these experimental findings. Initial assessments of subjective value, shown as a dotted line, can be transformed along the Y-axis. This indicates the rise in expectations that can be produced through effective interface design.

Conversely, an interface that indicated relatively low production values would have the opposite effect of reducing the absolute level of the anticipated utility. This can be shown by a transformation of the utility curve down the Y-axis.

This section has provided a brief overview of the ways in which utility curves can be extended from microeconomic consumer theory to model interaction with distributed systems. It is important not to underestimate the consequences of this analysis. Previous paragraphs have focused on the impact that subjective utility has for the presentation of information about download latencies and the production quality of remote resources. The introduction has also cited attempts to explicitly encode users' subjective utility as part of underlying network protocols and in the user models that are being developed to drive the next generation of Microsoft's help systems [10].

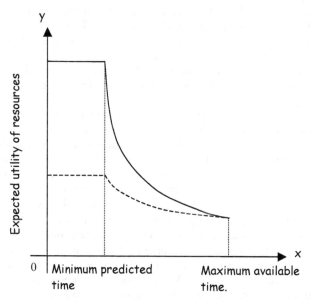

Fig. 3. Indications of Quality Raise Expected Utility

3   The Preference Relation and Axioms of Rationality

The previous section applied utility functions to represent and reason about interaction with distributed systems. It did not, however, provide any mathematical basis for these functions. Nor did it provide any of the axioms that might distinguish valid utility curves from those that characterise impossible preferences [6]. This is important because without these axioms it is possible to inadvertently represent a number of paradoxical situations. For instance, a user might prefer to allocate finite network connectivity to access a web page rather than read their email and at the same time prefer to read their email rather than access the same web page. This form of deadly embrace indicates a pathological form of inconsistency that cannot easily be explained using experimental observations about the way that real users choose to allocate battery life and radio connections. The following section, therefore, goes on to examine the theoretical foundations of consumer theory. These foundations are built on what are known as the rationality axioms of the preference relation. An analysis of these axioms helps to identify important differences between new applications of utility to support interface development and its more traditional uses in microeconomics.

Most work on consumer theory begins by defining a number of axioms that are assumed to hold over the consumption set X. A consumption set represents the set of all alternatives, or complete consumption plans, that a user can identify. For instance, they may choose to download a particular item of information over their wireless connection. The user chooses to sacrifice some portion of their available battery power and their communications bandwidth in order to "consume" this resource. It is, therefore, possible to identify the remote item of information as a potential element of the user's consumption set. It is important to emphasise that it may not be possible for the user actually to consume particular elements of X. They may attempt to access information that cannot be obtained given their current resources. This often arises when the users' PDA has insufficient power to access the wireless LAN or if they move beyond the boundaries of the cellular architecture. In such circumstances, the request must be cached until the batteries are recharged or the user moves back into a cell.

It is possible to define a number of preference axioms that are assumed to hold over the elements of X. These axioms form the basic premises that are assumed to hold for most of the more complex utility models that have been exploited by previous work in this area. The preference axioms are intended to be a minimal set of relations that must hold in order to provide a consistent model of users' preferences within a consumption set. A binary relation denotes consumer preferences over the elements of X. If $(x_1, x_2) \in \; >=$, or $x_1 >= x_2$, then "x_1 is at least as good as x_2". The $>=$ can, for example, be used to denote that a user prefers to allocate finite resources to retrieve one item of information, such as a web page, rather than another, for instance an email message. Although this relatively simple relationship only holds between two commodities, later sections will show how more complex topologies can be constructed from the initial formalization. We will also show how microeconomic theory tends to assume a partial ordering over the elements of X. We can also impose further constraints on the $>=$ relation to avoid the paradoxes that were introduced in previous paragraphs.

3.1   Completeness

The first of the preference axioms ensures completeness over the elements in X. People must have the necessary knowledge to discriminate between the different commodities that they are presented with. They must be able to state that for any two distinct consumption plans, x_1 and x_2, that x_1 is at least as good as x_2 or x_2 is at least as good as x_1.

Axiom 1   For any $x_1 \neq x_2 \in X$, either $x_1 >= x_2$ or $x_2 >= x_1$

As mentioned, the reason for examining the formal underpinnings of consumer theory is to uncover the implications that this model has for its application to human computer interaction. The Completeness Axiom makes a number of assumptions about the users of distributed applications. It is intended to ensure that users must be able to distinguish between the different strategies or plans that they can exploit during interaction. For example, if a user's task involves two remote items of information but they cannot determine whether they have sufficient power to retrieve either resource then it can be difficult to express a preference between them. In order to make an informed selection they will need more information about probable power consumption. It will be difficult to sustain the preference relation, $>=$, under these circumstances.

HCI Implication 1. *The Completeness Axiom makes an unrealistic assumption that the user will be able to distinguish between the different strategies or plans that they can exploit during interaction.*

Experience in the development of mobile applications shows that without significant training many users cannot accurately distinguish between the options that are available to them. Even relatively frequent users have only the crudest notion of caching or of cellular transmission protocols. As a result, a high number of relatively poor exchanges are made in which battery power is extinguished by attempts to transfer documents that could have been deferred until conventional network connectivity was restored.

3.2   Reflexivity

The second preference axiom also expresses an important principle for the rational decision-maker. In particular, it ensures that any good or service is at least as good as itself. Without such an axiom, it is possible to envisage a considerable number of paradoxes. The reflexivity axiom is, therefore, formalised as follows:

Axiom 2   For all $x \in X$, $x >= x$

In terms of human computer interaction, this ensures that the value associated with a remote resource is at least as good as the value of that remote resource. However, even this relatively benign axiom has certain problematic features when applied to interaction with distributed systems.

HCI Implication 2   *The Reflexivity Axiom states that the value of any good or service is at least as good as itself. This implies that each data source must be modelled as a distinct commodity even if the information that they contain is identical.*

The key point here is that there may be several different ways in which to obtain the same remote resource. Ideally, if information is cached then any request can be handled locally. However, if the same resource is not cached then the costs of accessing that resource are very different. Most people would prefer to access the locally cached version than the remote resource with its associated network connection and battery consumption. This leads us to the conclusion that we must be very careful about what we model as different commodities within any application of utility theory to distributed systems. The Reflexivity Axiom teaches us that local and remote versions of the same information are different resources. They must not be confused when applying models from microeconomics to represent and reason about human computer interaction.

3.3   Transitivity

The transitivity axiom helps to build up the partial ordering that reflect many consumer attitudes to the commodities that are available to them:

Axiom 3   For any x_1, x_2, $x_3 \in X$ if $x_1 >= x_2$ and $x_2 >= x_3$ then $x_1 >= x_3$

As before, it is possible to identify ways in which the transitivity axiom helps to model certain aspects of interaction with distributed systems. For instance, if a mobile user preferred to access their email account rather than download a web page and they prefer to download the web page rather than remotely print out the list of patients allocated to an operating theatre then it is also safe to conclude that they would prefer to cache their email than print the list. It is important to note, however, that this is the most controversial of the preference axioms. The previous example illustrates the point that these initial axioms characterise the notion of the "rational consumer". They describe an ideal that can be very different from the insights provided by empirical studies.

HCI Implication 3   *The Transitivity Axiom makes an unrealistic assumption that users act as "rational" consumers in a technical environment that they may not fully understand and which contains numerous distractions and delays.*

A number of experimental studies have shown that individuals do not always express preferences that are consistent with the transitivity axiom [3]. This is especially true when users hold only mild preferences between individual consumption patterns. Inserting a small delay or distraction before asking people about such orderings can lead users to express preferences that violate the transitivity axiom. Unfortunately, such delays and distractions are typical of the working environments of most mobile users. This has profound implications. Several mobile systems have been developed to automatically optimise users' caching and information transfer tasks [8, 11]. Such approaches, typically, assume a degree of rationality that is a key feature of the transitivity axiom but which is not always exhibited by observational studies of mobile human-computer interaction [12].

4   Preference Topologies and the Axioms of Taste

Previous sections have introduced the axioms that characterize the preference relation in microeconomic consumer theory. These axioms have been implicitly adopted by previous work that has sought to apply time dependent models of utility to user interface design [1]. In order to illustrate this connection, it is necessary to show how the previous axioms can be used both to constrain the $>=$ relation and also to develop topologies that form the more familiar utility curves shown in Figures 1, 2 and 3. This section also introduces further axioms that characterize and constrain these utility curves.

Definition 1

The $>=$ (preference) relation on the consumption set X is assumed to satisfy Axioms 1, 2 and 3.

We can use the Completeness, Reflexivity and Transitivity axioms to define a strict preference relation. This excludes the possibility that any two commodities might be equally preferred. It can be used to express total orderings amongst the elements of X.

Definition 2

$x_1 >> x_2$ (strict preference) if and only if $x_1 >= x_2$ and $\neg(x_2 >= x_1)$

This is important because there are often situations in which users are confident in expressing marked preferences between certain remote resources. For instance, we have developed a system that enables its users to express a strong preference that they receive messages from particular colleagues, such as their boss, before any other messages. The ability to express such preferences has important consequences for the effective deployment of finite bandwidth and battery power.

In contrast to strict preference, it is also possible to construct an indifference relation. This captures the idea that there will be some commodities for which the user cannot express a preference. Recall, however, that this need not violate the completeness axiom, which defines a partial rather than a total ordering. The indifference relation captures situations in which users do not care which of several remote servers might be chosen to address a particular information request.

Definition 3

$x_1 \sim x_2$ (indifference) if and only if $x_1 >= x_2$ and $x_2 >= x_1$

The previous definitions enable us to develop a topology with respect to any arbitrary commodity, x_0 that the user might select. In particular, we can define subsets of X such that the elements of that set are at least as good as that point, $\{x \mid x \in X, x >= x_0\}$. We can define a "no better than" subset, $\{x \mid x \in X, x_0 >= x\}$. Similarly, a "worse than" subset, $\{x \mid x \in X, x_0 >> x\}$. "Preferred to" is defined as follows: $\{x \mid x \in X, x >> x_0\}$. Finally, the indifference subset is given as: $\{x \mid x \in X, x \sim x_0\}$. It is, difficult to visualise the components of this topology if we think in terms of remote information resources that can be accessed over a wireless network.

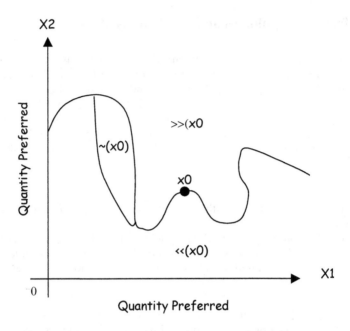

Fig. 4. Example Preference Topology Defined By Axioms 1, 2 and 3

Figure 4, therefore, shows X to be composed of 2D vectors of infinite real numbers $X = R^n_+[6]$. As can be seen, there is an area above the point $x_0 = (x^0_1, x^0_2)$ such that commodities in that region will be preferable to those represented by x_0. Conversely, the area below x_0 represents commodities that are no better than this point. Finally, there is an indifferent area to the left of x_0 that contains commodities that are valued as highly as the goods that are represented by this point. The key point here is that the first three preference axioms which help us to define preference relations also permit a number of anomalous topologies, such as that indicated in Figure 4. For example, there is a small region immediately to the left of x_0 where the user would actually prefer to have reductions in both x_1 and x_2. If we consider that x_1 and x_2 might represent a trade-off between using power to download incoming email messages and using power to transmit outgoing messages then this leads to a paradox where the user would prefer both to transmit and receive less messages. This situation can only be explained by enriching our notion of X to multidimensional vectors that consider wider resources implications; for example the user might choose not to access their mail because they want to conserve power for other applications. Alternatively, such paradoxes can be avoided by introducing further axioms that, like the others already presented, are often implicit in the concepts of utility that have been used in previous studies of human computer interaction. These axioms further constrain the preference relation to the point at which the resulting topologies will more closely resemble the conventional utility curves, such as those shown in Figures 1, 2 and 3.

4.1   Continuity

The continuity axiom ensures the closure of $>=(x)$, which is read as "at least as good as" and the $=<(x)$ relation, which is read as "no better than".

Axiom 4   For all $x \in R^n_+$, the "at least as good as" and "no better than" sets are closed in R^n_+.

Informally, a set in R^n is open if it does not contain any of the points on its boundary. It is closed if it does contain all points on its boundary. Stating that both "at least as good as" and "no better than" are closed, ensures that their complements are open. In other words, the boundary points between "at least as good as", $>=(x)$, and "worse than", $<<(x)$, are entirely contained within "at least as good as". Conversely, the boundary points between "no better than", $=<$, and "preferred to", $>>$, are entirely contained in "no better than".

HCI Implication 4   *The Continuity Axiom ensures topological nicety and is neutral with respect to Human Computer Interaction.*

Our analysis has failed to find any immediate implications of the Continuity Axiom for Human Computer Interaction. However, it does have important theoretical implications for the development of consumer theory. In particular, it helps to ensure that sudden reversals of preference do not occur [6].

4.2   Strict Monotonicity

The remaining axioms that can be applied to the preference relation are intended to reflect particular assumptions about consumer, or user, tastes. In most consumer theory there is an assumption that more is always better than less. This has become formalised by the axiom of strict monotonicity. It can be expressed as an assumption that if one bundle of commodity X contains at least as much of every commodity in y, then the first bundle is at least as good as the second.

Axiom 5   For all x_0, $x_1 \in R^n_+$ if x_0 is greater than or equal to x_1 then $x_0 >= x_1$ while if x_0 is strictly greater than x_1 then $x_0 >> x_1$. Note here that the $>=$ symbol stands for the preference relation.

This axiom and the continuity axiom also help to avoid the paradox in Section 4. If the elements of the consumption set were represented by vectors that modelled the amount of incoming and outgoing email then users would always prefer situations in which there were more incoming and outgoing messages. However, this interpretation again illustrates some of the concerns that arise when investigating the mathematical foundations of consumer theory.

HCI Implication 5   *The Axiom of Strict Monotonicity fails to characterise certain aspects of mobile interaction in which more communication can rationally be seen to be a worse situation than one in which connectivity is reduced.*

This observation might, at first, be seen to be paradoxical. However, a number of authors have written about the potential disruption that is caused by bringing mobile telephones and other networked computing devices into complex working environments [13]. Other authors have written about the social consequences of users being forced to reveal their geographical location in wireless LANs as they move from cell to cell [14]. These social and contextual factors can lead rational users to deliberately disconnect from a network. In other words, they may prefer less connectivity rather than more and hence may reject the Axiom of Strict Monotonicity.

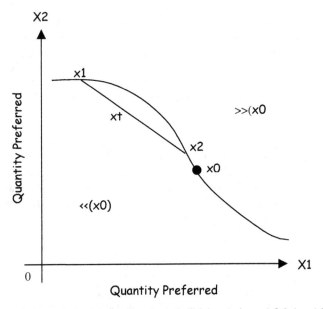

Fig. 5. Example Preference Topology Satisfying Axioms 1,2,3,4 and 5

Previous paragraphs have argued that the Axiom of Strict Monotonicity need not be regarded in the same way as the previous 4 axioms because its role in consumer theory is to model user tastes towards particular commodities. It should, therefore, not be surprising that it is inappropriate for certain aspects of human computer interaction with distributed systems. With this in mind, Figure 5 illustrates the impact that Axiom 5 has upon the topology that was introduced in Figure 4.

As can be seen, continuity and then mononicity first bound and then reduce the indifference region that was shown in the previous example. Axiom 5 ensures that that the indifference sets in R^2_+ cannot bend upwards or contain positively sloped segments and that all preferred sets are strictly above indifference sets.

4.3   Strict Convexity

The final axiom that is, typically, introduced to model preferences between commodities is known as Strict Convexity. It is intended to ensure that the resulting topologies assume the same "convex to the origin" shape that can be seen in the utility curves of Figures 1, 2 and 3. The impact of this axiom can be seen by looking at the indifference points x_1 and x_2 in Figure 5. These are indifferent because they lie on the same boundary between $>>(x)$ and $<<(x)$ that x_0 occupies [6]. From this we can conclude that $x_1 >= x_2$, however, convex combinations of these points, such as x_t will lie within $<<(x_0)$ and hence violate Axiom 6.

Axiom 6   If $x_1 \neq x_0$ and $x_1 >= x_0$ then $tx_1 + (1-t)x_0 >> x_0$ for all $t \in [0, 1]$

In terms of microeconomic theory, Axiom 6 leads to the principle of diminishing marginal rate of substitution in consumption. One way of thinking about the implications of Strict Convexity is that it reflects a predisposition or bias on the part of the user to prefer "mixed" bundles of consumables rather than the extremes that appear at either end of the curve in Figure 5. As a result, this axiom models users who take a balanced view of trading finite time or battery power for remote information. If they had little battery power left then they would be less likely to exhaust it with further network interaction than if they had a plentiful supply.

HCI implication 6   *The Axiom of Strict Convexity reflects a "balanced" approach to resource allocation or substitution. As one of the preference axioms of taste, however, it need not be appropriate as a model for all forms of human computer interaction.*

Again, however, it is possible to identify exceptions to this axiom. For instance, we have seen instances in which users will trade the last of their battery life to access a remote resource. This represents a novel form of what Reason has referred to as encysting within other domains of human computer interaction [15]. The user becomes so preoccupied with particular sub-tasks that they lose their overall awareness of the overall success or failure of their interaction.

5   Conclusion

A number of research groups have exploited utility curves to model interaction with distributed systems [5, 10]. However, much of this previous work has rested upon implicit assumptions about properties of the preference relation that underpins modern consumer theory. This paper has examined the mathematical basis of the preference relation. The analysis helps to identify the implications that preference axioms have for the application of consumer theory to interface development. In particular, we have argued that:

1. The Completeness Axiom makes an unrealistic assumption that the user will be able to distinguish between the different strategies or plans that they can exploit during interaction.
2. The Reflexivity Axiom states that the value of any good or service is at least as good as itself. This implies that each data source must be modelled as a distinct commodity even if the information that they contain is identical.
3. The Transitivity Axiom cannot easily be sustained because empirical studies have shown that preference paradoxes often arise when users do not fully understand their technical environment or when users are faced with numerous distractions and delays.
4. The Continuity Axiom ensures topological nicety and is neutral with respect to Human Computer Interaction.

5. The Axiom of Strict Monotonicity fails to characterise certain aspects of mobile interaction in which more communication can rationally be seen to be a worse situation than one in which connectivity is reduced.
6. The Axiom of Strict Convexity reflects a "balanced" approach to resource allocation or substitution. As one of the preference axioms of taste, however, it need not be appropriate as a model for all forms of human computer interaction.

There is, however, one important caveat. We have not argued for a one-to-one relationship between the preference relation, >=, and utility curves, such as those shown in Figures 1, 2 and 3. The preference relation defines an ordering over the elements of the consumption set, X. Utility functions simply represent those preferences by mapping preference rankings onto a simple numeric scale. More preferred commodities are assigned higher values while less preferred commodities are assigned lower numbers. Indifferent commodities are assigned equivalent values. Having raised this caveat, it is important to state that the utility function reflects the complete, reflexive, transitive, continuous and strictly monotonic properties of the preference relation. Hence our analysis applies both to the preference relation and to the utility functions that reflect that relation.

Utility functions are increasingly being used as a tool to model human computer interaction. Our analysis has shown that there are a number of theoretical issues that remain to be addressed before these techniques can accurately capture the diverse patterns of interaction that are observed in many mobile applications. In particular, our initial experience with developing interfaces for wireless LANs has shown that the axioms of rationality often do not apply to users who are struggling to come to terms with new styles of interaction. Similarly, the axioms of taste only go part of the way towards constructing valid models of the ways in which users choose to expend finite battery power and communications bandwidth in mobile environments.

This paper has assessed the theoretical foundations of utility theory as a means of supporting interface development. This research has helped to identify a number of areas for further work. For example, we have not discussed the factors that might directly or indirectly influence the individual preferences denoted by >=. Some of these factors stem from subjective attitudes towards the costs and benefits of particular interactions. Others can be influenced by systems engineering. For example, users may associate higher utility with a retrieval task if they can be sure that data has recently been updated. The interaction between these subjective attitudes and particular systems engineering architectures has not been widely explored.

There are other areas for further research. Our work has been motivated by a concern to improve our understanding of quality of service issues within a mobile environment. However, this research clearly has implications for other forms of human-computer interaction. Utility theory has been applied to represent and reason about the impact of retrieval delays over the Web. It has been used to develop the models of subjective value that support "intelligent" advice giving systems. It has also been integrated into ATM architectures to ensure that users' requirements are met by the underlying network protocols. Our work has begun to question the theoretical foundations of this related work. This does not imply that these applications are fundamentally flawed. It can, however, be argued that we only have a limited understanding of the reasons why certain utility curves offer such predictive value for these applications. Perhaps more importantly, our work has shown that these benefits cannot be relied upon to guide the detailed development of mobile human-computer interaction.

6   References

1. C.W. Johnson, Decision Theory And Safety-Critical Interfaces. In K. Nordby and P. H. Helmersen and D. Gilmore and S.A. Arnesen (eds.) Human Computer Interaction - Interact '95,Chapman and Hall, London, United Kingdom, 127-132, 1995.
2. J.G. March and H.A. Simon, Organisations, Wiley, New York, United States of America, 1958.
3. C. Puppe, Distorted Probabilities And Choice Under Risk, Springer Verlag, Lecture Notes In Economics And Mathematical Systems, No 363, Berlin, Germany, 1991.
4. E. Horvitz and G. Rutledge, Time-Dependent Utility and Action Under Uncertainty, Proc. 7th Conf. on Uncertainty in Artificial Intelligence, Morgan Kaufmann, San Mateo, CA, 1991, pp. 151-158.
5. C.W. Johnson (1995), Time and the Web: Representing and Reasoning about Temporal Properties of Interaction with Distributed Systems. In M. Kirby, A. Dix and J. Finlay (eds.), People and Computers X, 39-50, Cambridge University Press, Cambridge, United Kingdom.
6. G.A. Jehle and P.J. Reny, Microeconomic Theory, Addison Wesley, Reading, MA, 1998.
7. P. O'Donnel and S. Draper. How Machine Delays Change User Strategies. Adjunct Proceedings to HCI'95, British Computer Society, London. 1995.
8. M.R. Ebling, Translucent Cache Management for Mobile Computing. Doctoral Dissertation, School of Computer Science, Carnegie Mellon University, Pittsburgh, PA, March 1998.
9. C.W. Johnson, The Ten Golden Rules for Providing Video over the Web. In. C. Forsythe, E. Grose and J. Ratner (eds.) Human Factors and the Web, Lawrence Erlbaum, New York, United States of America, 1998.
10. E. Horvitz and T. Paek, A Computational Architecture for Conversation. In J. Kay (ed.), Proceedings of User Modelling 1999. Springer Verlag, 1999.
11. N. Davies, G. Blair, K. Cheverst and A. Friday, Supporting Adaptive Services in a Heterogeneous Mobile Environment. In L.-F. Cabrera and M. Satyanarayanan (eds.), Proc. Workshop on Mobile Computing Systems and Applications (MCSA) Santa Cruz, CA, U.S., IEEE Computer Society Press, Pages 153-157. December 1994.
12. K. Vaananen-Vainio-Mattila and S. Ruuska, User Needs for Mobile Communication Devices: Requirements Gathering and Analysis through Contextual Inquiry. In C.W. Johnson (ed.), Proc. of the First Workshop on HCI and Mobile Devices. Department of Computing Science, Glasgow University. Technical Report (GAAG-98-1), 1998.
13. P. Johnson, Exploiting Context in HCI Design for Mobile Systems. In C.W. Johnson (ed.), Proc. of the First Workshop on HCI and Mobile Devices. Department of Computing Science, Glasgow University. Technical Report (GAAG-98-1), 1998.
14. C.W. Johnson, The Impact of Time and Place on the Operation of Mobile Computing Devices, In H. Thimbleby, B. O'Conaill and P. Thomas (eds.), People and Computers XII: Proceedings of HCI'97, Springer Verlag, London, United Kingdom, 175-190, 1997.
15. J. Reason, Human Error, Cambridge University Press, Cambridge, UK, 1980.

A Framework for the Combination and Characterization of Output Modalities

F. Vernier and L. Nigay

CLIPS-IMAG, BP 53, 38041 Grenoble cedex 9, France
Tel. +33 4 76 51 44 40, Fax: +33 4 76 44 66 75
{Frederic.Vernier, Laurence.Nigay}@imag.fr

Abstract. This article proposes a framework that will help analyze current and future output multimodal user interfaces. We first define an output multimodal system. We then present our framework that identifies several different combinations of modalities and their characteristics. This framework assists in the selection of the most appropriate modalities for achieving efficient multimodal presentations. The discussion is illustrated with MulTab (**Mul**timodal **Tab**le), an output multimodal system for managing large tables of numerical data.

1 Introduction

The use of multiple modalities such as speech and gesture opens a vast world of possibilities in user interface design. The goal of multimodal interfaces is to extend the sensory-motor capabilities of computer systems to better match the natural communication means of human beings. The purpose is to enhance interaction between the user and the computer by utilizing appropriate modalities to improve:
- the information bandwidth between the human and the computer; that is the amount of information being communicated;
- the signal-to-noise ratio of conveyed information; that is the rate of information useful for the task being performed [20].

Although the potential for innovation is high, the current understanding of how to design, build, and evaluate multimodal user interfaces is still primitive. The power and versatility of multimodal interfaces result in an increased complexity that current design methods and tools do not address appropriately. This problem is exacerbated by the proliferation of new input and output modalities, such as the phycons [11] or ambient modalities [15].

In this paper, we focus on the design of output multimodal interfaces and we define a framework for characterizing output modalities and their combinations. This framework provides a better understanding of modality characteristics and of their combinations, and as such represents a step towards achieving the potential gain of multiple output modalities. Our unified framework coherently organizes the elements useful for the two key design issues of multimodal output user interfaces: the selection of modalities based on their characteristics and the combination of modalities for the design of a coordinated output interface. Combinations and characteristics of

P. Palanque and F. Paternò (Eds.): DSV-IS 2000, LNCS 1946, pp. 35–50, 2001.
© Springer-Verlag Berlin Heidelberg 2001

output modalities are useful for eliciting design rules, for classifying existing output systems and for evaluating the usability of a system.

The structure of the paper is as follows: First, we clarify the notion of modality using the concepts of interaction language and physical device. Indeed, as pointed out in [6], differences of opinion exist as to the meaning of the term "multimodal". Having defined an input/output modality, we present the main steps in the design of an output multimodal interface. After positioning our study in this design process, we present the two spaces of our framework: combinations of modalities and characteristics of a modality. The discussion will be illustrated with MulTab, a multimodal system that we developed.

2   Output Multimodality

Multimodality has mainly been studied for input (from user to system) interfaces [22, 23, 25], by utilizing multiple input devices for exploiting several human sensory systems. The "put that there" paradigm which emphasizes the synergistic use of speech and gesture is one such attempt. In addition to the fact that fewer studies focus on output multimodality, the related studies mainly investigate a single output modality including speech synthesis, natural language text generation and network diagram generation. There is consequently a crucial need for a model of output multimodal user interfaces. Indeed such output interfaces are very complex and nowadays their design and implementation rely on empirical skills of the designers and developers. Moreover, we believe that output multimodality is a more difficult problem to address than input multimodality. For the case of multiple input modalities, the user decides which modalities to employ and their function (complementary or redundant use) based on his expertise and the context. For outputs, the designer or the system itself must be able to perform such choices and combinations based on knowledge of the concepts to be presented, interaction context, available output devices as well information about the user.

In the literature, multimodality is mainly used for inputs (from user to system) and multimedia for outputs (from system to user), showing that the terminology is still ambiguous. In the general sense, a multimodal system supports communication with the user through different modalities such as voice, graphics, and text [7]. Literally, "multi" means "more than one" and the term "modal" may cover the notion of "modality" as well as that of "mode".
1. Modality refers to the type of communication channel used to convey information. It also specifies the way an idea is expressed or perceived [8].
2. Mode refers to a state that determines the way information is interpreted for conveying meaning.

In a communication act, whether it is between humans or between a computer system and a user, both the modality and the mode will come into play. The modality defines the type of data exchanged whereas the mode determines the context in which the data is interpreted. Thus, if we take a system-centered view, output multimodality is the capacity of the system to communicate with a user along different types of communication channels and to convey meaning automatically. We observe that both multimedia and multimodal systems use multiple communication channels. But in addition, a multimodal system is able to model the content of the information at a high level of abstraction. A multimodal system thus strives for meaning.

Our definition of. output multimodality is system-oriented. A user-centered perspective may lead to a different definition. For instance, according to our system-centered view, electronic voice mail is not multimodal. It constitutes a multimedia user interface only. Indeed, it allows the user to send mail that may contain graphics, text and voice messages. It does not however extract meaning from the information it carries. In particular, voice messages are recorded and replayed but not interpreted. On the other hand, from the user's point of view, this system is perceived as being multimodal: The user employs different modalities (referring to the human senses) to interpret mail messages.

In order to support our definition of output multimodality, we define an output modality as the coupling of a physical device d with an interaction language L: <d, L> [23].

- A physical device is an artifact of the system that delivers information. Examples of output devices include the loudspeaker and screen.

- An interaction language defines a set of well-formed expressions (i.e., assembly of symbols according to some convention) that convey meaning. The generation of a symbol, or a set of symbols, involves actions on physical devices. Examples of interaction languages include pseudo-natural language and graphical animation.

Our definition of an output modality enables us to extend the range of possibilities for output multimodality. Indeed a system can be multimodal without having several output devices. A system using the screen as the unique output device is multimodal whenever it employs several output interaction languages. We claim that using one device and multiple interaction languages raises the same design and engineering issues as using multiple modalities based on different devices.

Having defined an output multimodal system, we can now describe the different stages for achieving efficient multimodal presentations.

3   Output Multimodal Interface Design

The design of output multimodal interfaces requires the selection and the combination of multiple modalities. Such selection of atomic or composite output modalities can be performed:

1. by the designer while designing the system,
2. by the user while using the system,
3. by the system while running.

In case 2, we refer to the system as being *adaptable*. Case 2 must be related to case 1 because *adaptability* implies that the designer has previously selected a range of candidate modalities. In case 3 we call the system *adaptive (adaptivity)*.

Our discourse here is general and we present the steps for achieving a multimodal presentation. Three main steps are traditionally identified. These steps can be performed through design (by the designer) or through generation (by the system). These steps are:

1. content selection, which identifies what to say,
2. modality allocation, which identifies in what modalities to say it,
3. modality realization, which identifies how to say it in these modalities.

Within the design process or generation process, our framework is dedicated to the modality allocation step: i.e., the selection of an atomic or composite modality. In particular, our framework identifies a set of combinations of modalities and a set of characterizations of a modality. While the combination space enables the definition of new composite modalities, the characterization space helps in the choice of a modality, either atomic or composite. In the following paragraphs, we first present our combination space of output modalities and then our characterization space. We then illustrate our framework using our MulTab system.

4   Combination Space

Although each modality can be used independently within a multimodal system, the availability of several modalities in a system naturally leads to the issue of their combined usage. The combined usage of multiple modalities opens a vastly augmented world of possibilities in user interface design.

Several frameworks addressed the issue of relationships between modalities. In the TYCOON framework [18], six types of cooperation between modalities are defined, a modality being defined as a process receiving and producing chunks of information:

1. Equivalence involves the option of choosing between several modalities that can all equally well convey a particular chunk of information.

2. Specialization implies that specific kinds of information are always conveyed by the same modality.

3. Redundancy indicates that the same piece of information is conveyed by several modalities.

4. Complementarity denotes several modalities that convey complementary chunks of information.

5. Transfer implies that a chunk of information processed by one modality is then treated by another modality.

6. Concurrency describes the case of several modalities conveying independent information in parallel.

Each of these six types of cooperation is studied according to the usability criterion that it helps achieve. Such usability criteria are therefore called "goals of cooperation". The CARE properties define another framework for reasoning about multimodal interaction from the perspectives of both the user and the system: These properties are the Complementarity, Assignment, Redundancy, and Equivalence that may occur between the modalities available in a multimodal user interface. The notions of equivalence, assignment (or specialization), redundancy, and complementarity were primarily introduced by Martin [18]. We define these four notions as relationships between devices and interaction languages and between interaction languages and tasks. In [9], we formally define the CARE properties and showed how these properties affect the usability of the interaction. Finally, in our multi-feature system design space [23] and in our MSM framework [8], we emphasized the temporal aspects of the combination, a dimension orthogonal to the CARE properties.

Our combination space encompasses the types of combination presented in TYCOON, CARE and MSM, and identifies new ones. Our space is organized along two axes. The first axis considers the aspects that are combined. We first identify four aspects that can be combined:

1. Time: temporal combination
2. Space: spatial combination
3. Interaction language: syntactic combination
4. Semantic: semantic combination

Temporal and spatial combinations have been studied for combining output modalities [24]. We then introduce one aspect of combination, namely syntactic combination, which is based on our definition of a modality: an output modality being the coupling of an interaction language L with a physical device d: <d, L>. These three first aspects of combination (i.e., temporal, spatial and syntactic) focus on a modality as a vehicle of information. The last aspect that must be considered while combining modalities is the relationship between the meaning of information conveyed by the composite modalities. This last aspect is called semantic combination.

The second axis ranges over a set of combination schemas, as presented in Figures 1-5. These schemas use the five Allen relationships [1] to provide a means of combining multiple modalities into a composite modality.

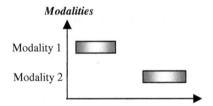

Fig. 1. Schema for distant modality combination.

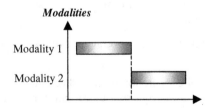

Fig. 2. Schema for modality combination with one point of contact.

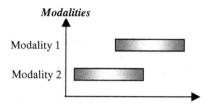

Fig. 3. Schema for modality combination with a non-empty intersection.

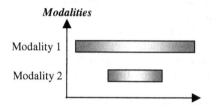

Fig. 4. Schema for modality combination with inclusion.

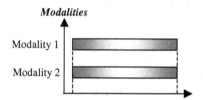

Fig. 5. Schema for modality combination with the same characteristics.

While the combination schemas define how to combine several modalities, the combination aspects determine what to combine. Our two axes (schemas and aspects of combination) are orthogonal: Table 1 names each type of combination obtained by blending these two axes. In the following paragraphs, we detail these combinations, our argumentation being based on the four identified aspects (i.e. (temporal, spatial, syntactic and semantic)).

Table 1. Applying the five combination schemas to the four combination aspects (temporal, spatial, syntactic and semantic).

Combination schemas

Combination aspects	Temporal	Anachronism	Sequence	Concomitance	Coincidence	Parallelism
	Spatial	Separation	Adjacency	Intersection	Overlaid	Collocation
	Syntactic	Difference	Completion	Divergence	Extension	Twin
	Semantic	Concurrency	Complementary	Complementary and Redundancy	Partial Redundancy	Total Redundancy

4.1   Temporal Combination of Modalities

As shown in Table 1, sequential and parallel combinations are two types of temporal combination that have been studied in the literature [8, 18, 22]. For example in [22], one dimension of the design space, called "use of modalities" primarily covers the absence or presence of parallelism at the user interface. We identify here three new temporal combinations: anachronism, concomitance and coincidence.

Two modalities are combined anachronously if there is a temporal gap between their usage. Anachronism and sequence are distinguished by the size of the temporal window between the usage of the two modalities. This size is defined by the designer. For example the designer can consider that two modalities are used anachronously if the temporal gap is longer than the perception time for causality (longer than a second). Concretely two sonic messages are perceived as independent if there is more than a second between the end of the first message and the beginning of the second one.

Two modalities are concomitant when one modality replaces another one with a time interval during which the two modalities coexist. As for anachronism, the designer must define the size of the time interval that we describe as transition time. This combination is important in helping the user understand the transition between two modalities and delegating part of the cognitive load to the perceptual human process. A concomitant combination implies that the two devices corresponding to the two modalities can function in parallel.

Finally, the coincidence of two modalities is when one modality is only used in the context of another one. Such a combination is necessary to implement a modality that can only be used with another one. If the main modality can be terminated, two design solutions are possible:

1. The main modality cannot be stopped if the included modality is in use.

2. Terminating usage of the main modality implies terminating usage of the included one.

For example let us consider a form, defining one modality, and a dialog box, defining a second modality. The dialog box is opened from the form. Two design solutions are possible. On the one hand, the form cannot be closed if the dialog box is not closed first. On the other hand, if the form is closed, all the dialog boxes opened from this form are automatically closed.

4.2   Spatial Combination of Modalities

Spatial combination is important for output modalities, especially when considering multiple graphical modalities on screen. Multiple modalities, using the same device (screen or loudspeaker, etc.) and sharing the same location, are possible design solutions because human perception is able to acquire several pieces of information in parallel using a single human sense (sight, hearing, etc.). Different sounds can be played in parallel and distinguished by the user [4]. Nevertheless for the user the perceptual space (source of the sounds and their propagation space) is the same. Likewise transparency is one mechanism for combining two graphical modalities sharing the same space on screen.

On the one hand, two modalities can be used separately, and consequently do not share a common space. Thus the user will perceive the two modalities as separate. On the other hand, the four other spatial combinations of modalities will likely be perceived as related, as explained in the psychological guide of perception presented in [19]. Adjacent modalities share one point or one edge in space. Intersected, overlaid and collocated modalities define three types of transparency. A magic lens [26] defines one modality overlaid on another modality used for displaying the background. Two magic lenses intersecting on top of a background illustrate the intersected combination. Finally our mirror pixel mechanism [27] is an example of collocated combination: Here two modalities are used at the same place (the full screen) to display a document and the video of the user (a camera pointing to the user).

While separate modalities are likely to be used as the vehicles of independent information, the four other spatial combinations will imply some dependencies between the conveyed information. The later combinations are also useful for saving space (limited space of the screen for example) but will also engender perceptual problems. In particular, visual continuity [24] is an ergonomic criterion that must be carefully studied when considering such spatial combinations.

4.3   Syntactic Combination of Modalities

In paragraph 2, an output modality is defined by the couple (physical device, interaction language). Syntactic combinations consider the interaction language of the modality (i.e., the logical form of the modality).

Two combined modalities can nevertheless have different syntaxes. For example in WIP [2], one modality is based on the English grammar (pseudo natural language) whereas another one is graphically depicted. An example of this syntactic combination (named difference) is seen in the following scenario: "The on/off switch is located in the upper left part of the picture" displayed above a picture.

Two modalities complete each other at the syntactic level when their corresponding syntaxes are combined to form a new syntax. The following generated sentence is one example of such a completion: "the date is 04/09/2000". Here two modalities are used, one based on pseudo natural language and one dedicated to displaying dates. The two corresponding syntaxes are combined to form a new syntax.

Two modalities are divergent when their corresponding interaction languages partially share the same syntax. For example speech synthesis and textual natural language generation correspond to two modalities that can be combined in a syntactically divergent way. Indeed the syntax of the two interaction languages is nearly the same, but spoken language is more informal than written language.

The syntactic combination named extension corresponds to two combined modalities where one modality has the syntax of its interaction language related to the syntax of the interaction language of the second modality. For example in [3], the generation of natural language text is combined with a text formatting modality, such as bullets corresponding to a sequence in the generated text.

Finally two syntactic twin modalities have interaction languages sharing the same syntax. This is the case of two modalities based on pseudo natural language: One of the modalities is related to the screen and the generated sentence is displayed while the other one is linked to the loudspeaker and the sentence is spoken. The CUBRICON system illustrates such a combination [21].

4.4   Semantic Combination of Modalities

The most studied aspect of combination is the semantic one, where one considers the meaning of the conveyed information along the modalities. The most common combinations are those of complementarity and redundancy. One example of complementarity can be seen in the following sentence, which is displayed above a picture: "The on/off switch is located in the upper left part of the picture". The meaning conveyed by the textual modality and the graphical modality are complementary. One example of redundancy consists of the same text, displayed on screen and vocally (speech synthesis) [21]. In contrast to complementarity and redundancy, concurrent combination of modalities implies that the conveyed information has no related meaning. In addition to the well-known complementarity, redundancy and concurrency, we introduce two new types of combination, namely Complementarity-Redundancy and Partial redundancy.

"Complementary-redundant" modalities convey information that is partially redundant and complementary. Multiple graphical views often use such a combination to display two different attributes of the same piece of information. One part is redundant to help the user understand the semantic link between the visual presentations. For example in the MagniFind system [16], two views of a hierarchy of folders and files are displayed on screen: one view (one modality) displays the folders and files as lists and sub-lists, whereas the second one depicts them in the form of a hyperbolic tree. The two modalities are redundant because they both display the same list of folders in different ways at the highest level of the hierarchy. But the modalities are also complementary because one displays the precise information about a subpart of the hierarchy while the other one displays the full hierarchy without details.

Partially redundant modalities describe two combined modalities where one conveys a subpart of the information that the second one conveys. This is for example the case of a thumbnail view combined with a global view.

4.5   Aspects and Schemas of Combination: A Unified Framework

The four identified aspects and five schemas that we have identified define a unified framework that encompasses the existing frameworks, including TYCOON, CARE and MSM. Each combination of modalities can be characterized in terms of the four aspects and the five schemas.

The combination of modalities gives birth to new composite modalities. We now need to characterize an atomic or composite modality in order to be able to select the most appropriate one. The next paragraph presents our characterization space.

5   Characterization Space

Characterization of atomic or composite modalities is necessary to be able to select them for an efficient multimodal presentation. As explained in paragraph 3, such selection is either performed by the designer or by the system itself (adaptativity). One characterization space of output modalities has been proposed in [5]. Four boolean properties, defined as modality profiles, are presented:

- Static or dynamic
- Linguistic or non-linguistic

- Analogue or non-analogue
- Arbitrary or non-arbitrary

Static/Dynamic property refers to the articulatory level (the physical form of the modality: the device d, part of a modality <d, L>) while the Linguistic/Non-linguistic property corresponds to the syntactic level (the logical form of the modality: the inter-action language L, part of a modality <d, L>). Analogue/Non-analogue and Arbi-trary/Non-Arbitrary properties are related to the interpretation process and therefore the semantic level. We introduce three new characteristics.

- Deformed or non-deformed

- Local or global

- Precise or vague

The deformed/Non-deformed property is related to the syntactic level. Indeed a de-formed modality is a modality that must be combined at the syntactic level as an ex-tension of a non-deformed modality. For example let us consider the written sentence "r u happy?". This defines a modality that is based on a pseudo natural language mo-dality "are you happy?" and a deformation modality, i.e. two modalities syntactically combined by extension.

The two other properties are related to the semantic level. For a given set of infor-mation to be presented, the Local/Global property refers to the range of information conveyed at a given time using the modality. If the user perceives all the pieces of information, the modality is global. If the user perceives only a subset of the informa-tion, the modality is local. In the software "PowerPoint", the slide by slide view is local while the slide sorter view is global. For each piece of information to be pre-sented, the second property, Precise/Vague, characterizes the precision of a modality. If the modality conveys all the information about one element necessary for the task to be performed, it is a precise one, otherwise it is a vague modality. For the editing task, the slide by slide view is precise whereas the slide sorter view is a vague modal-ity.

As shown by the seven properties, a modality can be characterized at three levels, the articulatory, syntactic and semantic levels (power of expression). One problem that we have still not addressed is the characterization of composite modalities: for example the characterization of an arbitrary modality combined with an analogue modality. Nevertheless, the seven properties define a starting point for characterizing modalities, in order to define design rules for their selection.

Neither our combination nor characterization spaces directly provide guidelines for the design of an efficient multimodal presentation. For example a semantic comple-mentary combination is not better than a semantic redundant combination, and an analogue modality is not better than an arbitrary modality. Our two spaces are the foundations for defining design rules. To identify design rules, we base our approach on ergonomic criteria [13].

For example let us consider the ergonomic observability criterion: Because of the limited size of the screen, observability of a large set of elements is impossible in its entire scope and detail. One interesting solution to the problem is to make observable one subset of the elements in detail while maintaining the global set of elements ob-servable without detail, using compression procedures: This approach is called "Focus + Context". It involves a combination of a local/precise modality with a global/vague one. The combination is defined as: (Temporal-Parallelism, Spatial-Adjacency, Syntactic-Difference, Semantic-Complementary).

Another example of design rules, related to the ergonomic insistence criterion, consists of an (Syntactic-Difference, Semantic-Redundancy) combination of modalities: The same information is conveyed twice by both modalities, which are based on different interaction languages. This design rule is closely related to the urgency rule[14].

Having presented our combination and characterization spaces, we now illustrate them using our MulTab system. MulTab (Multimodal Table) is an output multimodal system for managing large tables of numerical data.

6   The MulTab System

MulTab is dedicated to managing large tables (20 000 cells) of numerical data along several output modalities, all based on the same output device, the screen. One main modality displays the entire table, M1, as shown in Figure 6. Because the cells are too small, the numerical data cannot be displayed. Therefore this modality is global and vague. Another modality, M2, is used to color each cell according to the numerical data. This modality is again global and vague but less vague than the previous one, M1. In addition this modality is arbitrary, because it is based on an arbitrary mapping between the colors and the data values. A slider at the bottom of the table (Figures 6 and 7) enables the user to define which cells are colored. This slider is a non-arbitrary output modality, M3, that explains the mapping function between the colors and the numerical data. Let us now consider the combinations between these three modalities. The combination between M1 and M2 is defined as follows:

- Temporal-Parallelism
- Spatial-Collocation
- Syntactic-Difference
- Semantic-Complementary
  The combination of M2 and M3 is described as:
- Temporal-Parallelism
- Spatial-Adjacency
- Syntactic-Twin
- Semantic-Complementary

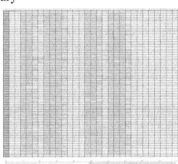

Fig. 6. Global view of the table and coloration of the cells.

In order to complement the vague modalities (M1 and M2), one local and deformed but precise modality is provided, as shown in Figure 7. This modality, M4, displays a part of the table with the numerical values of the cells. This modality is linguistic. The combination of modality M1 with modality M4 is described as:

- Temporal-Parallelism
- Spatial-Adjacency
- Syntactic-Extension
- Semantic-Complementary

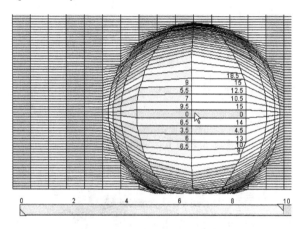

Fig. 7. A precise view (one modality) combined with the global view of the table (another modality).

Several precise modalities such as M4, can be used in parallel. As shown in Figure 8, multiple foci [17] within the table are useful for localization of a particular cell and comparison of the values of cells. A new focus is created from the main focus by direct manipulation. Each focus stems from the main focus. The foci move (lines and columns) as the main focus is moved. When the user moves the main focus, all the related foci are automatically moved accordingly (spatial constraints). Such combination is described as:

- Temporal-Coincident
- Spatial-Variable, depending on the user
- Syntactic-Twin
- Semantic-Complementary

Variability in spatial combinations ensures coverage of all five schemas. This allows us to define the intersection spatial combination shown in Figure 9.

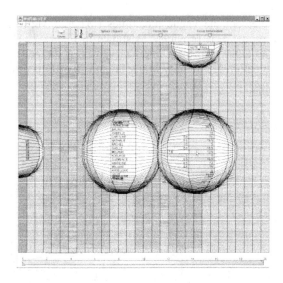

Fig. 8. Four foci within the table.

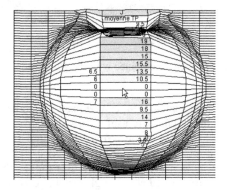

Fig. 9. Spatial intersection of two foci (two modalities).

In the design of MulTab we also studied the shape of the region of focus. The spherical shape of the focal region illustrated in Figures 7 and 8 is based on the fish-eye view study of [12]. In [10], two shapes have been experimentally compared in the context of the fovea system, shown in Figure 10. One focal region was circular (on the left in Figure 10) and one was rectangular (on the right in Figure 10). Results of the experiment showed that the users preferred the circular shape but were more efficient using the rectangular shape. In our system VITESSE [24], we also experimentally studied the deformed shapes. One main result is that the users preferred analogue deformation such as the spherical shape instead of non-analogue ones such as our cartesian modality that does not correspond to an existing shape in real life.

Fig. 10. Circular and rectangular focal regions in the Fovea system.

Such experimental results prompted us to display different shapes of the region of focus in MulTab and to let the user select the one of his choice. Using a slider, the user can smoothly change the shape of the focal region from spherical to rectangular. In Figure 11, we present three implemented shapes: spherical and pyramidal shapes respectively on the left and on the right, and a hybrid shape in the middle.

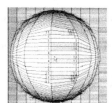
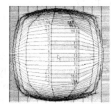
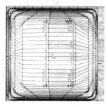

Fig. 11. Three shapes of the focal region in the MulTab system.

7   Summary of Contribution and Conclusions

We studied output multimodal interfaces from two points of view: the combination of modalities and the characterization of modalities. Our unified framework organizes in a coherent way the elements useful for the two key design issues of a multimodal output user interface: the selection of modalities based on their characteristics and the combination of modalities for the design of a coordinated output interface. Our framework is composed of two spaces. The first space, the combination space, is comprised of schemas and aspects: While the combination schemas define how to combine several modalities, the combination aspects determine what to combine. The second space, the characterization space, organizes the characteristics of a modality along three levels, articulatory, syntactic and semantic.

One contribution of our framework is to encompass and extend the existing design spaces for multimodality. However our combination and characterization spaces do not directly provide guidelines for the design of an efficient multimodal presentation. Our two spaces are the foundations for defining design rules. To identify design rules, we base our approach on ergonomic criteria. We have provided two design rules to illustrate our approach. Our future work will involve developing a coherent set of design rules based on our framework.

Acknowledgements. This work has been partly supported by the French Telecom-CNET Contract COMEDIR and by the French National Scientific Research Center (CNRS) with the SIIRI contract. Thanks to Emmanuel Dubois for his help in developing the MulTab system. Special thanks to G. Serghiou for reviewing the paper.

8   References

1. Allen, J.: Maintaining Knowledge about Temporal Intervals. Communications of the ACM, Vol. 26, No. 11, (1983) 832-843
2. André, E., Finkler, W., Graf, W., Rist, T., Schauder, A., Wahlster, W.:WIP: The Automatic Synthesis of Multimodal Presentations. In Maybury, M.T. (ed.): Intelligent Multimedia Interfaces. AAAI Press/MIT Press, Cambridge, Ma. (1993) 73-90
3. Arens, Y., Miller, L., Sondheimer, N.: Presentation Design Using an Integrated Knowledge Base. In Sullivan J., Tyler, S. (eds.): Intelligent User Interfaces. Frontier Series. New York: ACM Press (1991) 241-258
4. Beaudouin-Lafon, M., Gaver, W.: ENO: Synthesizing Structured Sound Spaces. Proceedings of UIST'94. ACM Press (1994) 49-57
5. Bernsen N.: A revised generation of the taxonomy of output modalities. Esprit Project AMODEUS. Working Paper RP5-TM-WP11 (1994)
6. Blattner, M.M, Dannenberg, R.G.: CHI'90 Workshop on multimedia and multimodal interface design. SIGCHI Bulletin 22, 2, (Oct. 1990) 54-58
7. Byte. Special Issue on Computing without Keyboard, (July 1990) 202-251
8. Coutaz, J., Nigay, L., Salber, D.: The MSM framework: A Design Space for Multi-Sensori-Motor Systems. Proceedings of EWHCI'93. Lecture Notes in Computer Science, Vol. 753. Springer-Verlag, Berlin Heidelberg New York (1993) 231-241
9. Coutaz, J., Nigay, L., Salber, D., Blandford, A., May, J., Young R.: Four easy pieces for assessing the usability of multimodal interaction: The CARE properties. Proceedings of Interact'95 (1995) 115-120
10. Coutaz et al.: CoMedi: Using Computer Vision to Support Awareness and Privacy in Mediaspaces. Proceedings (Extended Abstract) of CHI'99. ACM Press (1999) 13-16
11. Fitzmaurice, G., Ishii, H., Buxton, W.: Bricks: Laying the Foundations for Graspable User Interfaces. Proceedings of CHI'95. ACM Press (1995) 442-449
12. Furnas, G.: Generalized fisheye views. Proceedings of CHI'86. ACM Press (1986) 16-23
13. Gram, C., Cockton G. (ed.): Design Principles for Interactive Software. Chapter 2. Chapman & Hall (1984) 25-51
14. Hovy, E., Arens, Y.: On the Knowledge Underlying Multimedia Presentations. In Maybury, M.T. (ed.): Intelligent Multimedia Interfaces. AAAI Press/MIT Press, Cambridge, Ma. (1993) 280-306
15. Ishii, H., Ullmer, B.: Tangible Bits: Towards Seamless Interfaces between People, Bits and Atoms. Proceedings of CHI'97. ACM Press (1997) 234-241
16. Lamping, J., Rao R., Pirolli P.: A focus+context technique based on hyperbolic geometry for visualizing large hierarchies. Proceedings of CHI'95. ACM Press (1995) 401-408
17. Leung, Y., Apperley M.: A Review and Taxonomy of Distortion-Oriented Presentation Techniques. ACM Transactions on Computer-Human Interaction. Vol. 1, No. 2, (June 1994) 126-160.
18. Martin, J.C.: Six primitive types of cooperation for observing, evaluating and specifying cooperations. Proceedings of AAAI (1999)
19. May, J., Scott, S., Barnard, P.: Structuring Displays: a psychological guide. Eurographics Tutorial Notes Series. EACG: Geneva (1995)

20. Maybury, M.T. (Ed.): Intelligent Multimedia Interfaces. AAAI Press/MIT Press, Cambridge, Ma. (1993)
21. Neal, G., Shapiro, S. C.: Intelligent Multi-Media Interface Technology. In Sullivan J., Tyler, S. (eds.): Intelligent User Interfaces. Frontier Series. New York: ACM Press (1991) 11-43
22. Nigay, L., Coutaz, J.: A design space for multimodal interfaces: concurrent processing and data fusion. Proceedings of INTERCHI'93. ACM Press (1993) 172-178
23. Nigay, L., Coutaz, J.: A Generic Platform for Addressing the Multimodal Challenge. Proceedings of CHI'95. ACM Press (1995) 98-105
24. Nigay, L., Vernier, F.: Design Method of Interaction Techniques for Large Information Spaces. Proceedings of AVI'98. ACM Press (1998)
25. Oviatt, S.: Then myths of multimodal interaction. Communications of the ACM, Vol. 42, No. 11, (1999) 74-81
26. Stone, M., Fishkin, K., Bier E.: The Movable filter as a user interface tool. Proceedings of CHI'94. ACM Press (1994) 306-312
27. Vernier, F., Lachenal, C., Nigay, L., Coutaz, J.: Interface Augmentée par effet Miroir, . Proceedings of IHM'99. Cepadues (1999) 158-165

Specifying Multiple Time Granularities in Interactive Systems

Maria Kutar, Carol Britton, and Chrystopher Nehaniv

University of Hertfordshire
College Lane, Hatfield, Herts, AL10 9AB, UK
{M.S.1.Kutar, C.Britton, C.L.Nehaniv}@herts.ac.uk

Abstract. Time plays an important role in interactive systems, but can be difficult to specify, particularly where temporal properties exist at several different time granularities. The relationship between different time granularities is complex and translation between them can be difficult. In this paper, we discuss this relationship and highlight the way in which translation between different time granularities within a single specification may have important consequences for system behaviour. Using the notation TRIO≠, we provide examples from an interactive case study of the ways in which system behaviour may be influenced, and illustrate some of the potential difficulties which arise in the specification of temporal properties such as pace and regularity.

1   Introduction

'What then is time? If no one asks me, I know: if I wish to explain it to one that asketh I know not.'

St. Augustine's lament might equally be directed at temporal statements, as at the meaning of time itself. Such innocuous temporal expressions as 'every day' mask a number of potential meanings which are dependent on the exact context in which they occur. It is during the process of formalisation that the complexity of such temporal statements is revealed. This paper addresses the specification of interactive systems, where temporal requirements exist at multiple levels of granularity. It is recognised that time plays an important role in interactive systems [10] and that temporal properties of interactive systems have two main areas of relevance. Firstly, there may be temporal functional requirements which relate to system correctness, and in the second case, temporal properties of interaction can have an important bearing on usability issues. Temporal issues arise in interactive systems at a wide range of time granularities, from those at small scales such as what constitutes a double mouse-click, to larger granularities where we may be concerned with the rate of turnaround of messages over hours, days or even weeks [9]. The growth in interactive systems has resulted in increasing complexity with relation to time, and it is not uncommon for a number of granularities to be of importance in a single system. For example, in an e-commerce system we might be concerned with very small scale time constraints relating to system behaviour as the user browses the site, and also with turnaround times of minutes or hours for email messages. In addition we would need to consider peri-

P. Palanque and F. Paternò (Eds.): DSV-IS 2000, LNCS 1946, pp. 51–63, 2001.
© Springer-Verlag Berlin Heidelberg 2001

ods of days or weeks for goods to be delivered, and much longer time periods of many years relating to the customer and stock databases.

The specification of varied granularities of time may be achieved using a single granularity, but much of the natural understanding is lost. In addition, a number of issues relating to the relationship between different granularities must be considered. For example if I promise to telephone someone a week from today I do not mean that I will make the call in 7x24x60 minutes exactly, which is how I might (erroneously) represent the promise were I to consider only a single granularity of minutes. The way in which we move between different granularities can have important consequences for system behaviour, and this requires careful consideration of system properties. This is an issue which has been addressed in the field of real-time systems [2] [11][12], although it remains an emerging research area. In this paper we consider whether a notation developed for use in real-time systems, TRIO≠ [11], may be suitable for use in interactive systems, and suggests ways in which the notation may be enhanced in order to exploit the benefits in the field of interactive systems. In the rest of this paper we:

- Survey the relationship between time and interaction. (Section 2)
- Consider the relationship between different time granularities. (Section 3)
- Discuss how multiple time granularities may be combined in a single formal speci-fication, using a real-time notation. (Section 4)
- Highlight the ways in which system behavior is affected by the way in which we specify temporal properties, and on the way in which we translate between differ-ent time granularities. (Section 4)
- Identify directions for further research. (Section 5)

2   Time and Interaction

As we noted above, temporal issues can have a bearing on usability, as well as being relevant to a more specific notion of system correctness via the incorporation of strict time constraints. In this section we discuss the ways in which temporal issues can impact upon the quality of interaction, illustrating that it is important that we have a clear understanding of a system's temporal properties, in order to improve the quality of interaction.

Time plays a fundamental part in interaction between the user and system, and temporal properties of interaction should strongly influence interface requirements. An investigation into the way in which system delays affect user performance [18] suggested that users select different task strategies according to the length of the delay and concluded that "user performance is systematically affected by system delays". A follow up study [14] also concluded that delays alter user strategies, although this study did not confirm the ways in which strategies are influenced by delay. The sec-ond study suggested that the relationship between system delay and user strategy is more complex than a direct correlation between the length of the delay and the strat-egy selected.

The system's potential for supporting different user strategies (or goal trajectories), and the system's demand on user memory are significantly affected by timing, particularly system or user delay [15]. For example if the rate of interaction is too slow the user's execution/evaluation loop is broken [5]. This can lead to the user forgetting what must be done before the task is completed. The user generally expects feedback, informing him of what has happened, but at a very slow level of interaction it may be that nothing has yet happened. Thus, once a response finally arrives, the user must recall the appropriate context, which he may have difficulty doing. The relationship between time and interaction is of particular importance in multimedia applications, networked or distributed systems, and use of the World Wide Web. A small pilot study [1] surveyed and analysed the issues which Web users regard to be of central importance. The results indicated that users consider temporal issues to be intrinsic to usability. Below, we consider the ways in which time impacts upon interaction in more detail.

2.1   Two-Timing

Dix [3] has suggested that there may be no relation between the user's appreciation of time and the actual execution times of internal machine events. The traditional notion that increased computational power is all that is required to improve temporal qualities of interaction is questioned, and indeed in a further paper [6] it is noted that hardware insufficiencies have largely been overcome by advances in technology, only for us to be faced with similar temporal difficulties as a result of the increase in networking and its associated delays. Temporal issues are too entwined with usability for us to dismiss them on the assumption that technological advances will in themselves solve the problem. The fact that, in the user's view, the hardware hurdle has been overcome simply to be replaced by a network hurdle causing similar problems, emphasises the point that the user experience should be separated from hardware issues. In a technique referred to as 'two-timing', the temporal behaviour experienced by the user, at the interface, is viewed separately from the actual temporal behaviour of system computation [3]. This encourages us to think in terms of the realities faced by the user, rather than considering only those temporal performance issues that are directly under system control. If we consider the user's experience at the interface in isolation, we are forced to acknowledge the inadequacies present at the interface, and are able to consider what functionality might be included to help resolve the difficulties caused. This reinforces the need for usability issues to be considered in the early stages of development when such functionality can be smoothly integrated.

2.2   Pace and Rhythm

It has been argued that pace has an important bearing on the user's experience of interaction [4]. This is a temporal quality which is quite different to speed of response, the temporal property most often encountered in computer science. During interaction, channels of communication between the user and the computer are used not at a constant rate, but intermittently. Consequently, bandwidth, which assumes continuous transmission, is not necessarily an appropriate measure of communication. For example, when analysing the rate at which two individuals exchange emails, the pace of their interaction could be defined as the rate at which individual mail messages are produced. This would give us a somewhat different insight into the temporal properties of that relationship than if we were to consider bandwidth, which assumes continuous transmission, and could therefore tell us only about the average transmission of messages over a given period. Pace, the measure of the rate at which individual communications occur through a channel, is proposed as a primary property. This is an important issue with regard to interaction, which is both measurable and quantifiable, and may therefore provide a useful way of relating the pace, or potential pace, of the channels to the tasks the user must carry out.

Related to the notion of pace is the question of what time-scales humans can comfortably work to. It has been suggested [7] that our experience of whether timings are good or bad is affected by a combination of psycho-motor abilities and external stimuli. Rhythms are easier to deal with than occasional delays and it would seem that prediction is easier if we are dealing with regular time intervals. This means that regularity may be more relevant to the user's experience than the actual size of response time intervals. Thus a slower but consistent interface may be more effective than a generally fast but inconsistent one. The two studies which investigated the relationship between system delay and user strategy [18] [14] both found evidence that users adopt a pacing strategy, attempting to adjust their rhythm to match the system delay, although the studies were unclear as to how or why such a strategy is adopted. This confirms earlier evidence that where there is a predictable stimulus interval, which is relatively short, humans are able to reproduce that interval with a degree of accuracy [13] [19].

As we noted in the introduction to section two, a very slow pace of interaction can result in the user's execution/evaluation loop being broken. An alternative scenario to delayed feedback is that a response fails to arrive at all, requiring the user to both recognise that it has failed to arrive and to take appropriate action. Feedback is often delayed in open and cooperative systems. This obviously causes pace to slow and the user must therefore devise strategies to overcome the difficulties outlined. We must not only identify current user solutions for dealing with such problems, in order that new support strategies do not interfere with those (possibly subconscious) strategies currently in use, but also introduce new support systems to assist the user in overcoming these problems.

2.3   Granularity and Interaction

Temporal issues affect interaction at a number of different levels of granularity. At the fine-grained level we encounter issues such as status-status mappings [8], and the need for synchronisation of different multimedia modalities to ensure that audio and video channels perform in harmony. At the coarser-grained levels we may, for example, be concerned with the rate of turnaround of messages over a period of hours, days or weeks. Somewhere in between these two levels of granularity is the level at which the system makes demands on user memory: the recorded tolerance for response from command-line interfaces is 5 seconds [17]. We raise the issue of granularity of time here to illustrate that, when we consider the way in which temporal issues impact upon interaction, it is necessary to consider time scales which have not traditionally been seen as relevant in computer science.

Long-term interaction, where the rate of turnaround of individual messages may take hours, days or weeks, poses problems which are different from those found in higher pace interaction. People must remember that they have to do things, that other people should do things, and why things happen when they do [9]. A recurrent pattern of activity is identified - request, receipt, response, release (the four R's). To illustrate: someone sends you a message requiring your action (request), you receive the message (receipt), you perform some necessary action (response) and then file or dispose of things used in the process (release). The user may have difficulty in recalling the context of a delayed response, may forget to act themselves if they cannot react instantly to a request or, if an expected external response is not forthcoming, the whole interactive process may break down. This poses questions as to how the user may be assisted with coping strategies, particularly when automating a functioning paper-based system. If we identify the triggers for these different activities, and the areas where delays are likely to occur, we may be able to minimize the disruption caused, by incorporating support for alternative strategies.

2.4   Summary

It can be seen, therefore that temporal issues affect human computer interaction in a number of different ways. Temporal properties such as pace and rhythm may have a greater bearing on the user's interactive experience than simply speed of response, and therefore it is apparent that the temporal challenges in interaction may be quite different to those in other areas of computer science. The provision of alternative strategies for the user allows us to alleviate the difficulties caused by a lack of timeliness. This is of particular relevance where delays arise in areas which may be out of the control of the system owner, as is likely to be the case with e-commerce sites. Although we may be unable to eradicate such difficulties, we are able to minimise the disruption they cause through the introduction of further functionality.

If we are to provide solutions to the problems that the user experiences at the interface, arising from these temporal issues, then we must begin to give temporal issues higher priority than they are currently afforded in systems development. This is not to say that we should always try to incorporate strict temporal requirements, but that we must consider whether there are ways in we can reduce the impact on usability when delays and temporal inconsistencies are experienced. If this is to be done effectively then we must find ways in which we may fully analyse the temporal properties of a system in order to gain a greater understanding of the behaviour it will display to the user. This allows us to identify inconsistencies and likely problem areas, in order that they are rectified at an early stage in system development.

3   Time Granularity

The notion of time granularity describes the different levels of coarseness of time. At the finer grains we consider time to be measured in small levels such as seconds or milliseconds, and at the larger grains it consists of days, weeks or months and so on. So embedded into our lives is our notion of time, that we have no difficulty in understanding the relationship between the different granularities, and we easily switch between them. For example, arranging a meeting in the future, we might initially agree that the meeting should be *next week,* and then decide on a particular *day,* finally settling on a specific *'time'*, which will be defined in terms of hours and minutes (for both starting time and duration). In this case we have gradually come down through the various granularities until we have found one which is specific enough for our particular purpose. We are then likely to think of our future meeting in terms of the different granularities, depending on how far away it is. For example if today is Monday, and our meeting is arranged for *next week, Thursday, at 10am for one hour*, we might initially consider our meeting to be 'over a week' away. At this stage the finer granularities are of no real significance to when the meeting is with reference to today. Come next Monday however, we will be more likely to be concerned with a slightly finer granularity, and would consider our meeting to be three days away. On Thursday itself, we would think of the meeting as being *today, at 10am*, or perhaps, *an hour away (and potentially lasting for over an hour)*. By now, the coarser granularities do not convey the information about the time of our meeting in a form that is easily understood; it is very inconvenient for us to think of our meeting as being $1/168^{th}$ of a week away, when what we really mean is an hour, despite the fact that the same information is in fact being conveyed. It can be seen that we intuitively use the most appropriate granularity for a particular purpose and easily switch between the different granularities in our everyday lives. An investigation into the usability of electronic diaries [16] suggested that forcing a specific time granularity can have a negative effect on usability. For example, one diary studied required that meetings must be scheduled to the nearest minute, which may cause difficulties where the use of such a fine granularity is not considered appropriate by the user.

These different scales may be quite easily formalised using a real-time temporal logic, while conveying temporal information at appropriate levels of granularity. Here we are using TRIO≠ [2] [11], which is a fragment of first-order logic for specifying temporal properties of systems. In TRIO≠ one can quantify over times of varying granularity and constrain the occurrence of system events with respect to these, using operators such as *Futr* (in the future), *Past* (in the past), and so on. The notation incorporates a mechanism for translating between the various granularities, allowing the formulae specified in a larger granularity to be interpreted in a finer one. For example, we might represent our meeting being respectively, over a week away, three days away and one hour away as:

$$\text{Futr [Meeting, >1]}_w \qquad \text{Futr [Meeting, 3]}_d \qquad \text{Futr [Meeting, 1]}_h \qquad (1)$$

where the subscript denotes the level of granularity, such that $_w$ = week, $_d$ = day and $_h$ = hour. These statements show that there is a time point in the future, at which it will be true that there is a meeting, which is greater than one week / exactly three days / exactly one hour from the current time instant.

So representation of the different granularities may be quite easily achieved. Indeed, so long as we consider only one granularity at a time, there is no difficulty in reasoning about our formalisms. Moving from coarser, to finer granularities and vice versa can however cause some semantic difficulties. Whilst the transition may be achieved via simple multiplications and divisions, we need to build in some flexibility. For example if I agree to telephone someone a week from today, then this could be translated to the finer granularity of hours using the calculation 7x24. However, I do not really mean that I will make the call in exactly 168 hours, and so some flexibility should be incorporated, in this case perhaps 12 hours each way. This introduces a level of nondeterminism (or fuzziness – in the sense of fuzzy logic), but allows us to consider whether the promise is fulfilled with some degree of faithfulness to human practice.

There are however, some cases where this translation poses more serious semantic difficulties. Consider the example below (from [11]). The statement "every month, if an employee works, he is paid his salary", could be formalised in first order logic using the formula:

$$\forall \ t_m, \ \forall emp \ (work \ (emp, \ t_m) \rightarrow get\_salary \ (emp, \ t_m)) \tag{2}$$

where the subscript 'm' denotes the fact that 't' is measured in a time unit of months. The meaning of the statement is clear in relation to our understanding of the sentence. In a similar fashion we could formalise a requirement that whenever an employee is assigned a job, that job must be completed within three days:

$$\forall t_d \ \forall emp \ \forall j \ (get\_job \ (emp, \ j, \ t_d) \rightarrow job\_done \ (emp, \ j, \ t_d+3)) \tag{3}$$

If the two formulae were to be taken as comprising part of the specification of an office system, or the formalisation of a contract of employment, we would need a model that can include both formulae. Using the method we showed above we could translate our month into days – in this case terms labelled 'm' would become terms labelled 'd' whose constants are multiplied by 30 (assuming that all months have 30 days for simplicity of the example). But in this case this has the effect of altering the meaning of our statement. As a general rule we do not attach the same meaning to the two statements "every month, if an employee works he gets his salary", and "every day, if an employee works he gets his salary". We would expect, for example that working for a month means that the employee works on 20 or more days in order to be paid his salary, and that the salary is paid on only one day in the month. Thus, although we can attach the relevant meaning to such statements when they are given in English, there is important information which is conveyed purely by the context of the statement, including common sense cultural knowledge about working practices, payment schemes etc. Knowing the context allows us to attach the relevant meaning, but this information is not captured in the formalisms above.

In a similar fashion we would be unlikely to have difficulty in attaching temporal meaning to the following statements when they are given in English. Indeed it is quite easy for us to rephrase them with respect to a different time granularity:

1. Every year I have a birthday: *There is one day in each year which is my birthday*
2. Every day I eat: *There are a number of minutes in each day during which it is true that I am eating. (The minutes are unlikely to be contiguous.)*
3. Every night I sleep: *There are a number of hours in each night during which it is true that I am sleeping. (The hours are likely to be contiguous.)*
4. A train has been travelling at 30 mph for over two hours: *For all of the minutes in a two hour period, the train has been travelling at an average speed of more than 30 mph.*

The implicit information in sentences (i) and (ii) allows us to move to a finer granularity without difficulty. We understand that there is only one day on which it is true that it is a person's birthday, and that there are a number of minutes during each day that we are eating. Implicit information also tells us that there is likely to be more than one continuous set of minutes during which we are eating, whilst this is less likely to be true for the number of hours during which we are sleeping. In each case, examining the statement at a finer level of granularity reveals that formalisation at the finer level requires additional information that is not available purely from the coarser level formal description. In addition we must be aware that simple translation between the granularities, using multiplication and division, can alter the meaning of formal statements. This indicates that this is an area where automation is likely to be impossible, as each translation requires different implicit information. However, a person with appropriate domain knowledge, using a suitable notation can achieve this translation between levels of granularity. We show in the next section that where a system's temporal properties exist over a number of granularities, the relationships should be carefully considered because of the potential effect on system behaviour.

4   Specifying Granularity

In this section we show how the formalisation of temporal properties of a system containing multiple time granularities has revealed important information about potential system behaviour, and has highlighted aspects where the logic itself becomes difficult to use. With specification at a single granularity, the finer granularities are underspecified, but the way in which we translate between granularities may affect system behaviour. Moreover, we see that there is no one correct solution to the problem of translation.

The case study used is an interactive pet screen saver, MOPyfish. MOPyfish is a pet goldfish whose behaviour is dependent on the way in which it is treated over time. If it is fed and played with regularly it will develop into a happy, well-adjusted fish. Less attentive treatment results in a neurotic and unfriendly fish, whilst more serious neglect of its feeding requirements will lead to death. In this paper we use fragments of the feeding requirements to illustrate the complexity of the temporal requirements.

4.1   Feeding

If the fish is fed every day then it will behave as a happy fish. Its behaviour is determined by its treatment over the past seven days. We specify it in its happy state by the following TRIO≠ formula (at the day level of granularity):

$$\text{HappyF} \leftrightarrow ([\text{Past, Fed, 1}]_d \wedge [\text{Past, Fed, 2}]_d \ldots [\text{Past, Fed, 7}]_d) \vee \qquad (4)$$

$$(\exists\, t,\ 0 \leq t < 7,\ [\text{Past, Initialised, t}]_d \wedge (\forall u,\ 0 < u \leq t\ [\text{Past, Fed, u}]_d))$$

Here the fish has been fed on each of the last seven days, or has been initialised within the past seven days, and fed each day since then. As we noted above, in section 3, TRIO≠ incorporates a mechanism for translating formulae into a finer granularity. There are a number of ways in which the mapping to a finer granularity may be achieved, three of which are illustrated in figure 1 below.

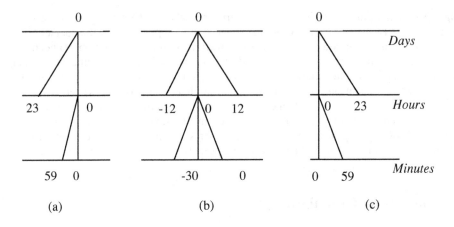

Fig. 1. Potential Mappings of Temporal Domains

The choice of mapping between the different temporal domains can influence system behaviour. For example, if we take the zeroes in figure 1 to represent midnight, and our fish is fed at 11:55pm, and again at 12:05am, then using mappings (a) and (c) would mean that our fish had been fed on separate days. Using mapping (b) however, our fish would still have been fed twice, but in this case it would have been fed on the same day. Consequently, it would display different behaviour.

4.2   Initialisation

A second temporal issue to consider is the way in which time is treated at initialisation of the fish. There are two viable possibilities – firstly, each day could be treated as a 24-hour time period from initialisation. In this instance, were the fish to be initialised at 3pm, a day would be considered to start at 3pm and end at 2:59pm. Alternatively, a day could be taken to initialise in tandem with the computer's clock, and run from midnight to 11:59pm. Here, the first day will be a short one. The choice made regarding initialisation would again potentially affect the behaviour displayed. If the first option is used, and the fish is fed at, for example 3:05pm on the day of initialisation, 2pm the next day, and 4pm on the day after, then it would effectively have not been fed on one day (as 26 hours elapse between the second and third feeding). Had the second option been taken, then feeding at these times would be counted as having happened every day. Although this allows periods of more than 24 hours to elapse between feedings, it is more in keeping with our understanding of 'daily feeding'. This is the more natural option, and is likely to be the one that is in line with the user's expectations, reflecting more faithfully their understanding of the temporal concept.

4.3   Regular Feeding

One aspect of the behaviour of the fish is that if it is fed at the same time each day, then it will begin to wait for it's food at the regular feeding time. This is dependent on this time at which it has been fed over the last seven days, and we allow a 10-minute 'window' for it to be fed in. This particular aspect concerns multiple granularities of time – we are concerned with whether it has been fed on each of the last seven days, and with the particular time, in hours, and minutes, at which it was fed. We need to refer to a specific time interval, measured in minutes, within each day. This means that the specification of this aspect appears at a flat granularity measured in minutes, and results in a very cumbersome formula specifying a regularly fed fish:

$$
\begin{aligned}
&\text{Regular\_feeding} \leftrightarrow \exists\, x_0,\, \ldots, x_6 \qquad\qquad\qquad\qquad\qquad\qquad (5)\\
&\quad 1440 \times 7 > x_0 \geq 1440 \times 6\\
&\wedge\ 1440 \times 6 > x_1 \geq 1440 \times 5\\
&\wedge\ 1440 \times 5 > x_2 \geq 1440 \times 4\\
&\wedge\ 1440 \times 4 > x_3 \geq 1440 \times 3\\
&\wedge\ 1440 \times 3 > x_4 \geq 1440 \times 2\\
&\wedge\ 1440 \times 2 > x_5 \geq 1440 \times 1\\
&\wedge\ 1440 \times 1 > x_6 \geq 1440 \times 0\\
&\wedge\ [\text{Past, Eats}, x_0]_m \wedge \ldots \wedge [\text{Past, Eats}, x_6]_m\\
&\wedge\ |\, x_0\,(\text{mod } 1440) - x_1\,(\text{mod } 1440)\,| \leq 5 \wedge \ldots \wedge |\, x_0\,(\text{mod } 1440) - x_6\,(\text{mod } 1440)\,| \leq 5
\end{aligned}
$$

That is, that feeding occurred on seven separate days in the past week, and that it ate when it was fed, and that the time at which this occurred was within the same ten minute time period on each day. We then need to specify that, having been fed at a regular time for the past seven days, the fish will wait for its food at the appropriate time:

$$
\begin{aligned}
&\text{Wait\_for\_food} \leftrightarrow [\text{Past, Regular\_feeding}, 5]_m \wedge \exists x_0\,(1440 \times 7 > x_0 \geq 1440 \times 6) \qquad (6)\\
&\wedge\ [\text{Past, Eats}, x_0]_m \wedge (x_0\,(\text{mod } 1440) \leq 5 \vee x_0\,(\text{mod } 1440) \geq 1435))
\end{aligned}
$$

The last disjunction specifies the five minutes on either side of the regular clock feeding time. This aspect of the behaviour of the fish can be formally represented, but the resulting expressions are awkward, and the fact that a single granularity has had to be used means that it is difficult to understand as a temporal statement. One purported advantage of TRIO≠ is that an element of naturalness is retained by specifying to the most suitable granularity, and this has been lost here. As we have seen in section 2.2 above, pace and regularity are important temporal concepts in interaction, and we highlight this section of the specification as it illustrates the difficulty in specifying such concepts where multiple time granularities occur.

It should also be noted that this formalisation will, over longer periods of time allow some 'drift' – if the fish were to be fed a minute late every day for a week, then the time 'window' which defines regular feeding will also become one minute later. It is arguable that this is more reflective of the user's likely expectations than if the time period were to be inviolably bound to the first time at which it was fed, given that behaviour is designed to reflect the way in which the fish has been treated over the past seven days. Another alternative would be to allow each day's feeding time to be bound to a ten minute window around the feeding time on the previous day. This would however allow the 'regular' feeding time to drift by over half an hour within a week, which may be less faithful both to our understanding of the notion of regular feeding, and to the actual behaviour we desire to be displayed.

4.4   Summary

The examples we have shown in this section have highlighted the way in which system behaviour may be affected by the way in which we denote the relationship between different time granularities. In addition we have found that even with a notation that can represent multiple time granularities, there are occasions where a flat granularity must nevertheless be used, resulting in a loss of natural understanding. In all of these cases, the information conveyed in relatively complex formal statements may be expressed very simply, (but on close inspection, ambiguously) in English. The process of formalisation reveals the ambiguity, and highlights the way in which a simple English temporal statement may carry a vast amount of implicit temporal information. The formalisation of 'regular feeding' has highlighted the way in which specification of regularity may lead to drifting. It has been found to be a desirable property for our purposes, but may be less so in other contexts, for example when considering the pace of interaction. Our current research is aiming to find ways to improve the expressiveness of TRIO≠, and similar specification languages. For example it would be useful if one could add predicates such as 'within x minutes of', referring to clock face time (avoiding the modulo 1440), or include predicates which make it easier to formulate specifications of pace, e.g. 'about every five minutes', 'every day at about the same time', and so on.

5   Conclusions

Time plays an important role in interactive systems, both through constraints on system behaviour, and because of the effect that temporal issues can have on the quality of interaction. Where systems have timing properties which consist of a number of different granularities, we must be very careful that we fully understand the relationship between the granularities. Temporal statements written in English may include a great deal of implicit information, much of which has great significance if we attempt to translate between the different granularities. Formalisation of a system's temporal behaviour can be difficult to achieve, even with a notation that has been designed to accommodate a number of different granularities. As our examples have shown however, formalisation of timing properties can yield significant information about potential system behaviour that might otherwise be overlooked, and therefore we feel that it has an important role to play in the development of interactive systems. It is clear that further research is needed in order that we may gain a greater understanding of the interaction between the different granularities. In particular, the development of notations that may be used to specify different granularities within a single specification is an emerging research area, and it may be possible to develop notations for this purpose which are aimed specifically at interactive systems. TRIO≠ has proved to be a useful notation for the specification of the temporal aspects of system behaviour, although as with many logical notations, there is a lack of guidelines for obtaining a modular structure and thus scalability, which can make larger specifications cumbersome. Therefore, we feel that it is best used to examine and specify the temporal aspects of system behaviour, perhaps alongside other notations which may be used to capture different system properties.

The specification of time granularity is a complex area and there are many potential directions for future work. It is possible that formal approaches other than real-time temporal logics, may be suitable for reasoning about time granularity. Potential notations include formalisms such as default logic [20] or preference logic [21], although investigation of such techniques is beyond the scope of this paper. An alternative direction for research is to consider whether there may be wider application for a notation which may be used to specify granularity in a more general sense. For example in CSCW systems it maybe desirable to reason about semantic as well as temporal granularity. Semantic granularity would allow consideration of, for example, different sized chunks of text, such as letters, words, paragraphs and so on. This may be of particular use in relation to coupling, where a shared artifact is inevitably out of date for some user (see, for example [22]). Current research is focussed on overcoming the difficulties presented by TRIO discussed in this paper.

6   References

1.   Byrne, A. and Picking, R. (1997) Is Time Out to be the Big Issue? Presented at *Time and the Web, Staffordshire University 19 June 1997*. Available at:
      http://www.soc.staffs.ac.uk/seminars/web97/papers/picking.html
2.   Corsetti, F., Crivelli, E., Mandrioli, D., Montanari, A., Morzenti, A., San Pietro, P., Ratto, E. (1991) " Dealing with different time scales in formal specifications", *10th IEEE-ACM International Workshop on Software Specification and Design, Como, Italy, October 1991*
3.   Dix, A.J. (1987) The Myth of the infinitely Fast Machine. In *People and Computers III* Diaper and Winder (Eds.) CUP
4.   Dix, A.J. (1992) Pace and Interaction. In *People and Computers VII*. Monk, Diaper and Harrison (Eds.) CUP
5.   Dix, A.J. (1994a). Que Sera Sera - The Problem of Future Perfect in Open and Cooperative Systems. In *People and Computers IX*. Draper and Weir (Eds.) CUP
6.   Dix, A.J. (1994b) Seven Years On, The Myth Continues. University of Huddersfield Research Report RR9405
7.   Dix, A.J. (1996a) Natural Time. Position Paper for CHI 96 Basic Research Symposium, April 1996, Vancouver, BC. Available at:
      http://www.soc.staffs.ac.uk/~cmtajd/papers/natural/natural.html
8.   Dix, A.J. (1996b) Temporal Aspects of Usability. Delays and temporal Incoherence Due to Mediated Status-Status Mappings. In *SIGCHI Bulletin, Vol. 28 No 3, April 1996* Available at: http://www1.acm.org:82/sigs/sigchi/bulletin/1996.2/Alan-Dix.html
9.   Dix, A.J., Ramduny, D. and Wilkinson, J. (1998) Interaction in the Large. In *Interacting With Computers, Special Issue on Temporal Aspects of Usability*
10.   Johnson, C. (1995) The Challenge Of Time. In *The Design, Specification And Verification Of Interactive Systems*", Palanque, P. and Bastide, R. (Eds.) Springer Verlag 1995 pp345-357
11.   Montanari, A. (1996) Metric and Layered Logic for Time Granularity. ILLC Dissertation Series 1996-02, Institute for Logic, Language and Computation, University of Amsterdam, 1996

12. Montanari A., Peron A. Policriti A., (1999) "Theories of Omega-Layered Metric Temporal Structures: Expressiveness and Decidability". The Logic Journal of IGPL, vol.7, no.1, January 1999, pp. 79-102.
13. Näätänen, R., Muranen, V. and Merisalo, A. (1974) Timing of Expectancy Peak in Simple Reaction Time Situation. *Actua Psychologica* 38(6), 461-470
14. O'Donnell, P. and Draper, S.W. How Machine delays Change User Strategies. In *Papers From A Workshop on Temporal Aspects of Usability*. Johnson, C. and Gray, P. (Eds) University if Glasgow GIST Technical Report G95-1.
15. Parker, H. (1997) The User's Experience of Time During Interaction. Technical Report CRC-97-1, Computing Research Centre, School of Computing and Management Sciences, Sheffield Hallam University, 1997.
16. Payne, S.J. (1993) Understanding Calendar Use. In *Human Computer Interaction, Vol 8 pp83-100, 1993*
17. Shneiderman, B. (1984) Response Time and Display Rate in Human Performance with Computers. In *ACM Computing Surveys, Vol. 16, No 3, pp 265-285, September 1984*
18. Teal, S. L. and Rudnicky, A.I. (1992) A Performance Model of System Delay and User Strategy Selection. In *Proceedings of CHI 1992 (Monterey, California, May 3-7, 1992)*. ACM, New York.
19. Wickens, C. D. (1984) Engineering, Psychology and Human Performance. Glenview, IL: Scott, Foresman and Company
20. Besnard, P. (1989) An Introduction to Default Logic. Springer-Verlag 1989
21. Brewka, G. (1989) Preferred Subtheories: An extended logical framework for default reasoning. In *Proceedings of the Eleventh International Joint Conference on Artificial Intelligence* 1989, pp 1043-1048
22. Dewan, P. and Choudhary, R. Coupling the User Interfaces of a Multiuser Program. *ACM Transactions on Computer Human Interaction*. March 1995, Vol. 2, No. 1, pp 1-39.

Verifying the Behaviour of Virtual Environment World Objects

James S. Willans and Michael D. Harrison

Human-Computer Interaction Group
Department of Computer Science, University of York
Heslington, York YO10 5DD, U.K.
e-mail:{James.Willans,Michael.Harrison}@cs.york.ac.uk

Abstract. Virtual environments are rapidly becoming more widespread and finding application outside specialised laboratories. However, there has been relatively little research developing tools and techniques to aid their development. This is particularly the case when defining the dynamics of the virtual world objects with which the user perceives and interacts. The complexity of these world objects can often mirror their real world counterparts, yet they are usually defined using program or macro application code. Consequently, there is no opportunity, beyond ad-hoc prototyping, of ensuring the world objects behave as required. Our work is focusing on the verification and refinement of abstract virtual environment behavioural specifications to an implementation. In this paper, we exemplify how the dynamics of these world objects can be specified using a hybrid formalism. We discuss and demonstrate how meaningful verification can take place on these specifications.

1 Introduction

In recent years the use of 3D virtual environments has become more widespread, partly as a consequence of diminishing technology costs and partly due to the availability of development environments such as the Maverik toolkit [8]. This class of interactive system is beginning to realise its potential in applications such as training [6.7], product prototyping [26] and data visualisation [20] outside the context of specialised laboratories.

Although there has been some work developing high level guidelines to promote usability in virtual environments [3,12] little effort has focused on developing tools and techniques to aid their development. This is particularly the case when defining the dynamics of the world objects that the user perceives and interacts with in the virtual world. The visual rendering and geometry of these objects are constructed using a 3D-modeller such as 3DStudio [1]. These renderings are then imported into a virtual environment toolkit such as Superscape [25] or Maverik [8] where the necessary dynamic behaviour is specified using program or macro code. There are two significant problems with this approach.

Firstly, the granularity of the world objects (the number of geometric components that constitute an object) is dependent on how the object will behave in the virtual environment [23]. This is because once the world object's visual appearance and

P. Palanque and F. Paternò (Eds.): DSV-IS 2000, LNCS 1946, pp. 65-77, 2001.

geometry are defined using a 3D-modeller, the rendering primitives constituting the description cannot be manipulated individually in the virtual environment toolkit. For instance, if a door with a knob is constructed as a rendered texture map, then there is no way that the knob can behave independently of the door. If a requirement of the environment is that the knob can turn, then the knob's visual rendering must be defined separately from that of the door. Consequently, unlike the current approach, the behaviour of the environment must be considered (at some abstraction) before the visual renderings can be defined. This problem does not exist for direct-manipulation interfaces because the visual renderings are pre-constructed in widget application programmers interfaces (APIs). The individuality of virtual environments means that API libraries cannot be constructed.

Secondly, defining the dynamics of the environment at code level does not offer an opportunity to verify that a world object will behave as required. The potential for error is further increased because virtual environment toolkits require the definition of an object's state, and the complex calculations describing the transformations between the state, to be defined at the same level of abstraction. These dynamics can often mirror the complexity found in an objects' real world counterparts[1]. Particularly, this is the case when a world object is made up of multiple geometric components because these inevitably have complex state dependencies on each other. With reference to the door knob example, the door itself should not be able to change to an open state unless the door knob is turned and pulled i.e. the door's behaviour is dependent on that of the door knob. We call objects that place such dependencies *complex world objects*. Successful definition of these currently relies on the developer's craft skill.

Given these two issues, it is reasonable to assume that ad-hoc prototyping must play a large part in the development process of virtual environments (this is confirmed in the case study presented in [13]). This is clearly undesirable and error prone. We can hypothesize that this results in world objects with complex visual renderings but limited behaviour (which may give false cues to interaction and result in usability problems [4]), or that the world objects fail to behave in a manner required or anticipated by the users of the environment.

Previous work [23] has demonstrated how the behaviour of world objects can be determined by examining the role that the object plays in the virtual environment. The key contribution of this work is that specifications are constructed that match the world object's geometric description and behaviour to the task requirements of the environment. Consequently, the granularity of a world object can be constructed with knowledge of the behavioural requirements, addressing the first issue outlined above. The behaviour of objects is specified using the hybrid formalism presented in [21,22]. This formalism uses Petri-nets [17] to describe the discrete (or state) behaviour of the world object and an extension to describe the continuous (or data-flow) behaviour.

The focus of our work is on the verification and refinement of these behavioural specifications to an implementation. The overall aim is to perform useful reasoning during the design of virtual environments dynamics and translate these designs (and reasoning) into working implementations. Previously [27,28] we have presented the Marigold toolset that supports the automatic refinement of the hybrid formalism to an implementation. Our contribution in this paper is as follows:

---

[1] if such exist, as in applications such as data visualisation this may not be the case.

- We present an example of specifying complex world objects using the hybrid formalism of [21,22].

- We show how meaningful verification can take place on the Petri-net part of the complex world object's specification and discuss how the Marigold toolset has been extended to facilitate this.

The paper is structured as follows. In section 2 we discuss related work. In section 3 we describe the Marigold toolset. In section 4 we examine the nature of virtual environment world objects and demonstrate how the hybrid specification presented in [21,22] captures these. In section 5 we discuss and exemplify verification of the specifications and describe extensions to the Marigold toolset to support this. Finally, in section 6 we summarise our conclusions.

2 Related Work

Palanque and Bastide have pioneered the use of Petri-nets for the specification and verification of interactive systems using the interactive co-operating objects (ICO) framework (see, for instance, [16,2]). Their focus has been on traditional direct manipulation interfaces. Petri-nets are also used in the work presented in [11] to specify the dialogue of interaction. Like the ICO approach, this deals with direct-manipulation interfaces. Our contribution concentrates on the value of Petri-nets for the verification of the dynamic behaviour of virtual environment world objects. This makes it possible to analyse different issues relating to the style of specification, verification and particularly refinement.

Jacob has contributed a great deal to the specification of virtual environments. He has developed a user interface management system (UIMS) [15,9] where the dynamics of virtual environment interaction techniques can be altered in a traditional UIMS manner. Our work is different from this in a number of ways. Firstly, in this paper we are considering the behaviour of virtual environment objects not interaction techniques. We consider interaction techniques to map the user onto the environment and control navigation, selection and manipulation. We believe that the behaviour of world objects should be independently specified from that of interaction techniques. This is because of their complexity and because of the need to reuse both the world objects and the techniques specifications. Secondly, and perhaps more significantly, because Jacob's notation is designed for interaction techniques it would be difficult to capture the behaviour of complex world objects because of its lack of support for concurrency (we will examine the need for this in the next section). Our work also addresses the issue of verifying the specification.

Other work has focused on the specification of virtual environment dynamics using techniques borrowed from the data-flow paradigm [19]. Visual representations of input devices, functions and output devices are connected together to define how data flows from the user, is manipulated and rendered back to the user. Steed [24] has shown how these definitions can take place while immersed in a virtual environment. Although such approaches provide an easier method of defining the dynamics than program code, it would not be possible to specify complex world objects because of the complexity of the resulting specification. In addition, such specifications offer no potential for verification.

3 The Marigold Toolset

In order to provide a context for the work presented in this paper, we will briefly describe the Marigold toolset [27,28]. This toolset was developed to aid in the specification and refinement to implementation of virtual environment dynamics using the hybrid formalism presented in [21,22]. Details of this formalism will be discussed in the next section. The main value of this refinement approach is that the semantics of the hybrid specification are automatically translated to an implementation. As well as preserving accuracy, this may reduce the transition time between design and implementation.

The toolset consists of three tools: the hybrid specification builder (HSB), the world object builder (WOB) and the prototype builder (PB). The HSB provides a means of visually specifying the dynamic behaviour independent of context (input and output devices and renderings, for instance). A small amount of code is added to some of the nodes constituting the specification. A stub of the interaction technique is generated from this specification. For interaction techniques, the stub is directly integrated into an environment using the PB. This process is performed visually by connecting the input and output attributes of techniques to devices and viewpoints, for example. For complex world objects, the WOB is first used to integrate the behavioural specification into the object's visual renderings. From this, another stub is generated which is also integrated into the environment with the interaction techniques using the PB. The world object encapsulates an object's behaviour and rendering into a single reusable component. From the PB specification, an implementation is generated for the virtual environment toolkit Maverik [8]. This can then be compiled and executed. Screenshots of the HSB and PB are shown in figures 1 and 2 respectively to give an overview of the nature of the toolset rather than a comprehensive description.

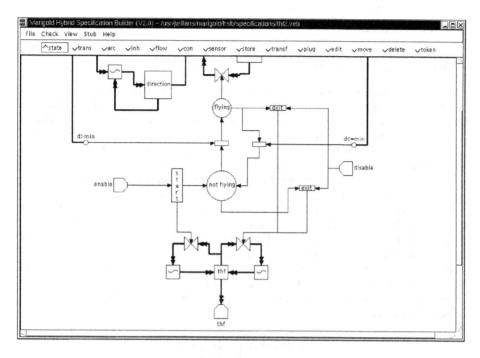

Fig. 1. The hybrid specification builder (HSB)

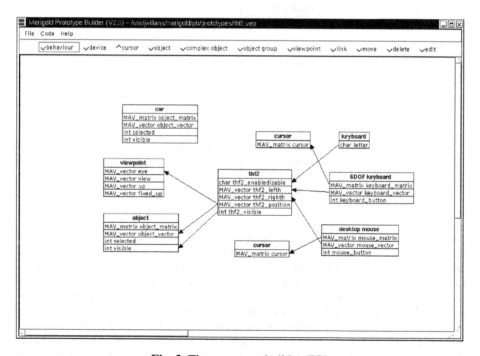

Fig. 2. The prototype builder (PB)

4 World Objects

4.1 World Object Behaviour

Previous work has shown that virtual environments can be thought of as consisting of a hybrid of discrete and continuous components [10]. Devices such as magnetic trackers produce continuous and discrete input information (position and button clicks), which enables and disables continuous updates of the virtual environment (through a viewpoint, for instance). This work primarily deals with interaction techniques where the state of the environment is minimal. For example, a virtual environment navigation technique usually has only two states *disabled* and *enabled*. However, complex world objects can be in many more states, for instance the virtual door may have the following states: door open, door closed, door locked, door unlocked, handle up and handle down. In figure 3 we present a model which conceptualises this behaviour. Continuous and discrete information is fed as input, thresholds are defined on the continuous information showing how it maps onto the state of the world object, the discrete information is mapped directly. The state of the world object then determines the enabling and disabling of continuous output to the virtual environment. In addition, it is possible to map discrete output directly from the world object's state space.

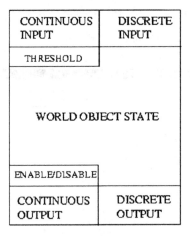

Fig. 3. Behaviour of a world object

The specification formalism discussed in the introduction [21,22] takes into account the hybrid characteristics of virtual environment behaviour. The discrete part of the specification is represented using traditional place transition Petri-nets (with places of one token capacity) with the added construct of an inhibitor arc. This notation is particularly suitable for capturing the state space of a complex world object because of its support for concurrency. Again considering the door example with a knob that turns, the door itself has a state (e.g. *open* and *closed*) and the knob has a state (e.g. *released* and *turned*) that are independent of each other. Therefore, there is a need to represent this concurrency. As we will demonstrate in the next section, Petri-nets easily capture the notion of state dependency between these concurrently active behaviours. Many state notations such as state transition diagrams are unable to capture concurrency, and those that do, such as Statecharts [5], describe the communication (dependency) between the independent states in a rather difficult way. The continuous part of the hybrid formalism maps continuous input and output within the Petri-net specification. This continuous description also defines when the data is transformed, and the data required to calculate the transformations. The complicated calculations themselves are black boxed.

4.2 Specifying World Object Behaviour

In this section we will demonstrate how the described hybrid formalism can be used to capture the dynamic behaviour of complex world objects. The example we will use is that of a gas hob that works as follows: in order to get a flame on the gas hob, it is necessary for the user to first turn on the gas knob and release the gas. The user must then press the ignition switch that creates a spark and ignites the gas. The ignition switch can then be released and pressed again (if desired) without any consequence. The flame remains on until the gas is turned off. To re-ignite the flame, it is necessary to repeat the process.

The resulting Petri-net specification for this world object is illustrated in figure 4. As can be seen, the marking of the net describes the ignition, knob and flame as initially off. When a *knob on* event is received, a token is moved from the *knob off* state to the *knob on* state. A token is then generated and placed in the *gas* state (the consumed *knob on* token is replaced). When an *ign on* event is received, a token is moved from the *ignition off* state to the *ignition on* state and, consequently, a token is generated and placed in the *spark* state (the consumed *ignition on* token is also replaced). When an *ign off* event is received, the tokens from *ignition on* and *spark* are removed and a token placed back in the *ignition off* state. If there is no token in the *gas* state, no further activity occurs. If there is a token in the *gas* state, then the tokens are consumed from the *gas*, *spark* and *flame off* states, and a token placed in the *flame on* and *gas* states. When a *knob off* event is received, the *knob on* and *gas* tokens are consumed, and a token placed in the *knob off* state. Consequently, the *flame off* state is no longer inhibited, and the *flame on* token is consumed and a token placed in the *flame off* state.

The continuous parts of the specification defines the continuous behaviour and its relation to the discrete Petri-net. Without this detail, the description would be useless as an implementation specification. This is because there is no indication of how the net maps to the predominantly continuous external environment. It is not possible to tell from the gas hob specification of figure 4 the causation of the events which trigger the interaction transitions.

Illustrated in figure 5 is an example of part of the net defined to contain the continuous detail. Here we have three external environment plugs, two inputs (the *ignition switch position* and the *selector position*), and one output plug (*the ignition switch position*[2]. Continuous information flows from plugs into, or from, transformers. Transformers perform some transformation on the data and yield some result which is placed in a store. In figure 5, the *ignition switch position* and *selector position* information are used to determine whether or not the ignition switch has been pressed by the *selector* (e.g. a virtual hand controlled by an interaction technique). This is calculated within the transformer and the result placed in the *selected* store. The *selected = true* sensor is fired when the value of the *selected* store becomes true. This enables the corresponding transition and, if there is a token in the *ignition off* state, moves this token to the *ignition on* state. When either of the two transitions in the Petri-net are fired, they enable a corresponding flow control. A flow control governs a continuous process. In the case of figure 5, the *position* store is updated and this value is passed to the *ignition switch position* plug. The *selected = false* sensor is fired when the value of the *selected* store becomes false, enabling the corresponding transition. Hence, when the state moves from either *ignition on* to *ignition off*, or *ignition off* to *ignition on*, the position of the ignition switch reflects this.

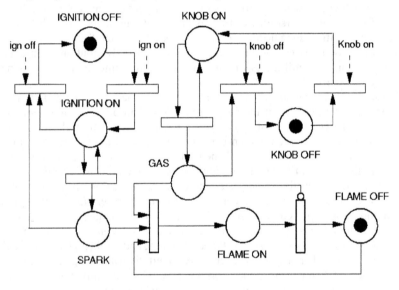

Fig. 4. Petri-net specification of the gas hob

This example illustrates how the dependency between the virtual environment components can be captured using the hybrid notation. In addition, it can be seen how these semi-formal semantics accurately describe the behaviour of the artifact in comparison to the textual description given at the beginning of this section.

---

[2] The two *ignition switch position* plugs are duplicated for clarity of presentation.

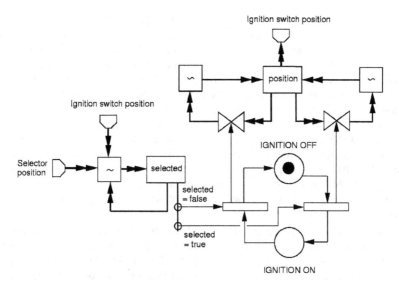

Fig. 5. Part of the hybrid specification for the gas hob

5 Verifying the Behaviour

One of the main motivations for specifying the behaviour in the described manner is to perform verification early in the design process. In this context, it is not necessary to consider the continuous part of the hybrid description. This is because, as illustrated in figure 3, the interesting states of the continuous behaviour maps onto (via. thresholds), and from (via. enabling/disabling), the discrete part of the specification. For instance in figure 5, the important part of the ignition behaviour is whether the continuous state of the *selector position* intersects with the continuous state of the *ignition switch position*. This state is captured in the discrete model. However, abstracting from the continuous behaviour means that an important assumption is made. That is, the continuous state captured in the discrete model can always be reached. For instance, in figure 5 this means that the *selected = false* and *selected = true* sensors can always fire. In reality this may not be true, for example the interaction technique may not have sufficient capability to move the *selector position* to the *ignition switch position*. Although this detail is out of the scope of the paper.

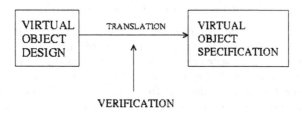

Fig. 6. The verification process

The main advantage of using Petri-nets from a verification perspective is the large body of previous research describing how desirable properties can be formally and automatically proved (see, for instance, [18]). Palanque and Bastide [16] demonstrate how traditional human-computer interaction principles can be verified in an ICO (interactive co-operating object) specification. For instance, undo-ability can be evaluated easily from such a specification and the design changed to reflect the result of such analysis if necessary. However, in a virtual environment context, changing the design of world objects to adhere to such properties is undesirable, rather we want to ensure that the specification is a faithful representation of the design. Even if the design does not satisfy the undo-ability principle, we may want to ensure that this is preserved in the design specification. Therefore, we are verifying the translation between an understanding of the behaviour of a design (often a real world phenomenon such as the gas hob) and the specification of this design (figure 6). In the gas hob example, we checked the following:

1. Whether dead-lock can occur. Dead-lock exists when no transition can be fired. This is a fundamental check of the specification because there is clearly no potential for deadlock in the real world gas hob. Failing this test would indicate that there is an error in the translation. Our verification concluded that the deadlock property did not exist.

2. Whether undesirable conflicts can occur, such as a token being in both the *ignition on* and *ignition off* state simultaneously. Similarly for the *knob on* and *knob off* states, and the *flame on* and *flame off* states. The physical characteristics of the real world gas hob ensure that knobs and switches cannot be in two distinct physical positions at any moment in time. However, in an abstract model an error in the translation could result in this being specified. Our verification concluded that these scenarios were not possible.

3. Whether it is possible to reach the *flame on* state. The aim of the gas hob is to make a flame appear. If the *flame on* state cannot be reached then the design is flawed. Our verification concluded that the *flame on* state can be reached.

4. Whether it is possible to have a token in the *knob on* state, no token in the *gas* state and a token in the *flame on* state. If the knob is on and the flame is on, then there should always be a token in the *gas* state, otherwise the inhibited transition would fire, and the *flame on* token moved to the *flame off* state. Our verification concluded that this could indeed be the case, consequently, proving a flaw with our original design of figure 4. The *gas* token is consumed when the transition is fired to switch the *flame on*. However, there exists the possibility that the inhibited transition could fire before the transition replacing the token in the *gas* state is re-fired. The amended specification for the gas hob is shown in figure 7.

These properties were checked from our Marigold hybrid specification builder (HSB). A screenshot of one of the dialogues to the verification is shown in figure 8, this checks whether a certain state can be reached. Other dialogues include the ability to check whether certain state progressions are valid. A reachability tree of the world object discrete specification is generated from the HSB. This lists every possible trace of place markings given a specification and an initial marking. The construction of the reachability tree involves converting any inhibitor arcs to states and transitions (this is a simple process for Petri-nets of the class we are using), and then recursively generating the tree itself (this process is well documented, see for example [18]).

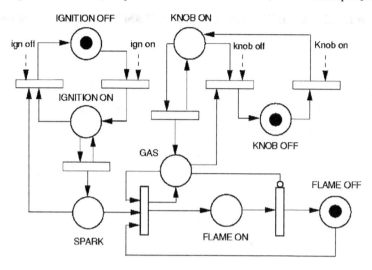

Fig. 7. Amended Petri-net specification of the gas hob

We are also exploring the potential for performing verification on a combination of the interaction technique specification(s) [27,28] and the complex world objects behavioural specifications. This combination enables us to consider the whole dynamic behaviour of a virtual environment. For instance, we may wish to consider the *complexity* of interaction required to perform a task in the virtual environment. This may be done by considering the demands made on the user by the interaction technique(s), and the consequent demands made on the interaction technique(s) by the complex world object. Additionally, we may wish to consider the *consistency* of interaction by examining whether there is a consistent mapping between the interaction technique(s) and the object's behaviour.

6 Conclusion

In the process of developing virtual environments, 3D-modellers are typically used to define world objects. Although they allow the refinement of visual rendering and object geometry, we have identified that there are no corresponding facilities for refining the behavioural requirements. Therefore, object behaviour is integrated within implementation phase prototyping of the application. This makes reasoning about the behaviour and determining how behaviour influences the granularity of the visual renderings difficult and error-prone. Potentially, this can lead to unusable environments that fail to meet requirements and confuse users.

In this paper we have demonstrated how our Marigold toolset has been extended to support the verification of complex world object's dynamics in the specification stage of development. We have demonstrated how this verification can be useful in identifying potential problems with the implementation. This is ongoing work.

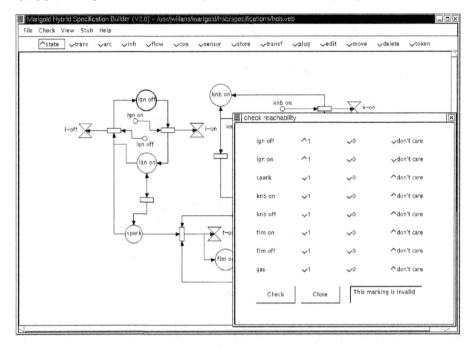

Fig. 8 Reachability analysis of a world object's behaviour

Acknowledgments. We are grateful to Shamus Smith for his comments on this paper.

References

1. Autodesk-corporation. 3Dstudio, 111 McInnis Parkway, San Rafael, California, 94903, USA.
2. Rémi Bastide and Phillipe Palanque. Petri net objects for the design, validation and prototyping of user-driven interfaces. In *Human-Computer Interaction – INTERACT'90*, 1990.
3. D.A. Bowman. *Interaction Techniques for Common Tasks in Immersive Virtual Environments – Design, Evaluation and Application.* PhD Thesis, Georgia Institute of Technology, 1999.
4. Kulwinder Kaur Deor, Alistair G. Sutcliffe, and Neil A.M. Maiden. Towards a better understanding of usability problems with virtual environments. In *INTERACT'99*, 1999.
5. David Harel. Statecharts: A visual formalism for complex systems. *Science of Computer Programming*, 8:231-274, 1987.
6. N. Higgett and S. Bhullar. An investigation into the application of virtual environment for fire evacuation mission rehearsal training. In *Eurographics 16th Annual Conference*, pages 87-96, 1998.
7. Larry F. Hodges, Benjamin A. Watson, Barbara O. Rothbaum, and Dan Opdyke. Virtually conquering fear of flying. *IEEE Computer Graphics*, pages 42-49, November 1996.

8. Roger J. Hubbold, Xia Dongbo, and Simon Gibson. Maverik – the Manchester virtual environment interface kernel. In Martin Goebel and Jacques David, editors, *Proceedings of 3ʳᵈ Eurographics Workshop on Virtual Environments,* SpringerVerlag, 1996.
9. Robert J.K. Jacob, L. Deligiannidis, and S. Morrison. A software model and specification language for non-WIMP user interfaces. *ACM Transactions on Computer-Human Interaction,* 1999.
10. Robert J.K. Jacob. Specifying non-WIMP interfaces. In *CHI'95 Workshop on the Formal Specification of User Interfaces Position Papers,* 1995.
11. Christian Janssen, Anette Weisbecker, and Jurgen Ziegler. Generating user interfaces from data models and dialogue net specifications. In *INTER-CHI,* pages 418-423, 1993.
12. Kulwinder Kaur. Designing virtual environments for usability. In *Human-Computer Interaction: INTERACT'97,* pages 636-639, 1997.
13. Kulwinder Kaur, Neil Maiden, and Alistair Sutcliffe. Design practice and usability problems with virtual environments. In *Proceedings of Virtual Reality World '96,* 1996.
14. Mieke Massink, David Duke, and Shamus Smith. Towards hybrid interface specification for virtual environments. In *Design, Specification and Verification of Interactive Systems '99,* pages 30-51. Springer, 1999.
15. S.A. Morrison and R.J.K. Jacob. A specification paradigm for design and implementation of non-WIMP human-computer interaction. In *ACM CHI'98 Human Factors in Computing Systems Conference,* pages 357-358. Addison-Wesley/ACM Press, 1998.
16. Phillipe A. Palanque, Rémi Bastide, Louis Dourte, and Christophe Silbertin-Blanc. Design of user-driven interfaces using petri nets and objects. In *Proceedings of CAISE'93 (Conference on advance information system engineering), Lecture Notes in Computer Science,* volume 685, 1993.
17. C.A. Petri. Kommunikation mit automaten. Schriften des iim nr. 2, Institut fur Instrumentelle Mathematic, 1962. English translation: Technical Report Report RADC-TR-65-377, Griffiths Air Base, New York, Vol. 1, Suppl. 1, 1966.
18. Wolfgang Reisig. *Petri Nets.* EATCS Monographs on Theoretical Computer Science. Springer-Verlag, 1982.
19. VPL. Research. Virtual reality data-flow language and runtime system, body electric manual 3.0., 1991. Redwood City, CA.
20. L. Sastry, D.R.S. Boyd, R.F. Fowler, and V.V.S.S. Sastry. Numerical flow visualisation using virtual reality techniques. In *8ᵗʰ International Symposium on Flow Visualisation,* 1998.
21. Shamus Smith and David Duke. Virtual environments as hybrid systems. In *Eurographics UK 17ᵗʰ Annual Conference,* 1999.
22. Shamus Smith, David Duke, and Mieke Massink. The hybrid world of virtual environments. *Computer Graphics Forum,* 18(3):C297-C307, 1999.
23. Shamus P. Smith, David J. Duke, and James S. Willans. Designing world objects for usable virtual environments. In *Design, Specification and Verification of Interactive Systems,* 2000.
24. Anthony J. Steed. *Defining Interaction within Immersive Virtual Environments.* PhD thesis, Queen Mary and Westfield College, 1996.
25. Superscape Corporation, Superscape, 1999. 3945 Freedom Circle, Suite 1050, Santa-Clara, CA 95054, USA.
26. M.R. Thompson, J.D. Maxfield, and P.M. Dew. Interactive virtual prototyping. In *Eurographics 16ᵗʰ Annual Conference,* pages 107-120, 1996.
27. James S. Willans and Michael D. Harrison. A toolset supported approach for designing and testing virtual environment interaction techniques. *Accepted for publication in the International Journal of Human-Computer Studies,* 1999.
28. James S. Willans and Michael D. Harrison. A 'plug and play' approach to testing virtual environment interaction techniques. In *6ᵗʰ Eurographics workshop on virtual environments,* pages 33-42, SpringerVerlag, 2000.

SUIT – Context Sensitive Evaluation of User Interface Development Tools

Joanna Lumsden[3] and Philip Gray

Department of Computing Science, University of Glasgow
17 Lilybank Gardens, Glasgow, G12 8RZ
{jo, pdg}@dcs.gla.ac.uk

Abstract. Developers of interactive software are confronted by a variety of software tools to help them design and implement user interfaces. They often resort to *ad hoc* means of tool selection and subsequently are dissatisfied with their chosen tool. In this paper we describe a framework, evaluation methodology, and associated tool for investigating the suitability of user interface development tools (UIDTs) for use in software development organizations and projects. We also present the results of two informal empirical studies carried out in support of the development of our framework and method.

Introduction

Developers of interactive software are confronted by a variety of software tools to assist in the process of designing and implementing the interactive aspects of applications. Not only do these tools fall into different categories in terms of gross functionality (widget toolkits, multimedia toolkits, rapid prototyping tools, full-scale UIDEs), but within each category, there is a growing number of competing tools with similar, but not identical, features. Choice of user interface development tool (UIDT) is fast resembling the choice of a car or a washing machine.

It is reasonable to expect that the quality of match between tool facilities and development project requirements will influence project results in terms of what can be accomplished as well as development cost and efficiency. Sometimes the effect will be large and easily identifiable – a tool may fail to support an important interaction technique (e.g. multimedia) – but more subtle effects are also possible. For example, the particular techniques used to produce some feature of the end user interface may be inefficient or ill-suited to the skills of the development team. This may result in the project team adopting sub-optimal design solutions to accommodate the tool, or their inability to use the tool effectively.

Developers often choose tools based on little more than an *ad hoc* inspection of marketing material, journal reviews, plus recommendations from colleagues. Although potentially adequate in some cases, this can clearly result in poor choices, especially when the information from brochures, friends, and reviews is not relevant to the context in which the tool will be used. Additionally, such an *ad hoc* approach

---

[3] nee McKirdy

P. Palanque and F. Paternò (Eds.): DSV-IS 2000, LNCS 1946, pp. 79–95, 2001.

is out of line with the more systematic, evidence-oriented approaches of modern software engineering.

In this paper we describe a framework, evaluation methodology, and associated tool for investigating the suitability of UIDTs for software development organizations and projects. The approach we take emphasizes the importance of the aims, practices, and constraints of the these organizations and projects in so far as they impact on tool evaluation. Section 2 outlines the setting and motivation for our work. Section 3 describes our evaluation framework and methodology in detail. This is followed, in Section 4, by an account of an evaluative study of their use. Section 5 sketches a recently-developed tool for supporting the UIDT evaluation process. We conclude with some observations on the current state of our research and plans for future work.

1   Background

The most substantial work on UIDT evaluation was conducted about ten years ago by Hix *et al* [1], [2], [3]. Their approach is based on functionality and usability-oriented checklists. Tools are assessed against an extensive set of criteria and cumulative ratings generated. These ratings serve as the basis for tool comparisons. While we believe the basic approach, based on an objective measure of functionality, to be appropriate, the method as it stands suffers from several problems:

- cumulative measures hide much useful evaluative information;
- their checklists are not adequately designed for extension as functionality increases and interaction techniques improve;
- and no account is taken of any factors other than functionality and usability.

Although other UIDT evaluation schemes and frameworks have used different sets of attributes of interest [4], [5], [6], [7], have made some effort to introduce tailorability [7], and have introduced performance benchmarks for some attributes [4], [5] – a situation which is reflected in evaluation methods for other CASE tools [8], [9], [10], [11] – they are all based on the common fundamental assumption that an evaluative judgement can be made regarding a tool largely independently of the context in which the evaluation takes place. That context includes the particular goals of the evaluation and constraints dictated by features of the project in which the tool will be used (including project requirements, staff abilities, financial limitations, etc.). In developing our approach, we have taken this context to be a core factor motivating and structuring the evaluation framework and method.

To confirm our belief that context is likely to introduce important factors in the evaluative process, we undertook a study of current industrial practice in UIDT selection. Via questionnaires, we asked 14 software developers about the tools they used, how they made their tool selections, and the context in which their selections were made [12]. We observed correlation between the type of application being developed and the type of tools used, and between tool type and other aspects of the project, including:

- team size;
- team member expertise;
- management structure;
- and the role of prototypes in the design process.

Additionally, we found that amongst our subjects there was little use of systematic evaluation methods at present, but a general desire to introduce appropriate methods if they were available. Overall, our study supports the notion that UIDT evaluation methods need to be developed which reflect the aims, practices, and constraints of the organizations (and project teams within those organizations) performing those evaluations.

2   SUIT

SUIT, a framework and methodology for the *s*election of *u*ser *i*nterface development *t*ools, was developed in response to the needs of user interface developers as described above. It provides a context-sensitive, extensible, and systematic means by which developers can determine the user interface development tool (UIDT) which best fits their needs. This section outlines the SUIT methodology and framework structure.

SUIT adopts a reference model-based approach to tool selection and can be used in three different ways:

- to select a UIDT based on a generic comparison of tools;
- to select the "best-fit" UIDT for a project based on the specific context and requirements of that project where the project has no precedent within the organization and hence no access to existing comparative data (see below);
- and to identify an appropriate UIDT for a specific project based on comparisons with previous projects.

The applicability of each approach is based on: the stage of design and/or development of the project; the precedence of the project within the context of the organization; and the intended specificity of the outcome of the use of SUIT. Each approach dictates the appropriate route through the SUIT methodology (see figure 1) and the manner in which the framework is manipulated.

The SUIT framework is an extensible reference model of all functionality and support features that might be found in a UIDT (see section 3.4 for greater detail on the framework itself). Guided by the appropriate methodological setting, the SUIT framework is tailored – that is, framework components are included or excluded from consideration – to provide a structure or pilot for data collection and thereafter a context for the interpretation of that data. The degree to which the framework *can* be tailored is determined by the amount of information which is available to the evaluator at the time of using SUIT. The degree to which the framework *is* tailored also depends on the intended use - e.g. generic comparison may require no tailoring.

The following sections illustrate the various uses to which SUIT can be put.

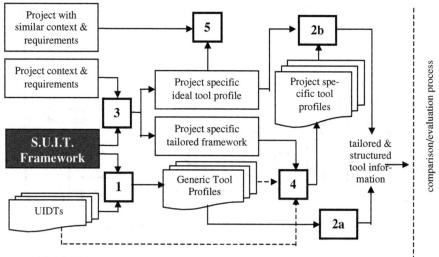

Fig. 1. The route map of the SUIT methodology showing all possible paths

2.1   UIDT Selection Based on a Generic Comparison of Tools

SUIT can be used to perform generic, i.e. non project specific, comparisons of tools. Such a comparison is independent of a project context, so no knowledge of the project or the context in which the project is taking place is required.

Figure 2 highlights the path which would be taken through the SUIT methodology in order to perform a generic comparison of UIDTs. In this case the SUIT framework is used as a complete reference model, i.e. every component in the framework is an active criterion for the comparison of the tools.

At step 1 in figure 2, each tool is examined in turn to determine which of the components listed in the SUIT framework are/are not present. For each tool, the information recorded during this process forms a generic profile of the individual tool – i.e. a profile of the tool in relation to the entire SUIT framework (or reference model) uninfluenced by the specifics of a project.

Generic profiles can be collated (step 2a) for use in the final stages of generic tool comparison or evaluation. It should be noted that SUIT provides the information, structure, and a means of data visualization for data comparison but does not stipulate the process by which the final comparison should be performed. This is the case for all uses of SUIT.

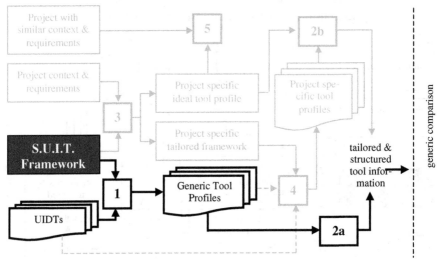

Fig. 2. Performing a generic comparison of UIDTs using SUIT

2.2   Project-Specific UIDT Comparison

SUIT is based on the hypothesis that, in most cases, effective tool selection for a specific project *must* consider: the purpose for which the tool is being selected – the functional requirements; and the context in which the tool will be used, including the institutional development process, technical resources, and human resources.   Generic comparisons highlight the differences between various tools, but it is in the context of a specific project that the significance of the differences becomes apparent. For example, if a given project requires a specific subset of UIDT functionality, a generic comparison does not *easily* highlight which of the tools examined best meets these requirements – a project specific comparison does.   Furthermore, a project-specific comparison can highlight the suitability of interaction style and interaction assistance provided by the tools with respect to the skills of project members.   Hence, in order to select the tool which best fits a specific project, the project's functional requirements and context of use have to be taken into consideration throughout the selection process.

Figure 3 highlights the methodological path designed for determining the best fit tool for an unprecedented project – that is, a project for which there have been, within an organization, no similar preceding projects which have themselves used the SUIT system to select a UIDT.

Given information about the project requirements, the basic SUIT framework is modified to produce a project-specific tailored framework which only considers data relevant to that project.   A copy of the tailored framework is augmented by adding contextual information to the functional requirements, creating a profile of the *ideal* tool for that project – see step 3 in figure 3.   It is against this profile that the data about *real* tools is compared in order to determine which tool best matches the ideal.

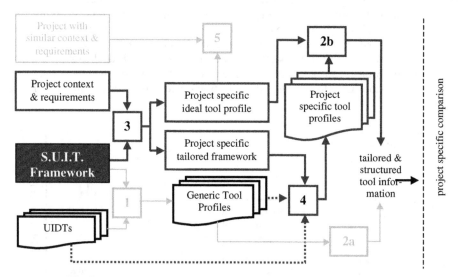

Fig. 3. Performing a project-specific comparison of UIDTs using SUIT

A project-specific tailored SUIT framework is essentially a project-specific reference model which is used to pilot the collection of (only relevant) data for the real tools. Step 4 in figure 3 shows that this data can be sourced in one of two ways: it can either be extracted (or filtered) from existing generic tool profiles; or it can be collected via direct examination of the actual tools. In either case, the result is a series of project-specific tool profiles, i.e. profiles of tools with respect to only those features which are of interest or relevance to the given project. These project-specific tool profiles can be collated with the ideal tool profile (see step 2b) for use in the final stages of the comparison process.

2.3   Project Specific UIDT Selection Based on Comparison with Previous Projects

The project specific ideal tool profiles, tailored frameworks, and associated tool information mentioned in the two previous sections, form a record of past UIDT selections using the SUIT system. Within a software development organization, it is often the case that "families" of projects are developed, for example, software solutions for financial institutions. Where this is true, and where SUIT has been used to inform previous UIDT selections, the "best-fit" tool for a new project can exploit the results of the tool selection from previous closely matching projects.

Figure 4 highlights the path through the SUIT methodology which would be followed if a tool selection is to be performed for a project which has predecessors with close similarities.

When drawing on information from tool selections for similar preceding projects, the new project context and requirements are examined to determine whether or not they would generate a project-specific ideal tool profile matching an existing project-specific ideal tool profile (see step 5 in figure 4). In this case, the tool recommendation as made for the preceding project would also be the best fit for the new project. If there are only slight differences between the ideal tool profile for a new project and an existing project, the project-specific tailored framework and ideal tool profile for the preceding project can be copied and tweaked (that is, minor changes made) and the altered versions used to complete the selection process as described in section 3.2, steps 4 and 2b.

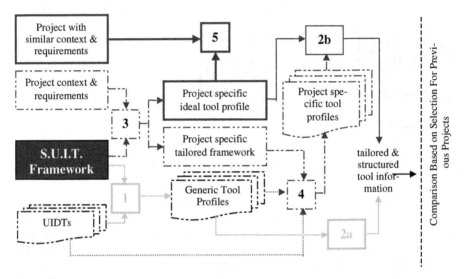

Fig. 4. Performing a project-specific comparison of UIDTs using SUIT where selection information is available for similar preceding projects

Given either of the above scenarios, the time and effort expended on previous tool evaluations reduces the cost of tool selection for new projects.

2.4   The SUIT Framework

The SUIT framework can be viewed as an extensible reference model of the functionality and support features that might be found in a typical UIDT. The list of components which comprise the reference model is a comprehensive extension and re-organization of the components which are included in the UIDT evaluation checklists published by Hix *et al* [3].

The SUIT framework contains three main sections: environmental context of use; user interface specific requirements; and developmental context of use.

Environmental Context of Use

A software development project takes place within an *environment* which SUIT models as: (1) human resources and (2) institutional goals or constraints. Failure to use these aspects of project development to inform and guide tool selection means that decisions regarding the suitability of tools are made without reference to the context in which the tool is to be used.   This can result in tool choices which are perhaps appropriate in terms of their functional provision, but are inappropriate in terms of the environmental resources and constraints that can affect the success or failure of the tool's use.

Human Resources

Software is usually developed by teams of people who, as individuals, have varied and perhaps very specific skills, different experiences of UIDTs, and who will work on varying amounts of the project as a whole.   As a group, they will provide a complex set of related resources and constraints that need to be carefully considered when selecting the most suitable UIDT for the specific project. SUIT provides the means by which the history or experience of each team member can be included in the selection or comparison process.   To accommodate the potentially different roles of individuals in the team, their experience of rapid prototyping and end-product implementation is considered separately.   In each case information is recorded concerning:

- the interaction mechanism(s) with which the team member is familiar (including specific programming languages where appropriate);
- the degree to which the team member's role in the project is routine;
- the level of semantic knowledge the team member possesses regarding the domain for which the application is being developed;
- the level of stress under which the team member is placed whilst working on the project;
- and the workload of the team member.

The information concerning the interaction mechanism(s) with which the team members are familiar is used directly in the generation of the project specific ideal tool profile (see section 3.2).   The remaining information can be used, if required, to assist in the comparison process if it is not immediately obvious from the project specific tool profiles which tool is most suited to the project.

Institutional Goals or Constraints

A software development company may have specific long-term institutional goals which are relevant to the acquisition or use of a UIDT, and must therefore be taken into consideration during the selection process.   SUIT captures constraining information such as the programming language which is supported by the UIDT; the staff training which is possible upon purchase of the UIDT; the universe of UIDTs from which the selection can take place; the financial costs involved with purchase and installation of the UIDT; the development platform(s) on which the UIDT must operate; and the speed with which the development must take place.

The principle role of these factors is to constrain the set of potential tools from which the evaluator can choose.   Obviously, if a tool cannot be found which conforms to these constraints, they would have to be negotiated in order to make a selection possible.   Initially though, they provide the boundaries within which the evaluator has to operate.   Although these environmental aspects are not directly involved with the actual evaluations, they can exert substantial influence over the process at the highest level.

User Interface Specific Requirements
The purpose for which an application is being developed and the design of the user interface to that application will generate certain concrete user interface specific requirements – for example, visual features which may be demanded by the client or external devices which may be fixed. If a UIDT is to be complete in its support of the user interface development for a project, each of these requirements must be catalogued (i.e. included in the project specific tailored framework) and then checked against the service provision of each potential UIDT. When choosing a tool for a specific project, the listed user interface components are selectively kept or rejected according to the requirements of the project, thus generating a project specific reference model (the project specific tailored framework) which is used for data collection and the creation of the project specific ideal tool profile against which the results are compared. In contrast, when performing a generic comparison of tools, the entire set of user interface specific components is used as a reference model for data collection and then comparison.

User interface specific features cover all those components which are likely to appear in an interface (including its associate peripherals). SUIT imposes a hierarchical categorization on the user interface specific aspects of its reference model. The list below demonstrates the two highest levels of classification. Reference should be made to the actual framework in order to obtain details about the lower levels of classification – that is, the actual concrete components or features [13].

- *General Properties of the User Interface*
  - Screen Navigation
  - Dialogue
  - Active Devices
  - Miscellaneous
- *Input/Output Devices*
  - Input Devices
  - Output Devices
  - Target Monitor
  - Other Hardware Devices
- *Output Presentation Types*
  - Text
  - Graphics
  - Animation
  - Audio
  - Video
  - Data Driven/Dynamic Objects

- *Combinations of Output Presentation Types*
  - One Screen/Different Windows
  - One Screen/Same Window

- *User Interface Features*
  - Boxes
  - Menus
  - Forms
  - Windows
  - Text Areas

Each of the above categories is extensible in order that technological advances can be introduced, ensuring that the SUIT framework remains up to date. Together the list of components provide a reference model of all possible interface associated features.

The hierarchical nature of these lists in SUIT serves two purposes: it makes navigation around the lists of features easier; and it enables the evaluator to select an entire category rather than have to consider each component within a category.

Developmental Context of Use
In addition to the environmental constraints mentioned in section 3.4.2, UIDT use is also constrained by aspects of the developmental context into which the UIDT must be integrated. These contextual aspects are primarily concerned with the integration of the UIDT into existing working practice and the ways in which the UIDT can enhance or support these practices, including the design and development methodology adopted by the organization for the completion of the project, and the technological support which must be provided by the UIDT.

On the assumption that a tool will be most easily adopted for use in an organization if it is compatible with, or enhances, the developmental needs and working practice of the organization, SUIT allows the evaluator to assess the degree to which the tools provide:

- user interface design and development steps
- evaluation assistance
- development aids
- project management
- tool characteristics
- quality attributes of the target system.

SUIT also imposes a hierarchical categorization on the developmental contextual aspects. As in the previous section, the following list shows the highest levels in the SUIT classification and reference should again be made to the actual framework for component level detail. During the evaluation process, the above aspects of a UIDT are treated in the same way as the interface specific features outlined in section 3.4.2.

General Layout of the SUIT Framework
The SUIT framework is organized around tables – an example of which is shown in figure 5. There is a separate table for each of the categories discussed in sections 3.4.1 to 3.4.3. The rows in the tables correspond to the various components within each category.

As can be seen in figure 5, the label for each component is preceded by a small box. Selection of these boxes registers the inclusion of their associated component in the evaluation process. Therefore, when performing a generic comparison, all of these boxes are selected. In contrast, when choosing a tool for a specific project, only those boxes which refer to components which are relevant to the project are selected. Tool user requirements usually vary in importance. Some software development tool evaluation methods enable components to be ranked or weighted according to their importance or significance [1], [2], [3], and [9]. However, as highlighted by Mosley, such mechanisms are time-consuming and complex, impeding *practical* UIDT evaluation [9]. For this reason, SUIT replaces weighting factors with tailorability in the framework, and data filters in the visualization environment (see section 5).

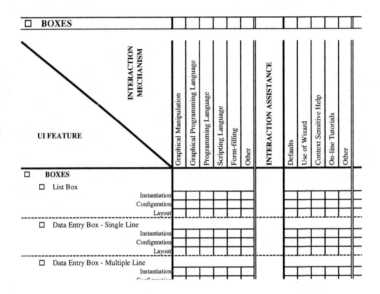

Fig. 5. A section of a typical SUIT framework page

The columns in the tables reflect the dimensions of the tools which should be recorded. These dimensions fall into the following five categories: the interaction mechanisms used; the interaction assistance provided; the cognitive demands placed upon the users; the quality of feedback from the tool; and other miscellaneous factors relating to the tool and its use.

Interaction mechanisms play a pivotal role in the selection of tools using SUIT – as was discussed in sections 3.2 and 3.3. Selecting a tool which lessens the disparities between the actual interaction mechanisms used and those which are appropriate for the anticipated tool users (as shown by the ideal tool profile) will in turn lessen the time taken for the users to learn the tool and hopefully increase the levels of acceptance of the new tool. Further, it can be seen that the examination of the interaction mechanisms and interaction assistance for each component is broken down into their instantiation, configuration, and layout (where appropriate) in order that potential differences in the three aspects of incorporating a component can be highlighted.

The remaining four categories play a secondary or supporting role in the selection of tools. Comparison of the project specific tool profiles with respect to the project specific ideal tool profile (i.e. functionality integrated with interaction mechanisms) will eliminate the most inappropriate tools from the selection process, but may not be sufficient to make a rational decision concerning the best fit tool for the project from the remaining tools. Instead, additional factors, such as these, may have to be taken into consideration in order to select one tool from a set of tools which may be similar in terms of functionality and interaction styles.

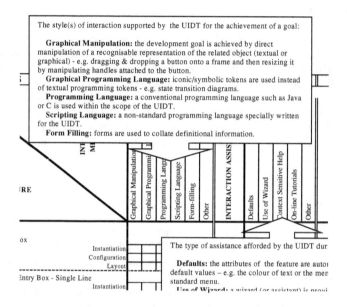

Fig. 6. A section of a SUIT glossary page

Finally, SUIT provides the facility to record miscellaneous information about a tool in order that particularly good or bad features of the tool can be noted and drawn upon during the selection process. Hence the supporting data in the additional columns provides the means by which the evaluator can make final judgement about (otherwise identical) tools and therefore make a rationalized recommendation of the best fit tool for a project.

Integrated Help in the SUIT Framework

For each page in the SUIT framework, there is a corresponding glossary page. These are annotated versions of the actual framework tables and describe what is meant by every term in each table. The glossary pages are located opposite the corresponding framework page for ease of reference whilst using the framework. An example of a part of a glossary page is given in figure 6.

3   Evaluative Study

Once completed, SUIT was the subject of an evaluative study.   The principal aim of this study was to assess the viability of SUIT as a paper-based mechanism for evaluation of UIDTs.   During this study, the use of SUIT was compared to that of the nearest alternative method – the checklist system developed by Hix *et al* [3] – but these findings are outwith the scope of this paper.   This section will briefly outline the nature of the study and summarize our findings related to SUIT's viability and potential value.

3.1   The Study

Twenty seven final year undergraduate computing science students were divided into pairs and allocated an evaluation method (either SUIT or the method developed by Hix *et al*).   They were taught how to use their allocated method and given a problem scenario outlining the requirements and context for a project.   Each pair was given 30 hours to complete an evaluation of two web page authoring tools and, with respect to the scenario, make a recommendation for the selection of one.   All subjects submitted an evaluation report, their evaluation forms, and a log sheet detailing their allocation of time to subtasks.   They also completed a questionnaire based on the NASA TLX workload measures [14].

3.2   The Results

Examination of the evaluation forms indicated that the subjects had, on the whole, correctly used the forms.   It appeared that they had been thorough and complete in their evaluation and there was noticeable intra-subject consistency in the use of the SUIT framework pages.

Although SUIT is designed to structure and guide UIDT data collection and not the actual *comparison* process, its structure and methodological emphasis may imply a possible approach to the latter.   In order to inform the design of a tool to assist in the *visualization* of the data, it was therefore essential to observe subjects' focus of attention during the comparison and decision making stages.   We identified, within the evaluation reports, occurrences of terms related to project requirements and context of use (e.g. "required attributes" and "team member").   The frequency, composition, and distribution of this term set indicated that use of the SUIT method directed the attention of evaluators to the project-specific and contextual aspects of UIDT evaluation supported by SUIT.   Any tool designed to aid the comparison of (SUIT related) tool information would have to provide the means to compare the data in the context of each of these aspects.   In particular the ideal tool profile was shown to play an essential role in the comparison process and should therefore be readily accessible within any visualization.

The evaluation reports were also examined in an attempt to gauge subjects' reactions to their evaluation method.   The following quote has been selected as representative:

"[SUIT] directed your considerations to specific things and ensured that you didn't overlook any details of user interface design. It proved to be hard to split the two packages we compared as they were very similar. In the end, the recommendation came more out of discussion and consideration of certain aspects of the scenario rather than from some metric derived from the framework."

Quotes such as that above highlight that the real difficulty in tool selection is deciding between two tools which are very close in terms of functionality and style. The variability and complexity of this task mitigates against offering a comprehensive and clearly defined approach to supporting the final comparison. It confirms the need for tools which provide the evaluator with the means to visualize and query the data during this examination and decision making process

The log sheets showed that subjects did not have to spend a large proportion of their time trying to understand and learn SUIT which would in turn suggest SUIT has the potential to be successfully adopted across a wider universe of subjects. It was noted that subjects spent the greatest proportion of their time using the actual tools to extract the required data. In order to reduce this cost, tool templates for some of the more common tools will be provided with the SUIT system – for example Visual Basic™ and Borland's Delphi™.

Encouragingly therefore, the results of the evaluative study were indicative of its viability as a paper-based evaluation methodology. There was evidence that the methodology is comprehensive and effective and that it directs the attention of the evaluator as it was designed to. The results also identified the principal requirements of any tool designed to visualize data gathered during a SUIT tool selection. In particular, the study highlighted the need to visualize the data for the ideal tool profile alongside the data for the individual tools. Further, it provided an indication of the manner in which the visualized data might need to be manipulated and/or queried – for example, the highlighting of differences/similarities with the ideal or the identification of the use of interaction mechanisms or interaction assistance types. Given the conditions under which the study took place, we were unable to avoid experimenter influence in terms of the anonymity of the two evaluation methods. Thus, we recognize that the Hawthorne affect may have influenced both the motivation of the subjects using SUIT, and their subjective assessment of the method. However, the subjects had no knowledge of what we were anticipating with respect to the relative importance of time versus quality of evaluation, or the content of their completed evaluation checklists, and therefore, this information is unlikely to be subject to method-oriented bias.

4   The SUIT Tool

The SUIT methodology, framework, and the observations outlined above informed the design of a visualization environment to assist in the comparison and analysis of data collected using the SUIT system. The tool has yet to be evaluated in any form, and therefore this section will simply introduce the tool and its core functionality. It makes no claims as to the effectiveness of its design.

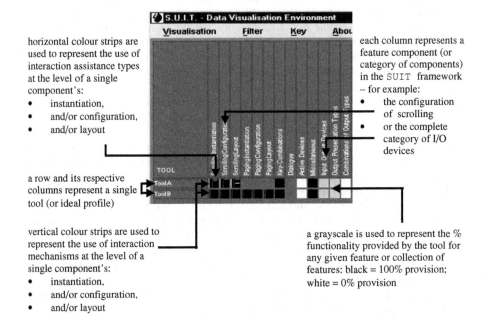

horizontal colour strips are used to represent the use of interaction assistance types at the level of a single component's:

- instantiation,
- and/or configuration,
- and/or layout

each column represents a feature component (or category of components) in the SUIT framework – for example:

- the configuration of scrolling
- or the complete category of I/O devices

a row and its respective columns represent a single tool (or ideal profile)

vertical colour strips are used to represent the use of interaction mechanisms at the level of a single component's:

- instantiation,
- and/or configuration,
- and/or layout

a grayscale is used to represent the % functionality provided by the tool for any given feature or collection of features: black = 100% provision; white = 0% provision

Fig. 7. An example of a SUIT Visualization

4.1   Introduction to the SUIT Visualization Environment

The SUIT tool is a research *data visualization* environment which extracts structure and data from external databases and represents their contents using a combination of location and color coding in order to allow analysis and interrogation of the data.   Figure 7 shows part of a visualization which has been created for a generic comparison of two fictitious tools, annotated to highlight the main features.

A SUIT data visualization explicitly represents most of the data which is contained within the SUIT framework.   The remaining data - that which is not visible above - is available on demand.   To simplify a visualization, the evaluator can chose to hide the information about interaction assistance.

Each of the categories in the SUIT framework is represented by a column in the visualization - for example, *Input/Output Devices* in figure 7.   The components within each of these categories are also represented by a column in the visualization, and can be examined by expanding the parent level column.   Similarly detail can be hidden by contracting a column and thus visualizing the data at the level of abstraction one above that which was selected.   In essence therefore, a row in the SUIT framework corresponds to a column in the SUIT visualization.   It is hoped that allowing the evaluator to select the level of abstraction at which to visualize data will enable greater control over, and flexibility of, analysis.   This aspect of the visualization is maximized by allowing the evaluator to vary the level of abstraction on a category-by-category basis such that some components can be viewed at the lowest level of abstraction whilst others can be viewed at the level of the complete category.

4.2   Interacting with a SUIT Visualization

Columns in the visualization can be re-ordered via drag-and-drop to allow selective juxtapositioning of the data during analysis. In this way, an evaluator can bring together components which are of greatest interest and therefore make visual comparison easier. In addition, columns can be hidden (or excluded) from the visualization to eliminate selected data and thus narrow the field of concern. At an instance level (i.e. the instantiation, configuration, or layout of a single component) the data concerning the interaction mechanisms used and assistance types provided can be viewed. If a feature is not provided by a given tool, these cells will appear blank in the visualization at this level - as exemplified by the columns for *Paging* in figure 7.

Aside from manipulating the visual appearance and location of the data within the visualization, the evaluator can also query the data. SUIT queries are essentially predefined filters which can be applied to the active data set. Initially, the active data set comprises all data which is in the visualization. This set becomes progressively smaller as filters are applied, such that all data components in the active set satisfy all of the applied filters. The SUIT maintains a textual record of the history of filter application in order that the semantics of the active data set can be viewed at any point in time.

In accordance with the results of the evaluative study discussed previously, SUIT provides a selection of basic filters. These include highlighting: all percentage functionality matches/mis-matches with the ideal tool profile; all interaction mechanism matches/mis-matches with the ideal tool profile; user defined uses of interaction mechanisms; user defined uses of interaction assistance types; user defined cognitive demands; user defined quality of feedback; user defined other miscellaneous aspects of the data; and all columns where there is a match/mis-match across all tools in the visualization. As previously stated, these filters can be applied solo or in combination. Together, data hiding and filter application enables the evaluator to focus on those issues which are of greatest significance in terms of identified requirements.

During the course of interaction with the SUIT visualization environment, an evaluator will potentially combine a number of the above facilities in order to interrogate the data or investigate a specific issue. At any point in time, the evaluator can chose to take a snapshot of the result of such manipulation in order that the state of the visualization can be maintained for reference during the comparison process. Once created, snapshots are independent of their source (i.e. the original visualization or another snapshot of which they are a copy) and so can themselves be further manipulated allowing the evaluator maximum flexibility for data analysis.

5   Further Work

Our work so far, albeit based on and informed by empirical investigations, still needs to be evaluated in terms of real UIDT assessments. We are currently embarking on a set of evaluative studies of the methodology and SUIT tool to find out if the methodology is practicable, the tool usable, and the results of their use beneficial and cost-effective.   The studies fall into two categories: (1) usability testing of the data visualization tool; and (2) observation of the SUIT system (and its outcome) used in two case studies, one industrial and one academic.

There are a number of potential directions for the extension of our approach.   Perhaps the easiest of these would be the modification of the SUIT method for other types of CASE tool.   This should only require generating a new reference framework based on the functionality of the tool type.   Moreover, as the framework, method, and tool begin to be exercised in real contexts of use, we anticipate that they will require elaboration and refinement.   In particular, we expect that heuristics will develop for managing the use of the SUIT tool, for doing the trade-offs necessary to turn an evaluation into a recommendation, and for integrating SUIT into software development practice.

6   References

1   Hix, D., Ryan, T.: Evaluating User Interface Development Tools. Proceedings of the Human Factors Society - 36th Annual Meeting (1992) 374 - 378
2   Hix, D., Schulman, R. S.: Human-Computer Interface Development Tools: A Methodology for their Evaluation. Communications of the ACM, Vol. 34(3). (1991) 74 - 87
3   Hix, D.: An Evaluation Procedure for User Interface Development Tools Version 2.0. Virginia Polytechnic Institute & State University (1991)
4   Bass, L., Abowd, G., Kazman, R.: Issues in the Evaluation of User Interface Tools. In: Taylor, R., Coutaz, J., (eds.): Workshop on Software Engineering & Computer-Human Interaction. Lecture Notes in Computer Science No. 896, Springer-Verlag, Berlin Heidelberg New York (1994) 17 - 27
5   Sundaram, S., Ramamurthy, K.: A Measurement Methodology for Evaluating User Interface Management Systems. In: Journal of Computer Information Systems. Vol. 37. (1996) 54 - 61
6   Myers, B. A.: UIMSs, Toolkits, Interface Builders. Human Computer Interaction Institute, Carnegie Mellon University. (1996)
7   Valaer, L.A., Babb, R. G.: Choosing a User Interface Development Tool. In: IEEE Software. August (1997) 29 - 39
8   Chikofsky, E. J., Martin, D.E., Chang, H.: Assessing the State of Tool Assessment. In: IEEE Software. May (1992) 18 - 21
9   Mosley, V.: How to Assess Tools Efficiently and Quantitatively. In: IEEE Software. May (1992) 29 - 32
10   Poston, R.M., Sexton, M.P.: Evaluating and Selecting Testing Tools. In: IEEE Software. May (1992) 33 - 42
11   Jorgensen, M., Bygdas, J.J., Lunde, T.: Efficiency Evaluation of CASE Tools - Methods and Results. Telnor Scientific Report TF R 38/95. (1995)
12   McKirdy, J.: An Empirical Study of the Relationships Between User Interface Development Tools & User Interface Development. University of Glasgow Technical Report TR-1998-06 (1998)
13   McKirdy, J.: S.U.I.T. - A Framework & Methodology for the Selection of User Interface Development Tools Based on Fitness Criteria.   University of Glasgow Technical Report TR-1999-34 (1999)
14   NASA-Ames-Research-Center, NASA Task Load Index (TLX) Version 1.0 Users Guide. Moffett   Field,   CA: NASA   Ames   Research   Center. http://csariac.flight.wpafb.af.mil/products/tlx.toc.htm

Structuring Interactive Systems Specifications for Executability and Prototypability

David Navarre , Philippe Palanque, Rémi Bastide, and Ousmane Sy

LIHS, Université Toulouse I, Place Anatole France,
F-31042 Toulouse Cedex, France
{palanque, navarre, bastide, sy}@univ-tlse1.fr
http://lihs.univ-tlse1.fr/{palanque, Navarre, Bastide, Sy}

Abstract. This paper presents structuring mechanisms for building executable specifications, in the field of interactive applications, using the Interactive Co-operative Object formal description technique. The design life cycle of the specification is presented as well as how PetShop (a software tool support the ICO formal description technique) can effectively support the various phases of the life cycle. The concepts and the tool are presented on a Range Slider case study. The Range Slider is a medium size component, used for instance, in the field of dynamic queries for information retrieval and visualisation.

1   Introduction

Following the classification of Ken Fishkin in [12], user interfaces (UI) have evolved from the first generation corresponding to keyboard UI to a fifth generation named embodied UI that might disappear with the "final" generation called invisible UI. According to this classification Graphical User Interfaces (GUI) only correspond to the second generation. However, looking at current practice in industry and at current toolkits for UI construction, a lot of design and implementation problems are still to be solved. However, a software engineer can find partial solutions, dedicated to the construction of interactive systems, such as:

- patterns for interactive applications that as described in [9]. In this book two design patterns for interactive systems are presented: PAC ([11]) and MVC ([14])
- metaphors for code structuring ([15]) for interactive applications. These metaphors propose generic structuring mechanisms for classes in a real size interactive application where hundreds of classes can coexist,
- software architectures for interactive applications such as Arch ([4]) or Pac-Amodeus ([17]) (as described and analysed in [3]) that propose generic structures with specialised components.

However, even though these proposals can provide useful hints, their use, from early design phases to implementation, still remains a challenge. The difficulties encountered by the developers for using these design concepts can be explained using the terminology of Norman's action theory ([18]). The difficulties arise from the fact that programmer's objects (user variables in Norman's terms) such as classes, instances and UI widgets available in the programming environment, are significantly

P. Palanque and F. Paternò (Eds.): DSV-IS 2000, LNCS 1946, pp. 97–119, 2001.
© Springer-Verlag Berlin Heidelberg 2001

different from the objects available in these proposals (system variables in Norman's terms) that are usually high-level (generally abstract) design concepts. In order to apply these concepts, the developer has to bridge an important distance both at the semantic and articulatory level and for the execution and evaluation phases.

The paper addresses this issue by presenting structuring mechanisms for a tool-supported formal description technique that aims to reduce both articulatory and semantic distance between the abstract concepts and their effective use. In order to reduce semantic distance, the formal description technique supports in a native way structuring approaches such as architecture and patterns. The reduction of articulatory distance is addressed through tool-support. Indeed, Petshop environment is able to interpret the formal specification and thus execute it as a prototype of the final application. The formal specification can then be decorated with instructions in a programming language (only JAVA binding is currently available) transforming gradually the formal specification into detailed design and consequently the prototype into a final interactive application. Even though presented on a simple but non trivial case study, the concepts presented here have been raised while applying the formal description technique to large scale Air Traffic Control applications within the Esprit Long Term Research project MEFISTO[4].

The problem of building executable specifications has already been addressed in the literature and one of the earlier structured discussions about it can be found in [16]and in [13].

The paper is structured as follow. Section 2 introduces the Range Slider case study that will be used throughout the paper to illustrate informally the formal description technique we defined (ICOs), the way it can be used as well as the design process that should be followed in order to fully exploit its advantages. Section 3 introduces briefly and intuitively the Interactive Cooperation Objects formalism. This formal description technique has been designed to address specific problems raised by the specification of interactive systems. The application of the formal description technique to the case study (introduced in section 2) is fully presented in section 4. After the presentation of the design process in section 0, section 6 explains and describes how this formal specification can be edited and executed within PetShop environment.

2   Presentation of the Range Slider Case Study

In order to present the ICO formalism and the Petshop environment supporting it, we use hereafter a case study. We also present, how using these tools it is possible to structure specifications for interactive applications in order to allow for executability.

---

[4] more information about MEFISTO is available on the following web site: http://giove.cnuce.cnr.it/mefisto

2.1   Global Presentation

Fig. 1 presents the window of the film application. This application has been generated using the SpotFire environment and can be downloaded from http://www.spotfire.com. This window is split into two main areas: the zoomable starfield display on the right and the set of query devices on the right [2]. This set of query devices can be manipulated by the user and the corresponding information in the starfield display is dynamically updated i.e. after each action of the user on the query devices.

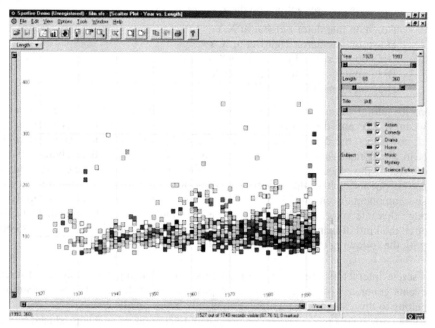

Fig. 1. Screen dump of the Film application from SpotFire.

2.2   Detailed Presentation

Two range sliders are located on the top right side of the picture. A Range Slider is an interactor that allows easily to select a range of values (RV) within a range of possible values (RPV). **Fig. 2** shows in detail the presentation part of a range slider interactor for selecting a range of lengths for Films. On this picture the current selection corresponds to all the movies which length is between 68 and 360.

The presentation part is made up of 5 interactors:

- A central part called *lift*, that allows the user to set both ends of the RV at a time,
- Two buttons called *LeftArrow* and *RightArrow*, that allow the user to set precisely the corresponding end of the RV.
- Two buttons called *LeftBar* and *RightBar*, that allow to set rapidly and roughly one of the values at the end of the RV.

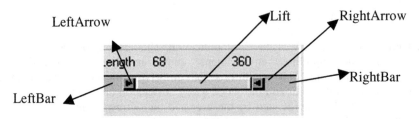

Fig. 2. The various elements of a Range Slider

The set of possible user actions on these interactors is:

Down on interactor LeftBar at X,Y
Down on interactor RightBar at X,Y
Drag on interactor LeftArrow at X,Y
Drag on interactor RightArrow at X,Y
Drag on interactor Lift at X,Y

From the initial definition of direct manipulation interfaces in [23], the difference between WIMP and direct manipulation interfaces has lost most of its interest. Indeed, nowadays, the distinction is less about the object manipulated (application objects in direct manipulation and UI interactors in WIMP ones) than about the manipulation of the objects themselves. For instance manipulating enhanced user interface components such as alphasliders [1] allows us to consider direct manipulation of these components even though the objects of the domain are still only manipulated through this interactor. For this paper we decide to address the classification of GUI through the kind of manipulation that can be performed on their interactors. This ends up with the following (for a more complete description please read [21]):

- discrete interactors: this kind of interactors is only manipulated through discrete events generated by the user acting on physical input devices. CommandButtons belong to this category as manipulation is only based on clic events.
- continuous interactors: these interactors react to streams of events produced by the user on continuous input devices
- hybrid interactors: they react to both continuous and discrete manipulations. Scrollbars belong to this category as the user can drag the lift or click on the arrows at top and bottom.

The Range Slider belongs to the hybrid category of interactors as it can be manipulated both in a discrete and continuous way. This is one of reason why we have chosen this case study. The reasons are

- the behaviour of the Range Slider is not trivial,
- it is made up of several more basic interactors,
- it belongs to the hybrid category
- this kind of compound quite complex interactors are more and more used in interactive applications and companies building user interface toolkits (such as Microsoft and Ilog) have already invested in component technology. However, the more complex the components the less reliable they are.

However, this case study does not represent concurrent behaviour. For concerns related to concurrency modelling in the ICO formalism please refer to [19].

These incorrect behaviours of interactors are even more critical as they can be reused widely and every time the same difficulties will arise. This shows the interest of validating carefully the design and the implementation of these ready-to-use, off-the-shelves components. This gives a new wide application area for formal specification techniques.

After this informal presentation of the range slider next section introduces the ICO formalism. For the readers already familiar with this formal specification technique, section 4 presents its application to the formal specification of the Range Slider.

3   Overview of the ICO Formalism

This section recalls the main features of the ICO formalism, that we use to model the case study in section 4. We encourage the interested reader should look at [7] and [5] for a complete presentation of the formal description technique.

3.1   Introduction

The ICO formalism uses concepts borrowed from the object-oriented approach (dynamic instantiation, classification, encapsulation, inheritance, client/server relationship) to describe the static (or structural) aspects of systems, and uses high-level Petri nets to describe their dynamic (or behavioural) aspects.

ICOs were originally devised for the modelling and implementation of event-driven interfaces. An ICO model of a system is made up of several communicating objects, where both behaviour of objects and communication protocol between objects are described by high level Petri nets. When two objects communicate, one is in the position of a "client", requesting the execution of a service and waiting for a result, while the other is in the position a "server" whose role is to execute the service. In the ICO formalism, an object is an entity featuring four components: behaviour, services, state and presentation.

3.2   Behaviour

The behaviour of an ICO states how the object reacts to external stimuli according to its inner state. A high-level Petri net, called the Object Control Structure (ObCS), describes the behaviour of the class. A Petri net is a directed bipartite graph whose nodes are either *places* (depicted as circles) or *transitions* (depicted as rectangles). Arcs connect places and transitions. Each place may contain any number of *tokens*. In high-level Petri nets, tokens may carry values. In our formalism, tokens may hold conventional values (integer, string, etc.) or references to other objects in the application. In that case, arcs are labelled by variables thus allowing representing the flow of tokens on the high-level Petri net.

A transition may feature a *precondition* that is a Boolean expression that may involve the variables labelling the input arcs of the transition.

A transition *is fireable* (may occur) if and only if:

(i)   each of its input places carries at least one token
(ii)   if the transition features a precondition; it exists tokens in the input places for which the precondition holds

When a transition is fired, it removes one token from each of its input places, and sets one token in each of its output places. A transition features an *action* part, which may request services from the tokens involved in the occurrence of the transition, or perform arbitrary algorithms manipulating the values of tokens.

3.3   Services

An ICO offers a set of services that define the interface (in the programming language meaning) offered by the object to its environment. In the case of user-driven application, this environment may be either the user or other objects of the application. Each service is related to at least one transition in the ObCS, and a service is only available when at least one of its related transitions is fireable. This relationship between transitions (T) and services is defined by the *availability function*:

$$Avail: \quad Services \quad \rightarrow \quad P(T) \text{ where P(T) is the power set of T:}$$

- $\forall s \in Services, Avail(s) \neq \varnothing$
- $\forall s, s' \in Services / s \neq s', Avail(s) \cap Avail(s') = \varnothing$

Using the ICO formalism, we distinguish between two kinds of services:

- services offered to the user, called *user services*, are represented in the ObCS by *user transitions*, and that directly relates to the presentation part of the ICO. Their graphical representation is a transition with a broken arrow and a greyed circle

- services offered to other objects that are graphically represented by a transition with an incoming broken arrow

3.4   State

The state of an ICO is the distribution and the value of the tokens (called the *marking*) in the places of the ObCS. As services are related to transitions, this allows defining how the current state influences the availability of services, and conversely how the performance of a service influences the state of the object.

3.5   Presentation

The Presentation of an object states its external look. This Presentation is a structured set of *widgets* organised in a set of windows. Each widget is described by a set of attributes and a set of presentation methods called in order to change the appearance of the widget. Each attribute represents part of its external look like its name, colour or bounds. Each presentation method is a way to modify one or several of its attributes.

The user → system interaction only takes place through these widgets. Each user action on a widget may trigger one of the ICO's user services. The relation between user services and widgets is fully stated by the *activation function* that associates to each couple (widget, user action) the service to be triggered.
More precisely the activation function is defined as follows:

$$Act: Widgets \; X \; Events \rightarrow Services$$

The system → user interaction is fully specified by the *rendering function* describing how to render information to the user. Rendering is state based [10], and thus the rendering function relates the call of presentation methods of the ICO class to the elements that represent state in the ICO i.e. places (see section 3.4). Two different operations can alter state in the ObCS of an ICO class: a token has entered in a place or a token has been removed from a place.

$$Rend: P \; X \; \{TokenEntered, TokenRemoved\} \rightarrow \wp(Widgets)$$

where $\wp(Widgets)$ is the power set of W and P is the set of places of the ObCS.

3.6   ICO and MVC Design Pattern

As stated in section 1, the ICO formal description technique supports the MVC design pattern natively. Up to three roles can be set for a class.
ICO class as a Model: in that case the ICO class has no presentation part. The class is not related to widget and thus both activation and rendering functions are empty.
ICO class as a Controller: in that case, the ICO class must be related to a set of widgets. The activation function describes how the user can interact with the class (by means of action on the widgets). The rendering function is empty.
ICO class as a View: in that case, the ICO class is also related to a set of widgets. The activation function is empty, as only a controller may be manipulated by a user. The rendering function describes precisely how, according to addition or removal of tokens in each place, the object triggers methods changing the appearances of the related widgets.
As we will see in next section, it is quite common that an ICO plays both the roles of controller and view at a time. In that case the class is a full-fledged ICO featuring all the presentation components (a set of widgets and both rendering and activation function).

If an ICO V is a view of a model this is denoted in the textual part of the class as
    View of Model1 **as** Model;
where Model1 is a variable holding a reference to an instance of the class Model.
    In that case the ICO V may feature a rendering function for the object for which it is a view. This rendering function is of the same type as the inner rendering function

of the ICO V. However, this external rendering function is defined over the set of places of the ObCS of the Class Model. An example of external rendering function will be given in section 0.

4   Formal Specification of the RangeSlider

The ICO-based specification of the case study consists in several object classes, pictured in **Fig. 3** using the UML diagrammatic notation [22]. This class diagram shows that the *RangeSlider* class is composed of elements from three other classes. More precisely it is made up of 5 instances: 2 *RangeArrows*, 1 *RangeLift* and 2 *RangeBars*. These three classes inherit from the same abstract class: *Button*. According to the software engineering principles for interactive systems construction, it is important to separate abstraction from presentation. For this reason a class *Range* representing the abstract data type of a range has been added to the set of classes.

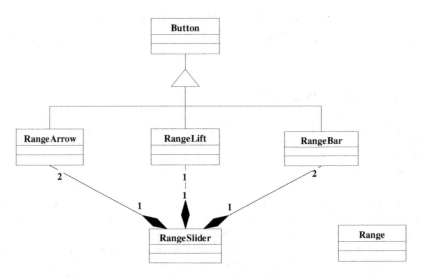

Fig. 3. Class diagram of the Range Slider

According to the Model View Controller design pattern [9] the *RangeSlider* class assumes both the Controller and View roles, while the *Range* class is only a Model, as illustrated in **Fig. 6**.

4.1   Specification of the *Range* Model

Hereafter (**Fig. 5**) we present the class *Range* as an ICO class. The Range class is the behavioural specification of the IRange interface given in **Fig. 4**.

```
interface IRange {
      float getMinimum( );
      void  setMinimum(float value);
      float getMaximum();
      void  setMaximum(float value);
}
```

Fig. 4: The *IRange* interface

The IRange interface is provided with operations to get and set the minimum and maximum values of the range. The ICO specification refines this interface by describing precisely the behaviour for the operations, in the form of a high-level Petri net. All the get operations are related to places by test arcs. These arcs play the role of validating conditions for a transition as the tokens are not removed by the firing of the transition but they are required for it fireability.

This net ensures an invariant on the consistency of the minimum and maximum values of the range, i.e.

$$absoluteMin \leq getMinimum( ) \leq getMaximum( ) \leq absoluteMax.$$

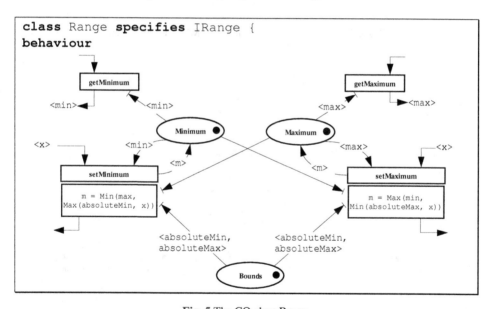

Fig. 5 The CO class Range

4.2   Software Architecture

The correct use of the design pattern MVC (see **Fig. 6**) helps ensuring the conformance between the model (the Range class) and the presentation (the RangeSlider class) as after any change in the model the view have to service a relevant notification. As the component classes (the arrows, the lift and the bars) are integrated in the Range Slider there is no need to represent them separately. However, the Range class must be represented as it is used by the Range Slider and is in charge of ensuring correct usage of the Range Slider (i.e. the constraints are always verified).

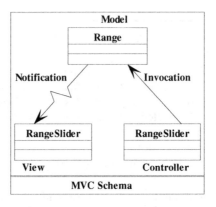

Fig. 6. Roles of classes according to the MVC design pattern

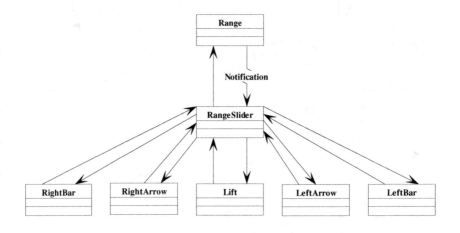

Fig. 7. Use relationship among classes

The RangeSlider class plays both roles of controller and view for the Range class. When it is a controller it converts user inputs into modification orders towards the

Range. On the contrary when the RangeSlider class plays the role of view of Range class, it receives notifications every time the Range is modified.

MVC design pattern makes the Range (the model) independent from any notion of presentation, so communication between RangeSlider (the controller) and Range only concerns abstract values. These abstract values correspond to the translation by the controller of low-level presentation information (at pixel level). To this end, the RangeSlider class delegates this computing to the set of integrated components (see five boxes at the bottom of **Fig. 7**).

Fig. 8 presents the sequence of actions that occur from the user input to the rendering to the user. It illustrates how user inputs are converted into modifications of the range by the RangeSlider and according to the MVC design pattern, how the RangeSlider renders these modifications.

Initially the Range Slider has a physical size in pixels. When associated to a Range, this number of pixel represents a range of values. The scale is defined by the ratio between the number of pixels of the RangeSlider and the number of values of the associated Range. For instance, if a RangeSlider of 100 pixels is associated to a range of [100 .. 1000] elements, then the scale is 9, i.e. each pixel represents 9 values.

When each of its components receives a user action, there is a need to compute the corresponding range modification. Following diagram in **Fig. 8**, a small example of manipulation of the Range Slider and the corresponding exchange of information between the various components:

- left arrow receives an event Mousedown,
- coordinates where the mouse event occurred (for instance at position (10, 10)) are stored,
- while it receives mouse event drag (for instance (30, 10)) it computes new offset in number of pixels (in that case 20),
- pixels are the converted into the corresponding value (here it is 180),
- this value is then communicated to the Range Slider that sets the left value of the Range.

The Range is then modified and notifies in return all its views i.e. the Range Slider. To render the new value it also notifies the corresponding components. For instance, after the RangeSlider has been notified for the modification of the left value of the Range, it sets its leftArrow, leftBar and lift to the new value. These components are then in charge of updating their graphical representation (in that case, only the bounding box property is concerned). For more details on the activation of these widgets, please refer to sections 4.4, 4.6, 4.7.

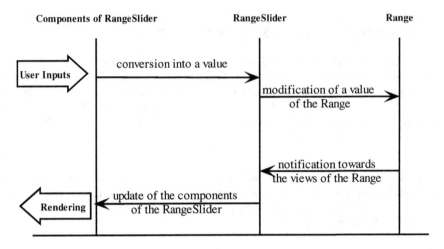

Fig. 8. Sequence diagram from user input to rendering

The following sections present the complete specification of the Range Slider at the end of the design process that is presented in section 5. This specification describes the four components of the class ICO as introduced in section 3. First, se present the set of services of the class (i.e. what is offered to the other classes of the application if any). Then the ObCS and the states are presented (i.e. the states of the application and the state changing operators). Lastly, the presentation part is described:

- The activation function (i.e. the actions the user can perform on the Range Slider and its reactions to these actions),
- The rendering function (i.e. the set of methods used by the Range Slider to render its state to the user)
- The widget (i.e. the set of attributes which identify the components as well as the methods which modify these attributes).

4.3   Services

For describing the set of services offered by a Class to its environment we use the Interface Description Language as defined by the Object Management Group for the CORBA standard Corba [24].

```
Interface IRangeSlider {
}
```

As it can be easily seen the IDL description does not represent the MVC mechanisms such as notification as this is closer to implementation with respect to the specification phase. As the RangeSlider is not used by other classes its interface is empty.

4.4   Behaviour (ObCS)

The behaviour of the Class Range Slider is fully described by its ObCS. The following describes the set of places (and their type) and the set of transition (and their action) of the Object Petri net defining the behaviour of the class.

```
Class RangeSlider
Specifies IRangeSlider {
            //Definition of Places
            Place CurrentRangeValue <Range> = {
1*<range> };
            Place UpdatingAllValues <Range>;
            Place UpdatingLeftValues <Range>;
            Place UpdatingRightValues <Range>;
            //Definition of Transitions
            Transition BeginUpdateAllValues {}
            Transition UpdateAllValues {
             Action {
               v.setMinimum(v.getMinimum() + x);
               v.setMaximum(v.getMaximum() + x);
             }
            }
            Transition EndUpdateAllValues {}
            Transition BeginUpdateLeftValue {}
            Transition UpdateLeftValue {
             Action {
               v.setMinimum(v.getMinimum() + x);
             }
            }
            Transition EndUpdateLeftValue {}
            Transition BeginUpdateRightValue {}
            Transition UpdateRightValue {
             Action {
               v.setMaximum(v.getMaximum() + x);
             }
            }
            Transition EndUpdateRightValue {}
            Transition DirectUpdateLeftValue {
             Action {
               v.setMinimum(x);
             }
            }
            Transition DirectUpdateRightValue {
             Action {
               v.setMaximum(x);
             }
            }
 }
```

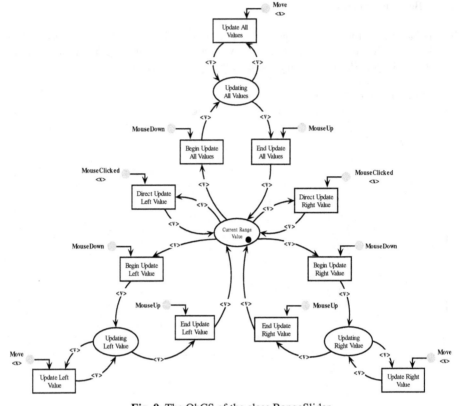

Fig. 9. The ObCS of the class RangeSlider

4.5   Widgets

The widget part described the external presentation part of the Range Slider. We describe hereafter (see **Fig. 10**) the set of basic attributes that characterise each instance of each component of the RangeSlider. For each attribute, a method *set* and a method *get* must be generated. For instance, the attribute range needs the two following methods:

1.   void setScale(float newScale);
2.   float getScale().

These methods must be used by other classes to access and modify the values of the attributes. We use inheritance between classes (here, RangeSlider inherits from JComponent defined by java swing), thus providing through inheritance a set of attributes. The attributes described hereafter are only new attributes or the ones that are overridden.

Another part of this widget part is the description of a set of methods used to produce rendering by the rendering function (see section 4.7).

```
Class WidgetRangeSlider
extends JComponent {
    Attributes {
        float scale
            //It is the value represented by one pixel
    }
    Rendering methods {
        ShowLeftValue(float v) {
            //Changes the position of the left arrow,
            //the size of the left bar and the lift
        }
        ShowRightValue(float v) {
            //Changes the position of the right arrow,
            //the size of the right bar and the lift
        }
        ShowLeftArrowWorking() {
            //Shows the left arrow as a pressed button.
        }
        ShowLeftArrowIddle() {
            //Shows the left arrow as normal.
        }
        ShowRightArrowWorking() {
            //Shows the right arrow as a pressed button.
        }
        ShowRightArrowIddle() {
            //Shows the right arrow as normal.
        }
    }
}
```

Fig. 10. The widget description part of the Range Slider

4.6   Activation Function

The activation function relates the events produced by a widget to the transitions of the ObCS. Thus if the transition is fireable and the event is produced (by a corresponding user action on the widget) then the transition is fired (and its action is executed).

As we can see, all the transitions of the ObCS in **Fig. 11** are related to user actions which means that only the user can trigger Range Slider functions (the class has no spontaneous behaviour and that does not offer services to other classes of the application). This can also be seen from the IDL description (see section 4.3) as no service is offered to the environment.

Widget	Event	Service
Lift	Down	BeginUpdateAllValues
Lift	Move <x>	UpdateAllValues
Lift	Up	EndUpdateAllValues
LeftArrow	Down	BeginUpdateLeftValue
LeftArrow	Move <x>	UpdateLeftValue
LeftArrow	Up	EndUpdateLeftValue
RightArrow	Down	BeginUpdateRightValue
RightArrow	Move <x>	UpdateRightValue
RightArrow	Up	EndUpdateRightValue
LeftBar	Click <x>	DirectUpdateLeftValue
RightBar	Click <x>	DirectUpdateRightValue

Fig. 11. The activation function of the Range Slider

4.7   Rendering Function

As sated in section 3.5 the rendering function describes how state changes are rendered to the user.

In the Range Slider specification, rendering is divided in two parts. The first part (see **Fig. 12**) is related to inner state changes of the Range Slider, while the second one (see **Fig. 13**) is related to the Range class as RangeSlider is a view of Range. Indeed, as Range Slider is a view of *range*, it needs to render state changes of this object. Variable range used in the method call to show the right and left value of the range refers to the object with which a Range Slider is instantiated (description of the initial marking of class RangeSlider 4.4).

Inner Rendering

ObCS element		Rendering method
Name	Feature	
Place UpdatingLeft-Value	Token Entered	ShowLeftArrowWorking()
	Token Removed	ShowLeftArrowIddle()
Place UpdatingRight-Value	Token Entered	ShowRightArrowWorking()
	Token Removed	ShowRightArrowIddle()

Fig. 12. The inner rendering function of the Range Slider

Rendering as view of *range*

ObCS element		Rendering method
Name	Feature	
`Place` Minimum	`Token Entered`	`ShowLeftValue(range.getMinimum())`
`Place` Maximum	`Token Entered`	`ShowRightValue(range.getMaximum())`

Fig. 13. The rendering function of the Range Slider as view of range

5   The Design Process

As one of the aim of this paper is to focus tool support for ICO formal description technique and to its link to implementation we only discuss here the lower phases of the design process that must be followed while specifying interactive application using ICOs. For more information about early phases (link with requirements, identification of classes, link with task descriptions, etc.) we would recommend the reading of [20].

Once the ICO specification is built, in order to execute it, the following steps have to be performed:

1. Edition of the four components of the ICO specification
2. Refinement by adding details to the specification

    - In the transitions (adding code)
    - In the rendering function (coding the rendering)

3. Execution of the formal specification. This can be done at the various stages of the development (only running the ObCSes)
4. Validation

    - Through the use of verification techniques and anlysis tools
    - Trough user testing of the execution of the specification

This process is detailed hereafter and its practical use, with the Petshop environment, is presented in section 6.

5.1   Edition of ICO Specification

Prototyping the presentation leads to the description of the layout of a set of components that must be described using the ICO formalism.

Editing an ICO specification is then the edition of the components (services, ObCS, widgets, activation function and rendering function) for each class of objects according to a prototype of the application's presentation part itself. This design process can be broke down to the following set of tasks:

T1. edit the ObCS of each ICO class: it requires the construction of the high level Petri net,

T2. prototype the application's presentation part: it requires to arrange the set of components that constitute the application's presentation part,

T3. edit the activation function: it requires to link components from the prototype to the user services,
T4. edit the rendering function: it requires the description of the impact of the ObCS's state changes on the presentation.

Task T1 and T2 can be performed independently, as T1 represents the edition of the dialog part of the interactive application and T2 the presentation part. Of course task T3 and T4 only occur when the relevant part of the two first tasks are performed.

5.2   Refinement towards Implementation

Thanks to the use of high-level Petri nets for the description of the behaviour of the classes, an ICO formal description is **executable** through a Petri net interpreter. Besides, high level ICO description can be refined by adding details like associating some extra code to the ObCS's transitions and coding the rendering methods in the widget part that are called by the rendering function. The scope of the code in the transition is strictly limited. Indeed, the only way for this code to interfere with the behavioural description of the Petri net is through the use of formal parameters (the input and output variables of the transition). Of course the content of the transitions is not taken into account in the verification process. When refined enough, an ICO specification becomes **prototypable** as at that stage the Petri net interpreter can also monitor application code while executing the specificaiton. Indeed, when running the ObCS it produces a sequence of events that describes the state changes of the application and when this sequence is handled it produces changes on the presentation part through the activation and rendering function.

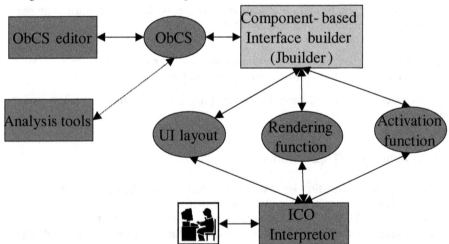

Fig. 14. Architecture of PetShop environment

5.3   Execution and Validation

Briefly, an ICO specification can be executed to provide a prototype of the application under design. It is then possible to proceed to a validation through user testing that, in that case, can be done more easily as, for instance, presentation is separated from the dialogue formal description. A formal validation occurs through the use of verification techniques and analysis tools. This validation is possible due to the algebraic foundation of the Petri nets [6].

6   Petshop Environment

In this section we present precisely how PetShop environment supports the design process presented in section 5. Some screen dumps are included in order to show what is currently available.

An environment that supports the ICO edition can be described by **Fig. 14**. More precisely, such an environment must support the four tasks described above.

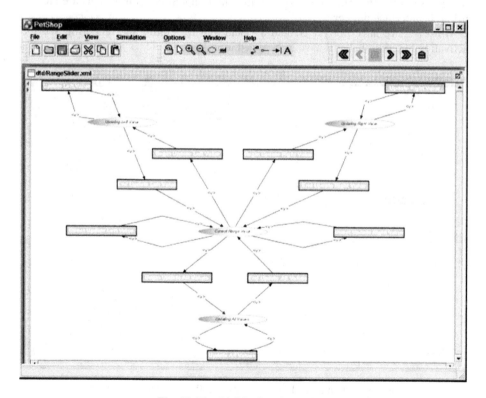

Fig. 15. The ObCS editor in Petshop

6.1   ObCS Editor

Our approach is supported by a tool call PetShop which includes a distributed implementation of high-level Petri net interpreter written in Java.

All the components of the ObCS can be directly built using PetShop. PetShop also
automatically generates an Object Petri net from the IDL description [25]. This Object
Petri net is not the final ObCS of the class but only the minimal set of places and
transitions corresponding to the IDL description.

The edition of the Object Petri net is done graphically using the Palette in the center of the toolbar. The left part of the toolbar is used for generic functions such as
load, save, cut copy and paste. The right hand side of the toolbar drive the execution
of the specification.

6.2   Edition of the Presentation

Currently, PetShop is linked to JBuilder environment for the creation of the presentation part of the ICOs. Thus creation of widgets is done by means of JBuilder interface
builder (see **Fig. 16**). This figure shows how the RangeSlider components are created
using the interface builder.

However, we have not yet created a visual tool for editing the rendering and the
activation function that still have to be typed in in Java.

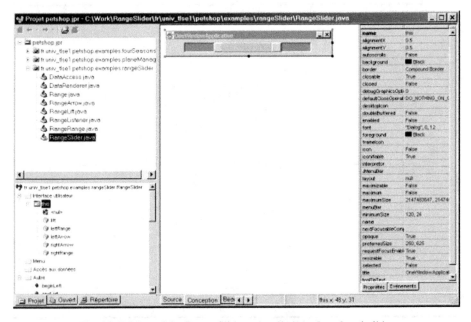

Fig. 16. Edition of the Range Slider using Jbuilder Interface builder

6.3   Execution Environment

A well-known advantage of Petri nets is their executability. This is highly beneficial to our approach, since as soon as a behavioral specification is provided in term of ObCS, this specification can be executed to provide additional insights on the possible evolutions of the system.

Fig. 17 shows the execution of the specification of the Range Slider in Petshop. The ICO specification is embedded at run time according to the interpreted execution of the ICO (see Bastide 95 and Bastide 96 for more details about it: both data structures and execution algorithms).

At run time user can both look at the specification and the actual application. They are in two different windows overlapping in **Fig. 17**. The window RangeSlider corresponds to the execution of the window with the Object Petri net underneath.

In this window we can see the set of transition that are currently fireable (represented in dark grey and the other ones in light grey). This is automatically calculated from the current marking of the Object Petri net.

Each time the user act on the RangeSlider the event is pass onto the interpreter. If the corresponding transition is fireable then the interpreter fires it, perform its action (if any) changes the marking of the input and output places and perform the rendering associated (if any).

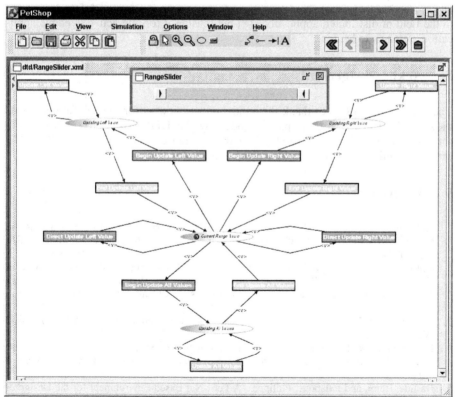

Fig. 17. The execution of ICO specification in PetShop

7   Conclusion

While the ICO formal specification technique has reach a maturity level allowing coping with real size dynamic interactive applications, the Petshop environment is still under development. A real size application has been completely specified in the field of the European project MEFISTO (http://giove.cnuce.cnr.it/mefisto.html).

However, the work done on this air traffic control application has also shown the amount of work that is still required before the environment can be used by other people than the ones that took part in its development.

In order to make it attractive to developers we are integrating additional features such as:

- tool-supported verification of properties,
- analysis of conformance with other representations such as tasks models
- performance analysis in order to support widgets selection and structuring

Another stream of research we are investigating is the generation of test cases from the formal specification in order to help developers checking whether an implementation is conformant with respect to the specification. This will allow development team to take the specifications, still use their favourite programming environment and later check whether their implementation is conformant with it. This work is more mature in the field of distributed applications [8] but reusing it for interactive dynamic applications remains to be done.

8   Acknowledgement

The authors would like to thank the anonymous reviewers for the helpful comments they provided. This work is partly funded by the LTR Esprit project MEFISTO (http://giove.cnuce.cnr.it/mefisto.html) and the France Telecom project SERPICO (http://lihs.univ-tlse1.fr/bastide/SERPICO.htm).

9   References

1. Ahlberg, Cristopher, and Shneiderman, Ben. "The Alphaslider: A Compact and Rapid Selector." *Human Factors in Computing Systems (CHI'94)* , Boston, Massachusetts, USA. USA,(1994) 365-71.
2. Ahlberg, Cristopher, and Truvé, S. "Exploring Terra Incognita in the Design Space of Query Devices." *6th IFIP Conference on Engineering for Human-Computer Interaction, EHCI'95*, Gran Targhee Resort, USA . Len Bass, and Claus Unger. Chapman & Hall (1995) 49-68.
3. Bass, Len, Clements, P., and Kazman, Rick. "Software Architecture in Practice."Addison Wesley
4. Bass, Len, Little, R., Pellegrino, R., Reed, S., Seacord, R., Sheppard, S., and Szezur, M. R. "The Arch Model: Seeheim Revisited." *User Interface Developpers' Workshop.* Version 1.0 (1991)
5. Bastide, Rémi, and Palanque, Philippe. "A Petri-Net Based Environment for the Design of Event-Driven Interfaces ." *16th International Conference on Applications and Theory of*

Petri Nets, ICATPN'95, Torino, Italy. Giorgio De Michelis, and Michel Diaz, Volume editors. Lecture Notes in Computer Science, no. 935. Springer (1995) 66-83.

6. Bastide, Rémi, and Palanque, Philippe. "Verification of an Interactive Software by Analysis of Its Formal Specification." *5ᵗʰ IFIP TC13 International Conference, Interact'95*, Lillehamer, Norway. Chapman et Hall (1995) 191-96.

7. Bastide, Rémi, and Palanque, Philippe. "A Visual and Formal Glue Between Application and Interaction." *Journal of Visual Language and Computing* 10, no. 3 (1999)

8. Bastide, Rémi, Sy, Ousmane, and Palanque, Philippe. "Formal Specification and Prototyping of CORBA Systems." *13ᵗʰ European Conference on Object-Oriented Programming, ECOOP'99*, Lisbon, Portugal. Rachid Guerraoui, Volume editor. Lecture Notes in Computer Science, no. 1628. Springer (1999) 474-94.Selection rate: 184 papers submitted, 20 accepted.

9. Buschmann, F., R. Meunier, H. Rohnert, P. Sommerlad, and M. A Stal. *System of Patterns: Pattern-Oriented Software Architecture*. West Sussex, England, John Wiley & Sons. (1996).

10. Campos, José C., and Harrison, Michael. "Formally Verifying Interactive Systems: A Review." in *4ᵗʰ Eurographics Workshop on Design, Specification and Verification of Interactive System (DSV-IS'97)*, Granada, Spain. Michael Harrison, and Juan Carlos Torres, Editors. Springer (1997) 109-24.

11. Coutaz, Joëlle. "PAC, an Implementation Model for Dialogue Design ." *Interact'87*, North Holland. (1987) 431-37.

12. Fishkin, Kenneth, Moran, Thomas P., and Harrison, Beverly. "Embodied User Interfaces: Towards Invisible User Interfaces." *7ᵗʰ IFIP Conference on Engineering for Human-Computer Interaction (EHCI 98)*, Crete. Kluwer (1999) 1-18.

13. Fuchs, Norbert. E. "Specifications Are (Preferably) Executable." *IEE Software Engineering Journal* 7, no. 5 (1992) 323-34.

14. Goldberg, A., and D. Robson. *Smalltalk-80: the Language and Its Implementations* Addison Wesley (1983).

15. Jacomi, Michele, Chatty, Stéphane, and Palanque, Philippe. "A Making-Movies Metaphor for Structuring Software Components in Highly Interactive Application." *Human-Computer Interaction'97 (HCI'97)*. Springer Verlag London (1997)

16. Jones, C. B., and Hayes, I. J. "Specifications Are Not (Necessarily) Executable." *IEE Software Engineering Journal* 4, no. 6 (1989) 320-338.

17. Nigay, Laurence, and Coutaz, Joëlle. "A Design Space for Multimodal Interfaces: Concurrent Processing and Data Fusion." *INTERCHI'93*. Amsterdam, The Netherlands, ACM press; (1993) 172-78.

18. Norman D. A. "The Psychology of Everyday Things."Harper and Collins (1988).

19. Palanque, Philippe, and Bastide, Rémi. "Formal Specification and Verification of CSCW Using the Interactive Cooperative Object Formalism." *HCI'95*, Huddersfield, UK. Cambridge University Press (1995) 213-30.

20. Palanque, Philippe, and Bastide, Rémi. "Synergistic Modelling of Tasks, Users and Systems Using Formal Specification Techniques." *Interacting With Computers* 9, no. 2 (1997) 129-53.

21. Palanque, Philippe, Bastide, Rémi, Navarre, David, and Sy, Ousmane. "Computer Discretised Interaction: From Continuous to Discrete and Back Again." *CHI 2000 Workshop on Continuity in Human Computer Interaction* , Den Haag, Netherlands. (2000)

22. Rational Software Corporation. *UML Notation Guide*. 1.1 ed.1997.

23. Shneiderman, Ben. "Direct Manipulations: a Step Beyond Prgramming Languages." *IEEE Computer* (1983) 27-69.

24. Siegel, Jon. "OMG Overview: CORBA and the OMA in Enterprise Computing." *Communications of the ACM* 41, no. 10 (1998) 37-43.

25. Sy, Ousmane, Bastide, Rémi, Palanque, Philippe, Le, Duc-Hoa, and Navarre, David. "Pet-Shop: a CASE Tool for the Petri Net Based Specification and Prototyping of CORBA Systems." *20ᵗʰ International Conference on Applications and Theory of Petri Nets, ICATPN'99*, Williamsburg, VA, USA. (1999)

A Toolkit of Mechanism and Context Independent Widgets

Murray Crease, Philip Gray and Stephen Brewster

Department of Computing Science
University of Glasgow, UK
G12 8QQ
{murray, pdg, Stephen}@dcs.gla.ac.uk

Abstract. Most human-computer interfaces are designed to run on a static platform (e.g. a workstation with a monitor) in a static environment (e.g. an office).
However, with mobile devices becoming ubiquitous and capable of running applications similar to those found on static devices, it is no longer valid to design
static interfaces. This paper describes a user-interface architecture which allows
interactors to be flexible about the way they are presented. This flexibility is defined by the different input and output mechanisms used. An interactor may use
different mechanisms depending upon their suitability in the current context,
user preference and the resources available for presentation using that mechanism.

1   Introduction

Szekely [1] describes four challenges that need to be met by human-computer interface technologies. Interfaces need to be able to automatically adapt themselves to
support the user's current task. Interfaces need to be able to support multiple platforms. Interfaces should be tailorable to the users current needs. Interfaces should be
able to handle both input and output using multiple mechanisms. This paper describes
a toolkit of interactors which are designed to provide a solution to the last three of
these challenges, with an implementation which supports adaptable and tailorable
output. An interface's support of multiple platforms and modalities combined with
ease of tailorability is gaining an increased significance due to mobile devices becoming ubiquitous. It is no longer sufficient to design a human-computer interface for
a static platform such as a workstation in an office. Rather, interfaces need to be able
to adapt to different contexts of use. The interface may adapt in the way it accepts
input, or in the way it is presented to the user. This adaption may occur for two reasons, a change in the resources available to the widgets (resource sensitivity) or a
change in the context the platform is situated in (context sensitivity). The resources
available to the widgets may vary due to a change in platform, for example from a
workstation with a large monitor to a personal digital assistant (PDA) with a limited
screen size; but it could also be due to the removal of a resource or greater demand
being placed on a resource. For example a MIDI synthesiser used to provide audio
feedback could be disconnected or have a reduced number of free channels due to the
play back of a MIDI sequence. The context of the platform, and therefore the widgets,

P. Palanque and F. Paternò (Eds.): DSV-IS 2000, LNCS 1946, pp. 121–133, 2001.
© Springer-Verlag Berlin Heidelberg 2001

could vary due to differences in the environment over time, for example the sun could gradually cause more and more glare on a monitor as the day progresses or a shared lab may have different ambient noise levels as the number of people in the room changes. The context may also vary as, for example, the location of a mobile device changes..

By using multiple mechanisms, the widgets can be more flexible in the way they can adapt themselves. The different characteristics of the different mechanisms, on both input and output, allow the demands made by the current context to be best met. Equally, with all the options available, it is important that users are able to tailor the widgets to their personal requirements. These requirements may be a high level preference, for example a preference for a particular colour, or may be based upon a need, for example if visual feed back is of no use to a visually impaired user.

2   Related Work

The Seeheim model [2] was one of the first user interface models to separate the user interface architecture into monolithic functional blocks. Three functional blocks were defined: the presentation system which handled user input and feedback; the application interface model which defined the application from a user interface's point of view and the dialogue control system which defined the communication between the presentation system and the application interface model. Like Seeheim, the toolkit architecture presented in this paper has a monolithic presentation component (albeit with separate blocks for input and output), although the dialogue control system is distributed through out the widgets. The toolkit architecture does not deal with application models because it is solely concerned with the input to the widgets and the output generated by the widgets.

MVC (Model View Controller) and PAC (Presentation, Abstraction, Control) [3] are both agent based models, where an agent is defined to have "state, possess an expertise, and is capable of initiating and reacting to events." [4]. An interface is built using hierarchies of agents. These agents represent an object in the application. In MVC, the model describes the semantics of the object, the view provides the (normally visual) representation of the object and the controller handles user input. In PAC, the abstraction describes the functional semantics of the object, the presentation handles the users interaction with the object, both input and output and the control handles communication between the presentation and the abstraction as well as between different PAC agents. The toolkit is object-oriented like both MVC and PAC, with each widget (or agent) encapsulated into different objects. Our toolkit, however, does not define the whole user interface in terms of a hierarchy of agents, but rather defines the individual widgets without specifying their organisation. Like the MVC model the toolkit separates input and output, although unlike MVC, the toolkit's widgets do not have a controller type object because it is concerned purely with input to and output from individual widgets. It would be possible, however, to build an MVC type architecture around the toolkit. Like PAC, the toolkit abstracts the widgets, but unlike PAC, the toolkit's abstraction is only aware of the widget's state but is not aware of the underlying application semantics. This is because the toolkit is designed as an extension of the Java Swing toolkit [5] allowing it to be easily incorporated into existing Java applications.

Previous solutions to the challenge of a toolkit suitable for multiple platforms have included virtual toolkits. These toolkits layer the user interface architecture, extracting the generic components into portable layers which sit on top of platform dependent layers. The SUIT system [6] was designed to run on three platforms, Mac, UNIX and Windows. The user interface was split into two layers on top of the platform dependent toolkits. The toolkit layer provided the tools necessary to implement the interface. The graphics layer provided a well defined graphical layer which could be easily ported between platforms. The XVT system [7] added a single, platform independent layer to the toolkits of the two platforms (Mac and Windows) supported. This layer mapped XVT commands into appropriate commands for the platform. These solutions provide a means to produce user interfaces for multiple platforms. Our toolkit relies on the portability of Java to ensure the interface can run on different platforms, but extends the notion of portability to include the resources available to the platform and the context the platform is running in

The Garnet system [8] is a set of tools which allow the creation of highly interactive graphical user interfaces, providing high level tools to generate interfaces using programming by demonstration and a constraints system to maintain consistency. The Garnet toolkit allows the graphical presentation of its widgets to be easily modified by changing the prototype upon which the widget is based. Doing this will update all dependent widgets. This is analogous to changing the design of output for a widget in an output module of our toolkit.

The HOMER system [9] allows the development of user interfaces that are accessible to both sighted and non-sighted users concurrently. By employing abstract objects to specify the user interface design independently of any concrete presentation objects, the system was capable of generating two user interfaces which could run concurrently for the same application. This allowed sighted and non-sighted users to co-operate using the same application. Unlike our toolkit, the HOMER system developed two interfaces, using two separate output mechanisms rather than have one interface which can switch between multiple mechanisms as and when required, using several concurrently if appropriate.

Alty et al. [10] created a multimedia process control system that would choose the appropriate modality to present information to a user. This would allow more information to be presented by increasing the bandwidth the interface could use. Additionally, if the preferred modality is unavailable if, for example, it is already being used for output, the system would attempt to present the information using an alternative. It was found, however, to be almost impossible to specify how these switches should be made due to their general nature. To limit the complexity of the system, a user-interface designer would supply it with valid options for output modalities. Our toolkit avoids this problem by avoiding generic solutions, but handling specific situations individually.

The ENO system [11] is an audio server which allows applications to incorporate audio cues. ENO manages a shared resource, audio hardware, handling requests from applications for audio feedback. This shared resource is modelled as a sound space, with requests for sounds made in terms of high level descriptions of the sound. Like ENO, our toolkit manages shared resources, although the toolkit extends the concept by switching between resources according to their suitability and availability. Similarly, the X Windows system [12] manages a shared resource, this time a graphics server. Again, our toolkit extends this concept by managing resources in multiple output mechanisms and switching between them.

Plasticity [13] is the ability of a user interface to be re-used on multiple platforms that have different capabilities. This would minimise the development time of interfaces for different platforms. For example, an interface could be specified once and then produced for both a workstation with a large screen and a mobile device with limited screen space. This is achieved by specifying the interface using an abstract model, and subsequently building the interface for each platform using that platform's available interactors and resources. Like the toolkit, plasticity allows user interfaces to adapt to available resources, although the mechanisms used are different. Plasticity allows an interface to be specified once and subsequently generated for multiple platforms. The interfaces for each platform may use different widgets to suit the resources available. For example, a chart may be used on a workstation monitor, but a label may be used on a PDA display. The toolkit, however, adapts the input and output of an existing widget to handle differing resources. For example, a widget may be reduced in size according to the available screen space. Additionally, the toolkit attempts to adapt the interface across multiple output mechanisms whereas plasticity is only aimed at visual feedback.

3   Toolkit Architecture

Here, we describe the architecture of the toolkit which allows the widgets to be resource and context sensitive. To enable this, the behaviour of the widgets is separated from the input and output mechanisms used. This allows the widgets to switch between mechanisms without affecting their behaviour. Similarly, the widget's presentation options are controlled by a separate module to allow the easy tailorability of the widgets. Initially, we describe how input to the widgets is handled. The second section describes how the widget are presented and finally, we compare input and output, highlighting any symmetries or differences, and describing how the two are combined in a consistent fashion.

3.1   Input Architecture

To be flexible the widgets need to be able to handle multiple input mechanisms, with the potential for new input mechanisms, such as speech or gesture, to be added dynamically. Fig. 1 shows the architecture employed to enable this.

The abstract widget behaviour describes the generic behaviour of the widget. For example, a button would have the generic behaviour described by the state transition diagram shown in Fig. 2.

This behaviour is expanded upon by the input mechanism behaviour(s) for the widget. These behaviours conform to the abstract behaviour for the widget, but may include sub-states which more accurately specify the behaviour of the widget for a given input mechanism. For example, Fig. 3 shows a simplified state transition diagram describing the behaviour of a button when using a mouse as the input mechanism.

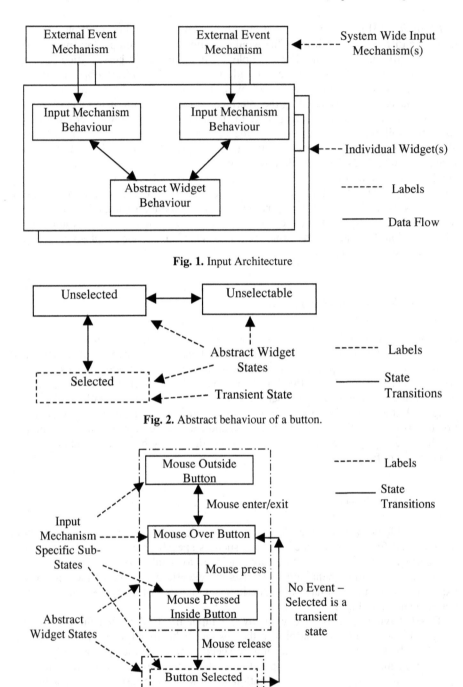

Fig. 1. Input Architecture

Fig. 2. Abstract behaviour of a button.

Fig. 3. Button behaviour for the mouse input mechanism (simplified).

The input mechanism behaviour(s) of a widget receive events from the relevant input mechanism(s). These events are then filtered appropriately according to the current state of the widget. If a relevant event is received, it is passed to the abstract widget state. If an event received by an input mechanism behaviour causes a change in the abstract state of the widget, the abstract widget state ensures that all input mechanism behaviours are notified so that the states of all the input mechanism behaviours are consistent.

For example, a button is in the unselected state, and it employs two input mechanisms, a mouse and speech input. If a user moves the mouse over the button, the appropriate event is received by the mouse input mechanism and is passed to the abstract widget behaviour. This event, however, does not affect the abstract state of the widget, so there are no concerns over the consistency of the states of the input mechanism behaviours. If the user was then to select the button using a speech command, this event would be received by the speech input mechanism behaviour and passed to the abstract widget behaviour. This event would change the state of the abstract widget to "selected", so the state of the mouse input mechanism behaviour would have to be changed to selected to remain consistent. As selected is a transient state, the abstract widget behaviour would automatically have to update the states of all input mechanisms to the unselected state. This differs from the notion of data fusion in the MATIS system [14] where pieces of data, from separate input mechanisms are fused into one command, for example a request for a plane ticket where the destination and departue locations are given in two different modalities. In the toolkit, the analogous situation is that the user moves the mouse over the graphical widget used to select one piece of data, but then actually selects the destination using speech input. Although two input mechanisms were used by the user, only one was used to make the selection. The use of the mouse in this case was redundant. If the user were to proceed with the selection using the mouse and selected the departure location using speech input, the toolkit would handle the two selections separately, and a mechanism such as data fusion would be required at the application level to determine the meaning of the pieces of data selected.

By separating the abstract behaviour of the widget from the input mechanism behaviour(s), the widget is insulated from any changes in input mechanisms. Indeed, the differences in input mechanisms are irrelevant to the abstract widget, and as such it is possible to replace one input mechanism with another, or even add a new input mechanism, providing multiple input mechanisms without affecting the widget in any other way. Which input mechanism(s) a widget uses is controlled by the user using a control panel (Fig. 4). This allows the user to add or remove input mechanisms to/from a widget.

3.2   Output Architecture

As with the input architecture, widget behaviour has been separated from the widget presentation, to allow the widgets to be flexible. Fig. 4 shows the output architecture.

The abstract behaviour of the widget requests feedback appropriate to its current state. This request is passed to the feedback manager which splits this request into multiple requests, one for each mechanism being used. Each new request is given three "weights", reflecting user preference for this mechanism, resource availability for this mechanism and the suitability of this mechanism in the current context. These mechanism-specific requests are passed to the appropriate mechanism mappers, where any user preferences are added to the request. These preferences may indicate, for example, a 3D effect graphical output style or a jazz audio output style.

These amended requests are passed on to the rendering manger. This monolithic component ensures that the feedback requested by different widgets will not conflict. Because it is monolithic, the rendering manager is able to oversee the requests made by all the widgets and consequently is able to highlight any possible conflicts. If the output mechanism is able to handle such clashes, then the requests are passed on, otherwise the rendering manager will change the request to a different, more suitable mechanism. As with the input mechanisms, the output modules are monolithic components. Consequently, it is possible to replace an output mechanism with a new one, or to add a new output mechanism without affecting the existing output modules.

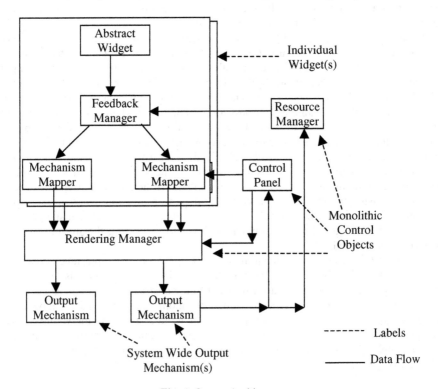

Fig. 4. Output Architecture

The widget's output can be modified in three ways. Users can specify a weight describing the importance they associate with a particular output mechanism for a widget. This could be set due to preference, the user prefers the audio feedback to be a little less intrusive, or user need, visual feedback is of no relevance to a visually impaired user. Output mechanisms can specify the resource availability weight. This could be affected by, for example, the screen size, or number of MIDI channels available. The suitability of a particular resource can be specified by external modules which can be added to the toolkit. These could, for example, measure the ambient volume, the brightness of the surroundings or the motion of a mobile device and adjust the feedback accordingly.

The control panel allows users to personalise the widgets output using parameters supplied by the output mechanisms. Users are also allowed to set a weight for their preference for each of the different output mechanisms here. The control panel also has an API allowing software control over these functions. The resource manager controls the values for the weights for the different output mechanisms. The user preference weight is received from the control panel. The resource availability weight is received from the respective output mechanisms, and the resource suitability weight is received from software components via the resource manager API. It is thus possible to build software modules to extend the toolkit which can detect the suitability of a particular output mechanism and inform the toolkit when appropriate.

3.3   A Comparison of the Input and Output Architectures

Although the input and output architectures are largely symmetrical there is one difference due to the fundamental asymmetry of input and output, namely the output architecture has a monolithic control structure, the rendering manager, whilst there is no analogous structure in the input architecture. Whilst it would be possible to include an input analogue in the architecture, it is difficult to see what purpose it would serve. The rendering manager is necessary on output because the output for different widgets could potentially clash. The rendering manager avoids this problem by tracking the feedback generated system wide. An input analogue is unnecessary because such clashes on input cannot occur given the way input is currently handled.

3.4   Ensuring Input and Output Are Consistent

Because both the input and output behaviours are not encapsulated within the widget, there is a danger that the input and output behaviours might not be consistent. For example, a widget's graphical representation could change size, but because the output behaviour is separate from the input behaviour, the area deemed to be valid for input to the widget may not be changed. To avoid this scenario it is necessary for there to be some communication between input and output mechanisms. This communication, however, needs to be controlled as there is little point in, for example, an audio output mechanism communicating changes in its presentation to a screen-based mouse input mechanism.

To ensure that the appropriate input and output mechanisms communicate, each mechanism is associated with an interaction area. These areas define the space in which a user can interact with the widget. For example, a mouse input mechanism and a graphical output mechanism would share the same 2½D interaction area. Each mechanism that uses a particular interaction area will share common characteristics. For example, mechanisms that use the 2½D interaction area described above will share the same co-ordinate system. The communication between input and output mechanisms is brokered by a communication object in each widget. This object controls the communication between all the input and output mechanisms ensuring that they are all consistent in their behaviour. The communication object would receive messages from all output mechanisms, and pass these messages on to input mechanisms that share the output mechanism's interaction space.

There is a potential danger that some input mechanisms may require analogous output mechanisms or vice-versa. For example, a gesture input mechanism where you point to the location of a spatialised sound source to select the widget requires a suitable output mechanism. Equally, some mechanisms may not be suitable for a a particular widget. For example, many current haptic devices which require the user to actively grasp the device would not be suitable for feedback indicating the state of a background task as it progresses. In this case, a haptic output mechanism would not be suitable. The solution provided by the toolkit is to supply it with default output mechanisms which are not platform dependent and are suitable for all widgets. A more generic solution would be to include constraints that mean all widgets must be able to be presented by at least one output mechanism, regardless of suitability or user preference.

4   Implementation

Java has been used to implement the toolkit. It was chosen due to its portability, adding to the flexible nature of the toolkit. The toolkit architecture has been fully implemented for the output, with three widgets (buttons, menus and progress bars) added to the toolkit so far. Output was implemented initially because we could take advantage of Java's built in event handling mechanisms. Although this isn't a suitable solution for the long term because it limits the use of different input mechanisms, in the short term it allows us to evaluate the effectiveness of the toolkit for output without the overhead of implementing the input architecture.

Rather than accepting events from independent input mechanism behaviour(s), the abstract widget encapsulates the input behaviour for the widgets using the Java AWT mechanism. The widget behaviours are specified using a state transition diagram which is hard coded into the abstract widget. Each node in the diagram listens for appropriate events, generating requests for feedback when the node is activated. When an appropriate event is received, the node is deactivated and the appropriate new node is activated. The requests for feedback are then passed to the widget's feedback manager where the request is split into multiple requests that are eventually received by the output mechanisms. Currently two output mechanisms are used, a graphical one based upon the standard Java Swing widgets and an audio one using earcons [15, 16]. Swing widgets are used as the basis for the graphical output because this allows us to use the AWT input mechanism, but it does have the disadvantage of not allowing as much flexibility in the way the widgets are presented. Additionally, this means that some of the output mechanism is encapsulated within the abstract widget along with the input mechanism.

The graphical presentation for the buttons and menus are generated in a similar way, by changing the size and colour of the widget appropriately. The progress bar, however, does not rely upon the AWT event system to receive events. The events are passed to it by the parent application. This allowed us to handle the graphical presentation of the progress bar in a manner more consistent with the design of the architecture, and to be more flexible in the way the widget is presented. The output module paints the progress bar from scratch in accordance with the request received, meaning the presentation can be changed in more interesting ways. Fig. 5 (a-c) show the same progress bar with different weights associated to the amount of resource available for graphical presentation.

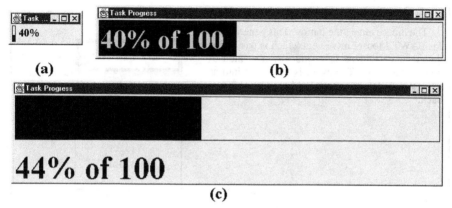

Fig. 5. Progress Bar Representations With Different Graphical Weights

The audio presentation for all the widgets is based upon previous work done on evaluating audio feedback in graphical user interfaces [17-19]. The audio presentation for all the widgets is flexible because it does not rely upon the Swing graphical output. Because of this it was possible to develop two different audio modules, which can be changed dynamically during use. The output modules are stored in Java jar files which are loaded as required. Should a developer wish to build a new output module, all he/she need do is build a java object which conforms to the API for an output module and load it into the toolkit.

An interesting issue that arose as a consequence of using Swing widgets and therefore the AWT event mechanism was that it became apparent that assumptions had been made by the designers of Swing regarding the importance different events to software engineers using their widgets. For example, if a user presses the mouse button outside a JButton, the JButton is in a different state than if mouse button remains unpressed. Similarly, mouse releases outside a JButton are of relevance to the JButton. These events, however are not deemed to be of relevance to software engineers using these buttons and consequently are not readily available. The solution used in the toolkit is to resolve this problem is to have a global listener for mouse presses and release which listens for such events occurring on all components and passes them on to all interested widgets.

To further enhance the flexibility of the toolkit, an external module has been developed which measures the ambient audio volume of the environment around the device running an application built using the toolkit and adjusts the weighting for the suitability of the audio feedback, for example reducing the volume of sounds played if the environment is quiet (and *vice versa*).

5   Worked Example

An audio/visual button is in its default state. The button is drawn as shown, with the cursor outside the area of the button. No sounds are played.

The mouse enters the button. This generates a Java AWT MouseEnter event which is passed to the abstract widget behaviour by the mouse input mechanism. The event is translated into a request for the appropriate, MouseOver, feedback.

The request is passed to the feedback controller. This widget has a weight of 30 for audio feedback, 50 for visual feedback and 0 for haptic feedback. Two requests are generated with appropriate weights, one for audio feedback and one for visual feedback. No request is generated for haptic feedback. Each request is passed onto the appropriate modality mapper.

Each modality mapper modifies the event in accordance with user preferences set in the control panel. In this case, the style Rectangular is applied to the graphical request and Jazz is applied to the audio request. Each request is passed onto the rendering manager.

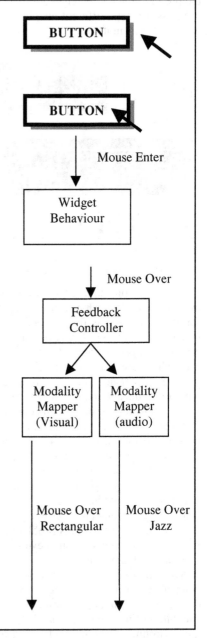

The rendering manager checks for potential clashes with these requests. In this case there are no clashes so the requests are passed onto the appropriate output modules.

Each output module receives the request and translates the request into concrete output. The visual module draws a rectangular button to match the user preference and shaded to indicate mouse over and the audio module plays a persistent tone at a low volume to indicate mouse over in a Jazz style to match the user preference.

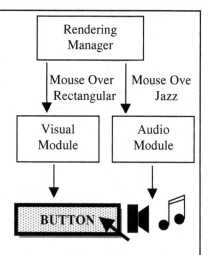

6   Discussion and Future Work

This paper describes a user interface architecture that we have implemented which allows widgets to be flexible in several ways, using multiple input and output mechanisms, with the ability to add or remove mechanisms dynamically. The widgets can adapt their presentation according to the resources available for presentation, the suitability of different mechanisms given the current context and in accordance with user preference. This is achieved by separating the input and output mechanisms from the behaviour of the widget, allowing the widget to be used regardless of the mechanism. With the increased use of mobile devices, being flexible in this way allows the toolkit's widgets to be suitable for multiple platforms in multiple contexts without requiring any changes to be made.

Because the input and output mechanisms are no longer encapsulated in the widget, but are separate objects outside the widget, there needs to be some communication between them to ensure that the input and output mechanisms remain in a consistent state. However, there is also a need to limit this communication so that it only occurs between appropriate input and output mechanisms. To ensure this is the case, each mechanism is defined to operate within an interaction area. Only mechanisms sharing an interaction area will need to communicate. The implementation, shows that the architecture is effective, with widgets being able to modify their feedback according to resource and context requirements.

Acknowledgement. This work was funded by EPSRC grant GR/L79212.

7 References

1. P. Szekely, "Retrospective and Challenges for Model-Based Interface Development," in Proceedings of DSV-IS, Namur, Belgique, 1996.
2. G. E. Pfaff, User Interface Management Systems: Proceedings of the Seeheim Workshop. Berlin: Springer-Verlag, 1985.
3. J. Coutaz, "PAC: An Object Oriented Model for Implementing User Interfaces," ACM SIGCHI Bulletin, vol. 19, pp. 37-41, 1987.
4. J. Coutaz, L. Nigay, and D. Salber, "Agent-Based Architecture Modelling for Interactive Systems," Critical Issues In User Interface Engineering, pp. 191-209, 1995.
5. Sun-Microsystems,   "The   Swing   Connection", http://java.sun.com/products/jfc/tsc/index.html, as on 10/01/2000.
6. R. Pausch, I. Nathaniel R. Young, and R. DeLine, "SUIT: The Pascal of User Interface Toolkits," in Proceedings of the ACM SIGGRAPH Symposium on User Interface Software and Technology, UI Frameworks, 1991, pp. 117-125.
7. R. Valdes, "A Virtual Toolkit for Windows and the Mac," Byte, vol. 14, pp. 209 - 216, 1989.
8. B. Myers, D. Giuse, R. Dannenberg, B. Zanden, D. Kosbie, E. Pervin, A. Mickish, and P. Marchal, "Garnet: Comprehensive Support for Graphical Highly Interactive User Interfaces," IEEE Computer, vol. 23, pp. 71-85, 1990.
9. A. Savidis and C. Stephanidis, "Developing Dual Interfaces for Integrating Blind and Sighted Users: The HOMER UIMS," in Proceedings of ACM CHI'95 Conference on Human Factors in Computing Systems, vol. 1, Papers: Multimodal Interfaces: ACM Press, Addison-Wesley, 1995, pp. 106-113.
10. J. Alty and C. McCartney, "Design Of A Multi-Media Presentation System For A Process Control Environment," in Eurographics Multimedia Workshop, Session 8: Systems, Stockholm, Sewden, 1991.
11. M. Beaudouin-Lafon and W. W. Gaver, "ENO: Synthesizing Structured Sound Spaces," in Proceedings of the ACM Symposium on User Interface Software and Technology, 1994, Speech and Sound, Marina del Ray, USA: ACM Press, Addison-Wesley, 1994, pp. 49-57.
12. R. W. Scheifler and J. Gettys, "The X Window System," ACM Transactions on Graphics, vol. 5, pp. 79-109, 1986.
13. D. Thevenin and J. Coutaz, "Plasticity of User Interfaces: Framework and Research Agenda," in Proceedings of Interact'99, Edinburgh: IFIP, IOS Press, 1999, pp. 110-117.
14. L. Nigay and J. Coutaz, "A Generic Platform for Addressing the Multimodal Challenge," in Proceedings of ACM CHI'95 Conference on Human Factors in Computing Systems, vol. 1, Papers: Multimodal Interfaces, 1995, pp. 98-105.
15. M. M. Blattner, D. A. Sumikawa, and R. M. Greenberg, "Earcons and Icons: Their Structure and Common Design Principles," Human-Computer Interaction, vol. 4, pp. 11-44, 1989.
16. S. A. Brewster, P. C. Wright, and A. D. N. Edwards, "An Evaluation of Earcons for Use in Auditory Human-Computer Interfaces," in Proceedings of ACM INTERCHI'93 Conference on Human Factors in Computing Systems, Auditory Interfaces, 1993, pp. 222-227.
17. S. Brewster and M. Crease, "Making Menus Musical," in Proceedings of IFIP Interact'97, Sydney, Australia: Chapman & Hall, 1997, pp. 389-396.
18. S. Brewster, P. Wright, A. Dix, and A. Edwards, "The Sonic Enhancement Of Graphical Buttons," in Proceedings of Interact'95, Lillehammer, Norway: Chapman & Hall, 1995, pp. 43-48.
19. M. Crease and S. Brewster, "Making Progress With Sounds - The Design And Evaluation Of An Audio Progress Bar," in Proceedings Of ICAD'98, Glasgow, UK: British Computer Society, 1998.

Integrating Model Checking and HCI Tools to Help Designers Verify User Interface Properties

Fabio Paternò and Carmen Santoro

Istituto CNUCE, Consiglio Nazionale delle Ricerche, Via V.Alfieri 1
56010 Ghezzano-Pisa, Italia
{F.Paterno, C.Santoro}@cnuce.cnr.it

Abstract. In this paper we present a method that aims to integrate the use of formal techniques in the design process of interactive applications, with particular attention to those applications where both usability and safety are main concerns. The method is supported by a set of tools. We will also discuss how the resulting environment can be helpful in reasoning about multi-user interactions using the task model of an interactive application. Examples are provided from a case study in the field of air traffic control.

1   Introduction

The importance of allowing an increasing number of users to access interactive software applications has stimulated a growing interest in methods for the design and development of effective user interfaces. The goal is to obtain applications able to support users, in a flexible and effective way, while they are performing their activities. Consequently, the part of an interactive software application dedicated to the control of dialogues with users and the generation of the presentation of the information is increasing thus raising the need for more structured methods to support its design. For example, Myers and Rosson [10] analysed a set of applications and found that on average, 48% of the code, 45% of development time, 50% of implementation time, and 37% of maintenance time was dedicated to user interface aspects.

The fact that it is actually quite easy to develop one user interface by using one visual environment such as Visual Basic or Visual Java may lead to misconceptions. Thus, one question can be posed: why should we spend time investigating new methods for developing user interfaces if they are already so easy to develop?

The problem is that what designers of interactive applications need is not just any user interface able to provide access to the application's functionality but one that can effectively support users while interacting with it. Thus, there is a need to understand what tasks users want to perform and how to represent them in order to better analyse their properties and interrelationships. This information is important for identifying an effective user interface. Here is where most current visual environments for user interface development fail to provide useful support.

If we consider UML [4], we can notice a considerable effort to provide models and representations to support the design and development of software applications. However, despite the nine representations provided by UML, the currently most

P. Palanque and F. Paternò (Eds.): DSV-IS 2000, LNCS 1946, pp. 135-150, 2001.
© Springer-Verlag Berlin Heidelberg 2001

successful model-based approach in software engineering, none of them is particularly oriented to support the design of user interfaces. Of course, it is possible to use some of them to represent aspects related to the user interface but it is clear that this is not their main purpose.

In model-based environments for user interfaces [13, 15] the basic idea is to identify abstractions and related tools that can support the work of user interface designers and developers. Particular attention has been paid to task models that are able to represent the design of activities that should be supported by an interactive application. Such models describe how activities should be performed and their possible relationships by integrating both functional and interactive aspects. They are the meeting point among all the important views involved in the design of an interactive application. Their development involves people with different backgrounds (software developers, user interface designers, application domain experts, end users, managers, ...). Usually, such task models are developed after an informal phase of task analysis and scenarios identification.

One of the advantages of using a formal approach is the possibility to rigorously reason about properties of the specification. This can be carried out by model checking techniques: the specification represents the model against which properties can be checked. Formal verification has been successfully used in hardware design where it is important to check that some properties are satisfied before implementing the specification into hardware. The HCI field is more challenging for verification methods and tools, since the specification of human-computer dialogues may be more complex than the hardware specifications. The main problems in applying model checking techniques to the design of user interfaces are:

- the identification of relevant user interface properties to check and their formalisation;
- the development of a model of the User Interface System which is meaningful and, at the same time, avoids the introduction of many low level details which would increase the complexity of the model without adding important information for the design of the user interface.

There are various motivations to carry out model checking for user interfaces:

- it is possible to test aspects of an application even if they have not been completely implemented;
- *user testing can be rather expensive*, especially in fields such as ATC (Air Traffic Control), the users (controllers in our case) are highly specialised personnel whose time has high costs. In addition, it can be very difficult to know how many tests are sufficient to have an exhaustive analysis. We are not proposing that users should not be involved in testing but we are indicating that model checking can decrease the need for empirical testing, even if it is always useful to have it.
- *exhaustive analysis*, the advantage of model checking is that the space of the states reachable by the specification is completely analysed. In user testing we just consider one of the possible sequences of actions, whereas a huge number of such traces may exist and even extensive empirical testing can miss some of them. This lack of completeness in empirical testing can have dangerous effects especially in safety-critical contexts.

However, there is another difference between model checking and empirical testing: in the former a model of the application is considered, in the latter the focus is on the concrete implementation of the application (or part of it). This means that the model should be a meaningful approximation of the application in order to support a useful analysis.

In [12] there is a discussion on how to approach the verification of user interface properties and examples of general properties are given. Other approaches to the same type of problems can be found in [1, 2]. However, despite the number of proposals for the use of formal methods in HCI [11], only a small number of applications to real case studies has been developed (see [7] for one example). The main reason for these limited results is that the use of formal methods is difficult and time-consuming. Even tools supporting them are often difficult to use and the results that they can provide sometimes do not justify the effort required.

Our approach aims to analyse multi-user interactive applications and how it can be applied to a real case study where the effort of using a formal approach is justified by the safety-critical context. To this end we have designed and developed a prototype environment that integrates a tool for task modelling with a tool for model checking. The overall goal is to understand how to ease the introduction of formal methods in the design cycle and to understand to what extent formal techniques can be useful in designing interactive applications.

In the paper, we first introduce the method that we propose and we discuss the motivations and the results of each of its phases. Then, we describe the prototype environment that we have designed and developed to support the integration of task modelling with model checking and the representations that it uses, and lastly we discuss examples of properties that can be verified with this approach. We also discuss examples taken from a case study that we have analysed concerning the design of a new interactive application for air traffic control in an airport.

2 Our Method

An interactive application is characterised by the dialogues it supports and the presentations of information that it generates for communicating information to the user. The description of both these aspects could be formally represented. However, the introduction of a formal representation has to be motivated. The effort to formalise presentation aspects does not seem to be justified because we obtain models that describe features that can be easily understood by direct inspection of the implemented user interface, as they are strictly related to how people perceive information. The case of user interface dialogues is different. There are aspects that are more difficult to grasp in an empirical analysis because when users navigate in an application they follow only one of the many possible paths of actions. In addition, interactive systems are highly concurrent systems because they can support the use of multiple interaction devices, they can be connected to multiple systems, they can support the performance of multiple tasks, they often can support multi-user interactions.

The current tendency is to increase such concurrency. On the one hand, this concurrency is a source of flexibility, usability, and interactive richness but, on the other hand, it generates a complexity that needs to be carefully considered, especially in safety-critical contexts. Thus, formal techniques can give a useful support to better understand dialogue models and their properties. Concerning when such a formalisation effort should be performed, we note that if just the lowest specification level of the task model (user actions and system feedback) was considered then many important aspects could be overlooked. A designer needs first to understand the logical and temporal relationships among the possible logical activities aspects (that to some extent depend on the artefacts available) and, consequently, a representation is required supporting such information. Formalising task models can allow designers to reach a number of results: a better understanding of logical activities to support; obtaining information useful for the concrete design of the user interface, the possibility of supporting usability evaluation of the application considered, the possibility of rigorously reasoning about properties. The last aspect has not sufficiently been considered and will be addressed in this paper on the assumption that *the dialogue aspects should be taken into account when formalising HCI aspects with particular attention to tasks and their performance.*

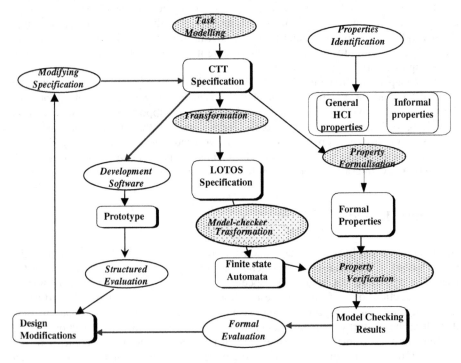

Fig. 1. Our Method

The method that we propose for the design of user interfaces with the support of formal methods is represented in Figure 1, where the processes are indicated with ovals and the results with rectangles. The ovals filled by points are tool-supported and are the phases that we mainly discuss in this paper. We have developed some of the tools involved in the method. We use model checkers developed by other groups [6] for the formal verification. More precisely, the method comprises the following activities:

- *Task Modelling*. After a first phase gathering information on the application domain, and an informal task analysis, designers should develop a task model that forces them to clarify many aspects related to possible tasks and their relationships. The task specification is obtained by first structuring the tasks in a hierarchical way so that abstract tasks are described in terms of more refined tasks. Next, temporal relationships among tasks are described using ConcurTaskTrees [13] which is a graphical notation allowing designers to describe hierarchies of tasks with temporal operators that have been identified extending the semantics of LOTOS [8] operators. In this way, we obtain a ConcurTaskTrees specification of the cooperative application with one task model for each role involved and one part specifying the relationships among tasks performed by users with different roles thus giving a clear indication of how cooperations are performed. For each task it is also possible to provide further information concerning the objects that they manipulate and attributes such as frequency, time requested and so on. The editor of task models in ConcurTaskTrees is publicly available at (http://giove.cnuce.cnr.it/ctte.html).

- *ConcurTaskTrees-to-LOTOS Transformation*. The ConcurTaskTrees specification can be used for two purposes. One is driving the development of a software prototype, in particular prototype presentation, consistent with the indicated requirements (for example, if we know that the application has to provide an overview of some information then presentation techniques suitable to summarise data should be considered). The other possibility is to transform the ConcurTaskTrees model into a LOTOS specification to analyse the dialogue of the user interface using model checking techniques. We have implemented a transformation tool where each task specification is translated into a corresponding LOTOS process. The motivation for this transformation is that there are various model checking tools able to accept LOTOS specifications as input. The LOTOS specification is the input for automatic tools (such as the CADP package [6]) that transform it into a finite state automata or Labelled Transition System (LTS). Since LOTOS has more expressive power than LTSs this transformation in some cases is not possible.

- *Property Formalisation*. The identification of the relevant properties of the user interface considers both general HCI properties, such as the continuous feedback property [12], and other properties that are specific of the considered application domain. To support user interface designers while editing formal properties, we have defined a set of templates associated to relevant properties so that the designer has only to fill some parameters for identifying the tasks involved in the property. Such tasks are directly selected on the graphical representation of the task model.

- *Model-checking*. After having formalised the identified properties with a formal notation, these properties are checked against the LTS specification, describing the Interactive System derived in previous steps, to verify which properties are valid in the system. Checking that the formal specification satisfies the relevant properties for the possible dialogues is useful to understand whether the design developed can support usability and safety aspects. The verification is performed by a general purpose automatic tool for formal verification and the results of the model checking are used for formal and informal evaluations that can lead to modify the ConcurTaskTrees specification thus re-starting the process.

3   The Case Study

The air traffic controllers' main task is to ensure flight safety and regularity: safety means that the minimal separation has to be maintained between aircraft, regularity means that the planes have to follow as much as possible the beforehand fixed flight plans. Currently, the air traffic controllers perform most of their activities using the following media and tools:

- Paper flight strips, automatically generated and printed by the system. Generally, there is one strip for aircraft and each of them contains flight information (type of aircraft, planned route, etc.) and it is used by controllers to annotate the flight's evolutions in the sector;
- Vocal communications: controllers communicate via voice by means of radio with pilots currently in the sector, via telephone and directly with other colleagues working respectively in other and in the same center;
- Other instruments such as the radar that allows them to monitor the current traffic situation, especially used when it is not possible to have the complete overview of the traffic with the naked eye.

As far as the management of the traffic in the proximity and within the airport concerns, there are two particular types of controllers that work elbow-to-elbow in the control tower and communicate with pilots using two different radio frequencies: the ground controller and the tower controller. In the MEFISTO project, a new interactive prototype application for air traffic control in the aerodrome area has been designed and developed. It uses communication by data link, a technology allowing asynchronous exchanges of digital data containing messages coded according to a predefined syntax. This means that controllers can provide commands by direct manipulation, graphical user interfaces. This type of technology is particular useful in bad atmospheric conditions where the controllers have difficulties in observing the movements of aircraft from the control tower.

The *Ground* controller has to look after movements "on ground", which means (for departing flights) to guide planes from the departure gate until the site immediately before the runway's starting point (holding position) and (for arriving planes) from the end of the runway until the arrival gate. In order to perform their activity controllers have to mentally build the current picture of traffic and decide who, when and how can go through the taxiways (that allow movements from the various airport areas from/to the runways), and so on, minimising the likelihood of conflicts. More specifically, when pilots are approaching the runway, they inform the ground controller, then the controller sends them the frequency for contacting the tower controller, because at that point the flight passes under the tower controller's regulation.

Tower controllers have to take care of maintaining the minimal separation between aircraft thus their duty is to allocate the access to the runway and decide about take-off and landing of aircraft. For instance, they receive the strip of a departing flight from the ground controller and, when they receive the pilot's request for taking off they can send the relative clearance depending on the current situation. Thus, they have to mentally calculate how to manage the separations in order to avoid conflicts and cancel the effects of the "wake vortex" between consecutive flights.

4   Task Models

4.1   Representing Task Models

The reason for introducing ConcurTaskTrees was that after first experiences with LOTOS [14] we realised the need for a new extension that allowed designers to avoid unnecessarily complicated expressions even for specifying small behaviours and to focus on aspects more important for user interface design. In addition, we noted that other notations for task models were lacking in precise semantics or missing constructs useful for obtaining flexible descriptions.

The notation we use for representing task models allow designers to obtain a hierarchical description of the possible activities with a rich set of operators to describe their temporal relationships. Different icons are used to indicate how the performance of a task is allocated. A task model of a cooperative application is obtained by designing the task model associated with each role involved in an application and the model related to the cooperative part. In the latter part, cooperative tasks are considered, they are tasks that require actions from two or more users and they are refined until we reach tasks performed by a single user. This allows designers to define constraints among tasks performed by different users. An example of cooperative task is driving an aircraft to the holding position as it requires actions from the pilot, the tower controller and the ground controller.

In Figure 2 we show an excerpt of ConcurTaskTrees specification taken from our case study. It considers the *Taxi to* task performed by the Ground controller when he receives a path request from a pilot in order to reach either the assigned runway and then take-off or to leave the runway and reach the arrival gate. The controller must first select the corresponding interaction technique (*Select taxi to* task) and then (>> is the sequential operator) choose ([] operator) between using the path automatically suggested or building a path manually. In the former case, the controller selects a predefined path and the system shows it graphically (the relative icon indicates a system task). In the latter case, the controller selects manual mode. Then, an iterative task (*Building Path*, * is the iterative operator) indicates that the controller can specify the next position and the system responds by graphically displaying the corresponding segment until the controller terminates the iterative building operation ([> is the disabling operator). Finally, the controller can choose between up-linking the path or cancelling it if he is not satisfied.

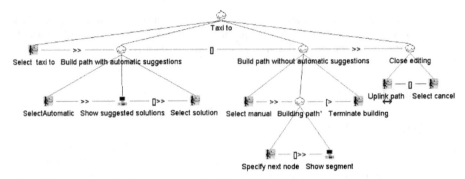

Fig. 2. An excerpt of a ConcurTaskTrees specification.

4.2   From ConcurTaskTrees to LOTOS

The first important aspect to consider is that the translation from ConcurTaskTrees to LOTOS is composed of two main steps: the translation of ConcurTaskTrees tasks into LOTOS processes, and the implementation of the ConcurTaskTrees temporal operators by means of the operators provided by the LOTOS language.

With regard to the former issue, the specification of each process implies that all the gates that are used in it have to be declared in its heading. The direct consequence is that in the specification of the root process all the gates have to be listed. Whereas in the specification of a process corresponding to a leaf task the translation is reduced to insert the associated gate and the *exit* action, in order to indicate when the successful end of the process occurs.

Some of the ConcurTaskTrees operators are derived from LOTOS, other operators (such as those   indicating optional and iterative tasks) need to be mapped onto LOTOS expressions. An example of the latter issue is in the translation of the ConcurTaskTrees iterative operator (*), that has not a direct correspondent in LOTOS. Referring to Figure 2, where the *Building Path* task is exactly iterative, its translation into LOTOS requires a recursive call of the LOTOS process associated with the task in order to simulate the behaviour of restarting an activity just after the completion of the previous execution.

4.3   Integration of Tools for Task Modelling and Tools for Model-Checking

The environment that we have designed to support this method allows an integrated use of two tools:

- CTTE (ConcurTaskTrees Environment) [3] that supports editing and simulation of task models of cooperative applications.
- A model checking tool, we have used that included in the CADP package [6] but our environment can be easily integrated with other similar model checking tools.

In this case the designer can edit a task model and then automatically translate it into a LOTOS specification that is the input for the model checking tool. The integrated environment allows designers to directly access to some functionality of the model checker (*Activate Model-checking tools* item in the *Tools* menu, see Figure 3).

Then, a new window appears (see Figure 4) showing all the possible functionality that can be accessed. The new window is mainly divided into two panels: one includes commands used to get and handle the LOTOS specification, and the other one provides commands to handle Labelled Transition System (LTS) associated with the current task model. Thus, depending on the particular panel that has been selected, the window shows different sets of commands. For example, if the user selects the possibility of handling commands for the LOTOS specification then the tool gives various options (as you can see from the picture): performing a simulation of the LOTOS specification (*Standard Simula...*button); performing a casual *execution (Random execution)*; producing the LTS (*Make LTS*) or finding deadlocks in the specification (if any), and so on.

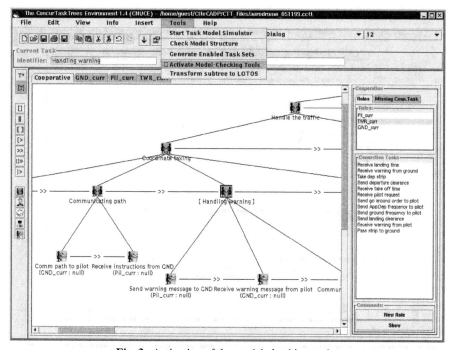

Fig. 3. Activation of the model checking tools.

In Figure 4 we show an example where the designer has activated the transformation into a LTS. After that, the editor of properties has been activated. In addition, through the *Transform* button appearing on the bottom of the *Check Tools* window, the designer can access further information, for example to get the LOTOS specification of the cooperative task model described in the CTT specification.

It is worth noting that, besides the possibility of having the entire task model translated into LOTOS, sometimes it could be useful to have the LOTOS expression correspondent to some subtasks. This can be obtained by selecting the *Transform subtree to LOTOS* item in the Tools menu (see Figure 3) after having selected in the editor the name of the root task of the subtree. For example, if we select a task in the editor window, and then activate the translation into LOTOS, then the CTT environment shows a window where it is displayed the corresponding LOTOS expression (see Figure 5) that can be saved in a file.

In addition, to facilitate the specification of the properties, the tool provides templates for predefined properties that can be filled interactively by directly selecting the tasks in the task model that define the specific occurrence of the property. The templates allow designers to specify general properties such as relative reachability (verifying if it is possible to enable the performance of task y after having performed task x), performing a task in any state, mutual awareness, and so on. Depending on the specific property that the user wants to verify, the user interface provides an indication of the information that designers should fill. For example, if users want to verify if it is possible to perform a specific task in any state, then they should be able to specify exactly one task. Whereas if they want to verify relative reachability they have to specify two tasks to check whether it is possible to perform the second task once the first one has been accomplished.

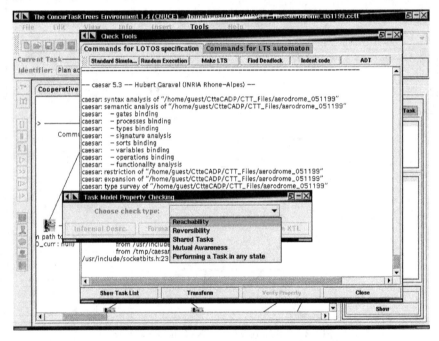

Fig. 4. Selection of the type of property to check.

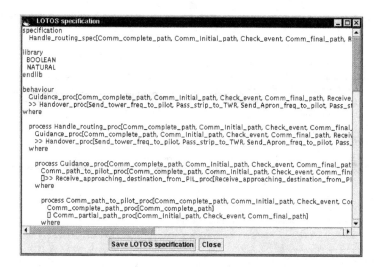

Fig. 5. An example of LOTOS specification automatically derived.

Templates help designers identifying the desired property while preventing them from doing syntax errors that occur often in this kind of activity. For example, if the user wants to verify, within the Ground controller's task model, if it is possible to reach the task for sending pilot the Apron frequency *(Send Apron freq to pilot)* from the task used to communicate the complete path *(Comm complete path)* then he has to select the *Reachability* item in the property list. After that, he has to graphically select in the task model the tasks involved in the property. In the case of reachability, two tasks have to be selected, so the left button of mouse allows designers to specify the first task and the right-button the second task: the associated fields are automatically filled, together with the correspondent roles (ground controller in the example of Figure 6).

The tool is able to provide the designers with both a formal and a natural language description of the property considered. If the designer decides to verify a property, then its formal specification is given to the underlying model-checking in order to verify if the specified property holds in the task model. In the negative case, the tool shows (one) execution that provides the counter-example for this property. It is possible to map the sequence of actions defining the counter-example given by the model checker to the corresponding tasks in the ConcurTaskTrees task model.

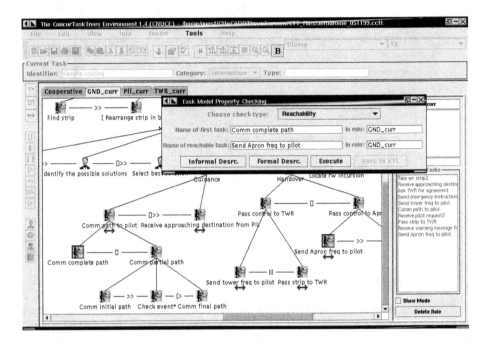

Fig. 6. Interactive Composition of a Property.

5   User Interface Properties

In a highly cooperative system as that considered in our case study we can focus on properties of the specific user interface customised for a particular user and look at properties related to the interconnections and communications between different users. We can consider both general properties indicated in the pre-defined templates and specific properties of interest in the case study under consideration.

In multi-user properties we bring out other properties that regard characteristics of the highly cooperative environment considered, such as "awareness" properties which allow designers to reason about the possibility of checking if one user can be aware of the results of activities performed by another user. Within the "single-user" category it is possible to indicate the properties that are related to only one user indifferently from the particular user we consider because they are common to more than one user's class.

We will use an extended version of ACTL [5], which considers data values in addition to action, to formalise examples of properties in the case study previously introduced. This type of extension can be easily converted in an XTL [9] expression that can be verified by the CADP tool. Some properties are instances of the general properties that have specific templates associated with them, other properties are specific to our case study.

5.1   Examples of Single-User Properties

We start with one example of single user property and then show other examples involving multi-user interactions.

Warning Message for Time-Out Expired. With datalink functionality, all the messages have a time-out indicating the time interval during which the associated answer has to be received in order to be appropriately considered and evaluated. When the time-out expires, an appropriate notification has to be shown on the message originator's interface, in order to signal either that the message has to be sent again, or that possible answers received after the time-out expiration have to be ignored. More precisely, the property can be expressed in this way:

If there is expiration of an operational time-out without reception of the operational datalink response message, the message originator shall be notified with an appropriate feedback. The related ACTL-like expression is:

AG [is_sent(controller, request)] **E**[true{~is_received(controller, answer} **U** {timeout} **A**[true{true} **U** {is_presented(controller,noanswer_feedback}true]]

This means that once the *controller* has sent a *request* to a *pilot*, then we have a temporal evolution during which no associated answer coming from the pilot to the controller has been received. Finally, as a result of the expiration of the fixed time-out, we reach a state from where for all the possible temporal evolution the desired effect of presenting an adequate feedback to the controller's user interface of the missed answer will be reached (*noanswer_feedback* in the above property).

This implies that only after the expiration of the time out we are sure that the desired effect (warning message for time-out expired) will be reached, thus allowing the controller to decide what is the best action to perform in order to make up for the error.

5.2   Examples of Multi-User Properties

In this paragraph we consider some examples of properties of multi-user interactions that we found important to formalise for verification: awareness property, that in this case mainly means that an action produced by one controller has to be shown to the other sector's controller and co-ordination properties.

Mutual Awareness Property. This property means that whenever a user performs an interaction, the associated effect has to be shown on the user interface of another user. We can use this property in our case study to be sure that the tower controller is aware of all the interactions performed by ground controllers which can have an impact on their activity. We consider both actions that controllers can perform directly on the system based on their decisions (for example the ground controller can change a previously fixed flight parameter), and actions that involve datalink dialogues with pilots. In other words, we want to pay attention to all the actions that might cause that controllers' activities clash each other, thus we do not consider the actions that the ground performs in order to get information on the system for monitoring it.

More precisely, we specify that whenever (AG operator) the ground controller performs a modification action on the user interface then for all the possible temporal evolutions (A operator) the event associated with the user interface modification reception will occur on the tower controller's user interface. The ACTL-like expression is:

AG[executed(ground, interaction)]**A**[true{true}**U**{presented(tower, feedback)}true]

With "executed" and "presented" wordings we want to distinguish when the system generates and undertakes the action from when the effects of the action are presented on the user interface. Of course, the property holds for the tower controller too. A direct consequence of the awareness is that the two controllers are more synchronised on these actions' sequences when (for example) a flight passes from one controller's handling to the other controller's. The most intuitive example is during the hand over from the ground controller to the tower controller for departure flights (whenever the pilot reaches the holding position, the ground controller performs a last contact and then the control is passed to the tower controller) and vice versa for arrival flights. In this case, the last contact message performed by the ground controller generates a feedback on the tower controller's user interface, so that the tower is aware of the performed action and he expects a pilot's message in the near future. In next figures we show an example of user interface in our prototype that supports this type of property.

In Fig.7 (left-side) there is the Tower controller's user interface (as you can see its focus is mainly on the runway) at a certain time. The information about the flight AZA2020 is greyed because this flight is not currently under the control of the Tower controller. In Fig.7 (right-side) the user interface of the Ground controller is shown at the same time. As you can see, the Ground controller (whose activities are mainly dedicated to managing taxiways) is sending the frequency to contact the Tower controller to the AZA2020 flight. In Fig. 8 the feedback of this action on the Tower controller's user interface is shown. The graphical technique that has been used to indicate that the Ground controller has sent the frequency of the tower controller to AZA2020 is an additional bold border around the flight label.

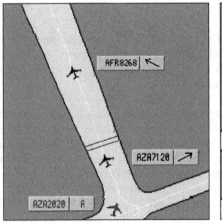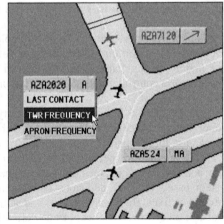

Fig. 7. User interface for tower controller (Left side), and for ground controller (Right side).

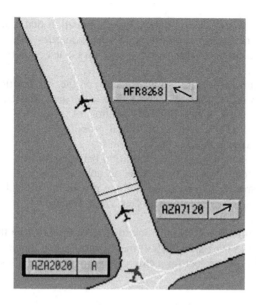

Fig. 8. Feedback for mutual awareness.

Location-Dependent Coordination Property. Here there is another case of proper controllers' *co-ordination*. In this case, different users are enabled to perform an interaction depending on the position of an object of interest: for example, this occurs when a departure flight has to cross an active runway in order to reach a different assigned runway. The ground controller gives the flight a path on the taxiways until the flight reaches the runway that he has to cross. Thus, on the one hand the pilots know that when they arrive at that point they have to wait for a message from a tower controller (who takes on responsibility for runways). In addition, and more importantly, the tower controller knows that, when the pilot has reached the crossing he has to provide clearance to go through the runway as soon as possible, without any explicit request from the pilot:

AG[sent(ground,   path)]   **A**[true{true}**U**{received(pilot,   path}   **E**[true{true}
U{stopped(pilot,   runways_crossing)}   **A**[true{true}**U**{sent(tower,   ok_crossing)}
true]]]

This means that once the ground controller has sent the path to a pilot in order to reach the assigned runway, we have a temporal evolution during which the message has been received by the pilot. Then, we reach a state, by performing the pilot's action of stopping at the crossing of the taxiway with the runway, from where for all the possible temporal evolutions the desired effect (the tower controller sending the authorisation to cross the runway) will occur.

6   Conclusions

In this paper we have presented and discussed a method that introduces the use of formal support in the design of interactive safety-critical applications. We have explained what the main aspects to consider in such formalisation efforts are and how we build a formal task model of a cooperative application that is then used to reason about single and multi-user properties. Such properties are identified through multidisciplinary discussions that involve end users, user interface designers, and software developers.

This approach has been applied to a case study in the Air Traffic Control field: the management of aircraft in the aerodrome area with data link communication. Our method is supported by a set of tools (editor of task models, translator from ConcurTaskTrees to LOTOS, editor of formal properties of user interfaces) that can be integrated with existing model checking tools.

Further work is planned on better integration between our tools for task modelling and existing model checking tools in order to achieve, for example, more effective user interfaces for specifying properties and the possibility of analysing the results of the model checker directly in the ConcurTaskTrees model.

Acknowledgements. We gratefully acknowledge support from the European Commission for the MEFISTO Esprit LTR Project (http://giove.cnuce.cnr.it/mefisto.html) and our colleagues in the project for useful discussions on the topics of the paper.

References

1. B.d'Ausbourg, C.Seguin, G.Durrieu, P.Rochè, Helping the Automated Validation Process of User Interfaces Systems, Proceedings ICSE'98 pp.219-228.
2. G.Abowd, H.Wang, A.Monk, "A formal technique for automated dialogue development", Proceedings DIS'95, ACM Press, pp.219-226.
3. G.Ballardin, C.Mancini, F.Paternò, Computer-Aided Analysis of Cooperative Applications, Proceedings Computer-Aided Design of User Interfaces, pp.257-270,, Kluwer, 1999.
4. G.Booch, J.Rumbaugh, I.Jacobson, *Unified Modeling Language Reference Manual,* Addison Wesley, 1999
5. R.De Nicola, A.Fantechi, S.Gnesi, and G.Ristori. An action-based framework for verifying logical and behavioural properties of concurrent systems, Computer Network and ISDN systems, 25, 1993, 761-778
6. J. Fernandez, H. Garavel, A. Kerbrat, R. Mateescu, L. Mounier, M. Sighireanu, CADP (CAESAR/ALDEBARAN Development Package): A Protocol Validation and Verification Toolbox, Proceedings of the 8th Conference on Computer-Aided Verification, LNCS 1102, Springer Verlag, pp. 437--440, 1996.
7. A.Hall, "Using Formal Methods to Develop an ATC Information System", IEEE Software, pp.66-76, March 1996.
8. ISO (1988). Information Processing Systems - Open Systems Interconnection – LOTOS - A Formal Description Based on Temporal Ordering of Observational Behaviour. ISO/IS 8807. ISO Central Secretariat.
9. R. Mateescu and H. Garavel, XTL: A Meta-Language and Tool for Temporal Logic Model-Checking. Proceedings of the International Workshop on Software Tools for Technology. Transfer STTT'98 (Aalborg, Denmark), July 1998.
10. Myers, B., Rosson, M.B., "Survey on User Interface Programming", *Proceedings CHI'92*, pp. 195-202, ACM Press, 1992.
11. P.Palanque, F.Paternò (eds.), Formal Methods in Human-Computer Interaction, Springer Verlag, 1997.
12. F.Paternò, Formal Reasoning about Dialogue Properties with Automatic Support, Interacting with Computers, August 1997, pp.173-196, Elsevier.
13. F.Paternò, Model-Based Design and Usability Evaluation of Interactive Applications, Springer Verlag, ISBN 1-85233-155-0, 1999.
14. F.Paterno', G.Faconti, On the Use of LOTOS to Describe Graphical Interaction, in Monk, Diaper & Harrison eds. People and Computers VII: Proceedings of the HCI'92 Conference, pp.155-173, Cambridge University Press.
15. A.Puerta, A Model-Based Interface Development Environment, *IEEE Software*, pp. 40-47, July/August 1997.

More Precise Descriptions of Temporal Relations within Task Models

Anke Dittmar

Universität Rostock,
Fachbereich Informatik, D-18051 Rostock
ad@informatik.uni-rostock.de

Abstract. Task models are more and more accepted as a prerequisite for a good design of interactive systems. In the existing approaches, the description of temporal relations between the subtasks corresponds to the hierarchical decomposition of a task. This paper proposes a separate specification of actions and goals constituting tasks where an action model called *simple action model* describes the hierarchical and sequential character of the task. An extension of the simple action model by additional temporal constraints is suggested. Thus, a more general models can be specified which can be adapted to actual conditions. The *adapted action model* allows a more precise modelling of temporal relations between subactions. This approach can contribute to a more flexible task modelling.

1   Introduction

The need of considering the real tasks of the potential users is more and more accepted by developers of interactive systems (IS). "There is no point in building a system that is functionally correct or efficient if it doesn't support user's tasks or if users cannot employ the interface to understand how the system will achieve task objects"[4].

In [9] the need of a well-defined theory of tasks is emphasized. There is an underlying assumption that such a theory can support the modelling of the conceptual knowledge a user requires to perform a task. Several task analysis techniques were developed, e.g., TAKD [2] supplying task models of the users. Model-based approaches like [19], [13], or [5] use task models in connection with other models to derive an appropriate specification of the IS. In general, these methods distinguish between the description of the existing (task) situation and the envisioned one which will be influenced by the introduction of the new IS. In most cases one can find a description of the working environment or domain of the users (domain model), a specification of their task structures (task model) and a model of the user characteristics (user model). Of course, close relationships exist between these models. How a user acts, depends on his own characteristics and the current state of his environment. Vice versa, a person changes his environment and himself (his abilities, skills, or attitudes) by acting upon the world.

P. Palanque and F. Paternò (Eds.): DSV-IS 2000, LNCS 1946, pp. 151–168, 2001.

There is a general agreement that people own hierarchical representations of their tasks (e.g., [14]). Because of his limited working memory a person is not able to survey more complex tasks. Consequently, he forms intermediate tasks from subtasks [6]. A further, very important aspect of a task representation is the behavioural one. Whereas a task hierarchy says something about the subtasks which have to be executed to fulfil the whole task (*what* to do), a behavioural representation takes into consideration the conditions for performing a subtask (*when* to do things [15]). Following [6], we say a task has both a *hierarchical* and a *sequential character*.

In this paper, a brief overview of existing modelling approaches (Sect. 2) is followed by the explanation of our basic understanding of relevant concepts in Sect. 3. The simple action model is defined and its temporal relations are more precisely. After showing some limitations of this model Sect. 4 proposes the adapted action model which allows a more precice description of temporal relations within task models. Finally, Sect. 5 gives some conclusion.

2   Brief Overview

The *H*ierarchical *T*ask *A*nalysis (HTA), developed by Annett and Duncan 1967, is an early attempt to analyze and describe cognitive as well as motor tasks. Fig.1 depicts a part of a task representation from [15]. The example illustrates the hierarchical breakdown of operations (written in boxes) and *plans* as the most important elements of a HTA. "...plans should be considered to be units of descriptions which specify the conditions under which each of the constituent subgoals [operations] needs to be carried out in order that the overall goal is attained successfully" (Duncan 1974, in [15]).

It can be seen that the description in Fig.1 contains hints to the operations a human subject has to perform (e.g. set up projector) as well as to objects of the domain in which he acts (e.g. lecture, overhead projector). Plans are also described in a semiformal way. Typical elements of plans are fixed sequences of operations, cued actions, choices, and cycles. The if-statement *OK?* in the example refers to states of domain objects. According to Shepherd a plan P is attached to an operation O which is represented as a node in the hierarchy. It contains all suboperations which are subnodes of O.

"The use of a formal approach is innovative in the practice of task modelling where often people use available operators [to describe the sequential character] without paying sufficient attention to their exact meaning ..." [11]. A possible animation of task models and their smoother integration into the design process can be enumerated as further reasons for formal, and even constructive task models.

TKS [9] can be seen as a first attempt to formalize the aspects of a task model. The User Task Model (UTM) contains a goal structure. Each (sub-)goal is represented by a unique node in a tree and at the same time it is considered as a CSP-process [8]. Process equations describe the sequential character of tasks.

Shepherd remarks quite rightly in [15] "There are many ways in which suboperations can be carried out to attain different goals and, for most practical purposes,

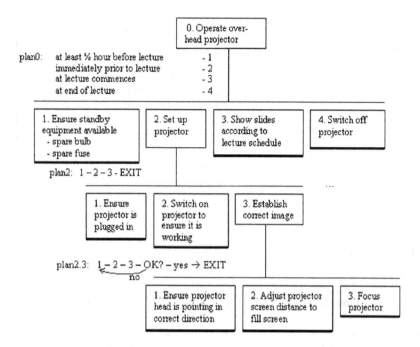

Fig. 1. Part of a Shepherd HTA

we gain little by trying to standardize them." This view can be formalized by the parallel operator (‖) resp. interleaving operator (⫴) of CSP which do not enforce useless temporal constraints on processes.

In [1], a similar approach to [9] but with more emphasis on the constructive nature of task models can be found. ''A task model contains a task hierarchy, where the subtasks are linked by temporal relations ...''. In addition to the temporal relation between subtasks, ''external ('world') conditions'' are mentioned which influence the execution of tasks. UAN [7], ConcurTaskTrees [12], MDL [16] go also in this direction concerning task modelling. An advantage of the latter approaches is their support of operators which allow the specification of more specific temporal relationships among subtasks. Operators for the deactivation and the interruption of a task are the most interesting ones. Fig.2 gives an overview of some operators describing the sequential character of tasks in MDL, ConcurTaskTrees, and UAN.

Except the UAN all other mentioned formal temporal notations base on some kind of process algebra with synchronous message passing. As to be seen later this "tradition" will be continued.

Before more flexible behavioural descriptions of tasks are proposed in Sect. 4, the simple action model is defined in Sect. 3.2. The model is based on modelling concepts outlined in Sect. 3.1. The formal definition of the simple action model allows a precise analysis of the temporal relations which can be described within this model (see Sect. 3.3).

MDL	ConcurTaskTrees	UAN	Name
$P_1 >> P_2$	T1 >> T2	A B	enabling/ sequence
$P_1 [] P_2$	T1 [] T2	A I B	choice
$P_1 \| \| \| P_2$	T1 | | | T2	A & B	interleaving/ indepent concurrency/ order independence
$P_1 [> P_2$	T1 [> T2		disabling/ deactivation
$P_1 \Delta P_2$	T1 I> T2	A → B	interruption/ suspend-resume/ interruptibility
P^{opt}	[T]		optional task
P^*	T^*		loop/ iteration
$P_1 \sqrt{} P_2$			symmetry

Fig. 2. Some temporal operators

3   The Simple Action Model

3.1   A Basic Understanding of Task Modelling

As mentioned in the introduction, a general consensus of the need for basic concepts like task, goal, operation, or task hierarchy has been reached. But there is no unique use of these terms. Some authors call it goal structure or task tree what others name, for example, hierarchy of operations. We can find the terms basic task, simple task, action, primitive, procedure for "somewhat" that a subject "performs without any 'planning' activity taking place" [9] or "which, by definition, [is] not further decomposed" [7]. As [17] we feel not very satisfied with this situation. Here only a short explanation of our view on task modelling and related basic concepts is given. A full description is beyond the scope of this paper.

A *task* is considered as a unity of *goals* and *actions* serving these goals. In Fig.3, the hierarchical concept of activities as used within the activity theory (e.g., [10]) is outlined.

A human being carries out *activities* to satisfy his needs or motives which can concern objects of the 'real world', ideas and others. Activities are realized by goal-driven *actions*. A *goal* serves as a mental anticipation of an intended or desired result. An action, again, is performed by a sequence of *operations* which are not in the consciousness of a human being and depend only on the *actual conditions*. Of course, no static or strict borderlines exist between activities, actions, and operations.

The concepts surrounded by the dotted line and their relations affect our understanding of a task. Thus, a *task model* has to contain at least

- an *action model*,
- a model of the environment (*domain model*),
- a *goal model*, and last but not least
- relations between these models.

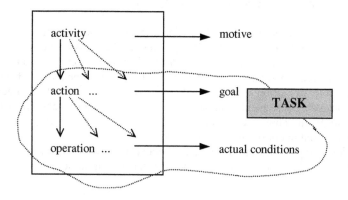

Fig. 3. Hierarchical concept of activities [18]

We consider a task as a process which is characterized by a planning, an execution, and an evaluation phase which normally overlap each other. During the planning phase the task model is created. It will guide through the execution of the task. Evaluation means the comparison between effects of actions and their goals. Consequences of a less successful evaluation could be a repetition of actions or changes   of the task model itself.

In our approach an explicit distinction between action structures and goal structures is made. Goals are set by subjects in their environment. They are descriptions of intended states of the environment. In [3], a nice characterization of goals is given expressing that they can be clear or unclear, specific or general, simple or complex, explicit or implicit. It is emphasized that humans have not only hierarchical organized goals but they can also be confronted with a net of sometimes contrary goals. Dörner [3] says that the actions are goal-oriented. But this is one aspect only. Goals can also be established afterwards by looking at the actions and their effects. Hence, the construction of the action model and the goal structure is woven.

The action model is comparable with the models introduced in Sect. 2. It consists of a hierarchical decomposition of the action combined with temporal relations between the nodes of the tree describing the sequential character of the action. Actions, and more precisely their operations, can only be performed under certain conditions. In [1], and [11] the term *precondition* is used. The execution of an action has *effects* on the actual conditions. A task is fulfilled if its goal structure is *satisfied* by the execution of its action model. The satisfaction of goals is related to the actual conditions and is decided in the evaluation phase.

This model associates subjects with an own will with tasks only. They can use instruments to fulfil them. A machine or a software system can perform operations only. A human action or a system operation can, under certain conditions, activate a system operation which supplies a certain effect. It is the responsibility of the human to evaluate whether the effect meets his goal(s).

The rest of this paper concentrates on the exploration of the action model.

3.2   The Definition of the Simple Action Model

An action model consists of a hierarchical decompostion of the action into subactions. This is specified by the *action tree*. The root refers to the action itself, all other nodes to subactions. The leafs are called *basic actions*. A basic action is associated with an operation. Furthermore, there exist temporal relations between the subactions describing possible execution sequences. A process algebra is used to specify these temporal relations. Consequently, an action is to be seen as a process. An operation is mapped to an event. Thus, we abstract at this stage from all details of an operation which is carried out unconsciously by a subject.

For the following definition of the action model the definition of a tree as directed and cycle-free graph and terms like subnode, root, leaf, parent node, or child of a tree are assumed.

Let T be a tree, then the function
- *root/1* supplies the root of T,
- *children/2* supplies the set of child nodes of a node N of T, if N is a leaf the result is the empty set,
- *sub/1* supplies all descendant nodes of a node of T.

Let P be a process, then αP is the alphabet of P as the set of all event names used within P.[5] P can be described by a set of equations where for each process P_i occurring on the right-hand side (RHS) of an equation there is an equation with P_i on the left-hand side (LHS). In the sequel, an equation with P on the LHS is written equ_P.

- The function *procs/1* takes a process expression Pexpr and supplies the set of processes occurring in *Pexpr*.
- Let equ_P a process equation, then $rhs(equ_P)$ supplies the RHS of equ_P.

Definition 1.   (Simple action model) *Let AH be a tree with root(AH) = A and sub(A) = {$A_1, A_2, ..., A_n$}. Let AS = {$equ_A, equ_{A_1}, ..., equ_{A_n}$} be a process specification for the action A. Further, let OP be a set of operations. The tuple AM(A) = (AH,AS,OP) is called* simple action model *for action A if the following conditions hold:*

- $\forall A_i \in sub(A)$ and A_i is not a leaf: $procs(rhs(equ_{A_i})) = children(A_i)$,
- $\forall A_i \in sub(A)$ and A_i is a leaf: equ_{A_i} is of the form $A_i = op.Done$ $(op \in \alpha A,$ *Done is the skip process)*
- $\alpha A \subseteq OP$

AH is called the hierarchical *and AS the* sequential description *of A.* For reasons of simplicity a bijective mapping of nodes of *AH* to processes of *AS*, a bijective mapping of operations to events, and the appropriate identity of names is assumed in Def.1. In the process expressions the following operators can be used:

|	(parallel) composition	;	sequence (enabling)
+	choice	[]	option
*	iteration	[>	deactivation
|>	interruption.		

---

[5] For brevity we do not make a distinction between processes and their names (beginning with capitals) as well as events and their names (beginning with small letters).

An abstract example of a small simple action model is illustrated in Fig.4.

The next section shows the limitations of the sequential descriptions of a simple action model by considering explicit and implicit temporal relations.

3.3   An Exploration of the Temporal Relations in the Simple Action Model

An action can be performed by the execution of a sequence of operations which is in tune to the sequential description of the task. In the sequel, sequences of basic actions instead of sequences of operations are considered. Hence, events and process equations with basic actions on the LHS can be neglected. This is possible because basic actions are mapped to operations (see Def.1). Then, the alphabet of an action (process) A is to be seen as the set of all basic actions of A. In Fig.4, αA would be the set $\{A_1, A_{21}, A_2\}$.

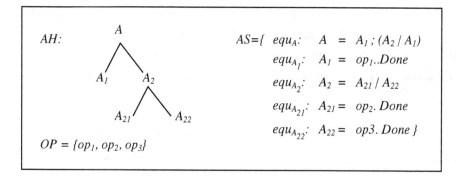

Fig. 4. A simple action model

A process can be defined as the set of all traces of its possible behaviour. In other words, the behaviour of a process A is the set of *execution sequences* in which A is capable of engaging. This set is referred to as Beh_A.

(1) $\langle\rangle \in Beh_A$,

(2) if $s^\frown t \in Beh_A$ then $s \in Beh_A$ (see e.g. [8]), s is called *prefix*, $s^\frown t$ is the concatenation of s and t.

Sequences of basic actions are considered as traces. An action A is fully completed by

$tr = \langle A_{i_1}, A_{i_2}, ..., A_{i_n} \rangle$ $(A_{i_j} \in \alpha A)$ if $A \xrightarrow{tr} Done$, tr is said to be a *maximal* trace. All other execution sequences of A are prefixes.

Every subaction $A_i \in children(A)$ of an action A can occur more than once in $equ_A \in AS$ (e.g., A_1 in Fig.4). Let A_i^{oc} be the notation of an *occurrence* of A_i where oc is the occurrencing index. There are two kinds of occurrencing. Whereas the relative occurrencing refers to a single equation, the absolute occurrencing takes into consideration all equations from which the occurrence is derived. A relative occurrencing index is denoted by a tuple of numbers. An absolute index is a list of relative indexes. Occurrences are treated like subactions with new names. The function

$$occ_{rel}: \ PEXPR \rightarrow PEXPR$$

enumerates the relative occurrences of subactions of an expression (*PEXPR* is the set of process expressions). In Fig.4, $occ_{rel}(rhs(equ_A))=A_1^{\ 1};(A_2/A_1^{\ 2})$. A_i is short for $A_i^{\ ()}$.

If A^{oc} were an absolute occurrence of A $A_1^{\ oc^\wedge<1>}$, $A_2^{\ oc}$, and $A_1^{\ oc^\wedge<2>}$ would be the absolute occurrences of A_1 and A_2 derived from AS (see Fig.4).

$A_i^{A_j^{oc}}$ refers to all occurrences of A_i which can be derived by AS from a (relative or absolute) occurrence A_j^{oc}. Further, let $trans_{max}$ be a function which replaces options and iterations in expressions (with occurrences) in the following way

- *[Pexpr]* is transformed to $trans_{max}(Pexpr)$,
- *Pexpr** is transformed to $(Pexpr^{x(1)}; Pexpr^{x(2)}; ...; Pexpr^{x(n)})$ $(n \in Nat)$ where $Pexpr'=trans_{max}(Pexpr)$ and $Pexpr^{x(i)}$ is obtained from $Pexpr'$ by replacing all $A_k^{\ oc} \in procs(Pexpr')$ by $A_k^{\ (oc,i)}$.

Then, every equation $equ_A \in AS$ defines a maximal set of temporal relations $(A_i^{\ oc_i} op A_j^{\ oc_j})$ between each pair $(A_i^{\ oc_i}, A_j^{\ oc_j})$ of occurrences on the RHS where $op \in \{/, ;, +, [>, />\}$. 'Maximal' means that if $A_i^{\ oc_i}$ and $A_j^{\ oc_j}$ are executed, they are not allowed to injure the specified temporal relation between them.

Definition 2. (Explicit temporal relations)   *Let equ_A be a process equation, $B,C \in PEXPR., A_i^{\ oc_i} \in procs(B), A_j^{\ oc_j} \in procs(C)$.*

$$TR_{rhs(equ_A)} = \begin{cases} \{(A_i^{oc_i}opA_j^{oc_j})\} \cup \{(A_j^{oc_j}opA_i^{oc_i}) \mid op \in \{+,|\}\} \cup TR_B \cup TR_C \\ \qquad ,if \quad trans_{max}(occ_{rel}(rhs(equ_A))) = BopC \\ \varnothing \qquad \qquad ,otherwise \end{cases}$$

is the maximal set of temporal relations *imposed by equ_A.*

$$TR^{AS} = \bigcup_{equ_{A_i} \in AS} TR_{rhs(equ_{A_i})}$$

is the maximal set of explicit temporal relations *of a simple action model $AM(A)=(AH,AS,OP)$.*

The maximal set of explicit temporal relations in Fig.4 is $TR^{AS}=\{(A_1^{\ 1}; A_2), (A_1^{\ 1}; A_1^{\ 2}), (A_2 | A_1^{\ 2}), (A_1^{\ 2} | A_2), (A_{21} | A_{22}), (A_{22} | A_{21})\}$.

If two subactions are related by the composition-operator this temporal relation can be omitted because | is the weakest operator which sets no temporal constraints at all, $Beh_{(A_i|A_j)} = \{tr \mid tr \in (\alpha A_i \cup \alpha A_j)^* \wedge (tr \nmid \alpha A_i) \in Beh_{Ai} \wedge (tr \nmid \alpha A_j) \in Beh_{A_j} \}$ $(\alpha A_i \cap \alpha A_j=\varnothing).$[6] A subject can perform any specified basic action at any time. If A_i and A_j are related by another operator op, e.g. by the sequence operator, this imposes a restriction of $Beh_{A_i \ op \ A_j}$. It is interesting that this restriction can be found between all

---

[6] tr $\restriction$ X is obtained from tr by omitting all symbols outside X

subtasks of A_i and A_j. This phenomenon is called 'inheritance' in [8]. 'Inheritance' says that if $(A_i^{oc_i} \; op \; A_j^{oc_j}) \in TR^{AS}$, then $\forall \; A_{i'} \in sub(A_i)$, $A_{j'} \in sub(A_j)$:

$$Beh_{(A_{i'} \, op \, A_{j'})} = \{ \; tr \, |(\alpha A_{i'} \cup \alpha A_{j'}) \, | \, tr \in Beh_{(A_i \, op \, A_j)} \}.$$

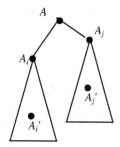

Fig. 5. Context of subactions Ai' and Aj'

Fig.5 sketches out the region of transmission of explicit temporal relations between two subactions A_i and A_j to subnodes A_i' and A_j'. The least common anchestor A of A_i' and A_j' is called *context of A_i' and A_j' $(A=context(A_i',A_j'))$*. Consequently, TR^{AS} defines a set of implicit (or inherited) temporal relations with respect to A.

Definition 3.(Implicit temporal relations) Let TR^{AS} be the maximal set of explicit temporal relations of a simple action model $AM(A)=(AH,AS,OP)$. Let $(A_i^{oc_i} \; op \; A_j^{oc_j}) \in TR^{AS}$ be an explicit temporal relation.

$$TR^{AH}_{(A_i^{oc_i} op A_j^{oc_j})} = \{(A_i^{A_i^{oc_i}} \; op \; A_j^{A_j^{oc_j}})\} \; \cup \; \{(A_i^{oc_i} op \, A_j^{A_j^{oc_j}})\} \; \cup \; \{(A_i^{A_i^{oc_i}} \; op \; A_j^{oc_j})\}$$

is the set of implicit temporal relations *imposed by* $(A_i^{oc_i} \; op \; A_j^{oc_j})$ with $A_i \in sub(A_i)$ and $A_j \in sub(A_j)$

$$TR^{AS,AH} = \bigcup_{etr \in TR^{AS}} TR^{AH}_{etr}$$

is the maximal set of implicit temporal relations *of AM(A) imposed by AS and AH.*

In Def.3 all occurrences in the temporal relations are relative to their context. For example, Fig.4 defines $TR^{AS,AH}=\{(A_1';A_{21}), (A_1';A_{22})\}$.

$TR^{AM(A)}=TR^{AS} \cup TR^{AS,AH}$ is the set of all temporal relations specified in $AM(A)$ $(TR^{AS} \cap TR^{AS,AH}=\varnothing)$.

To conclude, in the simple action model temporal relations are described explicitly between subactions at the same hierarchical level only. All methods of Sect. 2 have chosen this approach to connect the hierarchical description of an action with the sequential one. In other words, the sequential decomposition 'corresponds to' the hierarchical decomposition. Thus, restrictions of the set of execution sequences can take place exclusively between subactions of local subtress. (By the way, this is the reason why a process specification AS of a simple action model can never produce a dead-lock situation.)

4   An Extension of the Simple Action Model

4.1   Motivation

First example
Let *AM(A)=(AH,AS,OP)* be a simple action model with *AH* as illustrated in Fig.6. Two temporal relations $(A_{11};A_{12})$ and $(A_{12};A_{22})$ should be fulfilled by *AM(A)*. The first one can be specified explicitly by $equ_{A_1}: A_1 = A_{11};A_{12}$. This is not possible for the second relation because the context *A* of A_{12} and A_{22} is not their parent node. But equ_A: $A=A_1;A_2$ can transmit the requested relation. There are no constraints between A_{21} and A_{22}. Thus, $equ_{A_2}: A_2=A_{21}/A_{22}$ is fine.

Fig.7 shows *AS* and the resulting explicit and implicit temporal relations. As to be seen the requested temporal constraints are satisfied by *AM(A)*. But there are some more. *AS* is too restrictive because explicit temporal relations are possible between subactions only which have the same parent node.

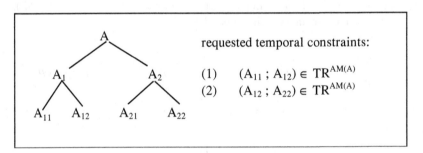

requested temporal constraints:

(1) $(A_{11} ; A_{12}) \in TR^{AM(A)}$
(2) $(A_{12} ; A_{22}) \in TR^{AM(A)}$

Fig. 6. The first example – Part 1

More decriptive power would be useful in order to specify a *refinement AS'* of *AS* according to the requested temporal constraints but with less additional constraints than *AS* ($Beh_A^{AS} \subset Beh_A^{AS'}$).

$$AS = \{ \ equ_A: \ A=A_1 ; A_2,$$
$$equ_{A}1: A_1=A_{11};A_{12},$$
$$equ_{A}2: A_2=A_{21} \mid A_{22} \}$$

$$TR^{AS} \ = \ \{(A_1;A_2), \ (A_{11};A_{12})\}$$
$$TR^{AS,AH} \ = \ \{(A_1;A_{21}), \ (A_1;A_{22}), \ (A_{11};A_{21}),$$
$$(A_{11};A_{22}), \ (A_{12};A_{21}), \ (A_{12};A_{22})\}$$

Fig. 7. The first example - Part 2

Second Example

Let us have a look at a second example to put a different perspective on the problem. Let us assume that someone wants to prepare a 'classical meal' (at least in Germany). Potatoes, some vegetable, and (most important) meat have to be prepared. Fig.8 illustrates a simple action model as explained. Imagine that only one pan is at disposal to 'Steam vegetable' and to 'Roast meat'. One of the goals or desires is to have a hot meal. It could be decided to steam the vegetable in the pan and, then, to roast the meat *'immediately afterwards'* in the same pan.

There is a general conceptual model about cooking a meal. But this model cannot consider all possible situations or, in terms of Fig.3, all actual conditions. Thus, in order to cope with the actual situation, in this case with the one and only pan, additional information has to be asserted to the model. An extra temporal relation between the subactions 'Steam vegetable' and 'Roast meat' adapts the simple action model to the actual conditions.

From our point of view, people use very rarely a big monolithic action model to fulfil a task. They have a general conceptual model and use mechanisms to adapt this model to concrete situations instead. Several adaptation mechanisms seem to be possible, for instance a combination of model parts.

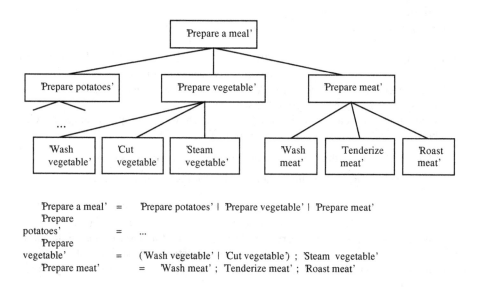

'Prepare a meal'	=	'Prepare potatoes' I 'Prepare vegetable' I 'Prepare meat'
'Prepare potatoes'	=	...
'Prepare vegetable'	=	('Wash vegetable' I 'Cut vegetable') ; 'Steam vegetable'
'Prepare meat'	=	'Wash meat' ; 'Tenderize meat' ; 'Roast meat'

Fig. 8. The second example - preparation of a meal

This paper concentrates on the exploration of temporal relationships between subactions and their more flexible modelling.

4.2   The Adapted Action Model

The idea is to take a more general 'simple action model' like in the second example and to assert temporal constraints to the sequential description leading to a refinement of the original sequential description. Fig.9 illustrates this approach for the example of Fig.7.

$$
\begin{aligned}
AS \ &= \{ \ equ_A{:}A \ = A_1 \mid A_2, & TR^{AS} \quad &= \{(A_{11};A_{12})\}, \\
& \quad equ_{A_1}{:} \ A_1 = A_{11} \ ; \ A_{12}\}, & TR^{AS,AH} \ &= \varnothing \\
& \quad equ_{A_2}{:} \ A_2 = A_{21} \mid A_{22} \ \} & & \\[2mm]
equ_c{:} \ \ & C = A_{12};A_{22} & TR_{rhs(equ_c)} \ &= \{(A_{12};A_{22})\}
\end{aligned}
$$

Fig. 9. An adaptation of the first example

Definition 4. (Adapted action model) *Let $AM(A)=(AH,AS,OP)$ be a simple action model for action A. Further, let $AS_{add}=\{equ_{C_1},...,equ_{C_n}\}$ be a set with*

- *C_i are fresh process names,*
- *$rhs(equ_{C_i})$ are process expressions which do not contain events,*

$$A'_{i_j} \in \left\{ A_{i_j}, A^{oc}_{i_j}, A^{A^{oc}_k}_{i_j} \right\} \ - \ procs(rhs(equ_{C_i}))=\{A'_{i_1},A'_{i_2},...,A'_{ni_j}\} \text{ with and } A_{i_j} \in sub(A)$$

(oc is a relative occurrencing index).

Then, $AAM(A)=(AH,AAS)$ with $AAS=(AS,AS_{add})$ is called an adapted action model, AS_{add} are additional temporal constraints.

The advantage of adapted action models is that they allow explicit temporal relations between (occurrences of) subactions of different subtrees.

- If $(A_i \ op \ A'_j) \in TR^{AS_{add}}$ then this relation holds for all occurrences of A_i.
- If $(A_i^{oc} \ op \ A'_j) \in TR^{AS_{add}}$ then this relation holds for the occurrence A_i^{oc}.

- If $(A_i^{A^{oc}_k} \ op \ A'_j) \in TR^{AS_{add}}$ then this relation holds for all occurrences of A_i which are derived from A_k^{oc} $(A_k \in sub(context(A_i,A_j)))$.

A simple action model is a very simple mechanism for descriptions. Extensions should not give up this feature completely. The question is what kind of additional constraints is reasonable. In this paper, equations $equ_C \in AS_{add}$ are allowed only which fulfil the following conditions.

1. For all $A'_i \in procs(rhs(equ_c))$: A'_i occurs only once on the RHS.
2. The operators $;, +, |>, [>$ are used only.
3. For all $(A'_i,A'_j) \in TR_{rhs(equ_c)}$: AS contains no iteration and option of A_i and A_j within their context. More exactly, let $A=context(A_i,A_j)$, then

    - $not \ \exists tr \in Beh_A{:} \ (tr \upharpoonright \alpha A_i) \in Beh_{A*_i} \ \wedge \ (tr \upharpoonright \alpha A_i) \notin Beh_{A_i}$
    - $not \ \exists tr \in Beh_A{:} \ A \xrightarrow{tr} Done \ \wedge \ (tr \upharpoonright \alpha A_i) = \langle\rangle$ (analogous for A_j).

To repeat, every additional constraint $equ_{C_i} \in AS_{add}$ imposes new temporal relations between subactions of A. It is possible that they are in contradiction to the rest of AS_{add} itself or to $TR_{AM(A)}$. There exists e.g. a cyclic dependency if $(A_i;A_j) \in TR^{AS}$ and $(A_j;A_i) \in TR^{AS}{}_{add}$. How can it be proved that the sequential description of an adapted action model is *sound* ?

The soundness can be shown by adding single temporal relations from $TR^{AS}{}_{add}$ step by step to existing explicit and implicit temporal relations TR^{expl} and TR^{impl} and by checking the resulting relations TR'^{expl} and TR'^{impl}. Thus, contradictions between the equations of AS_{add} can be excluded too.

Let '<' be a relation between operators: $op1 < op2$ if $Beh_{(A_i\, op1\, A_j)} \subset Beh_{(A_i\, op2\, A_j)}$ for subactions A_i and A_j. The following operators fulfil the demand of $op1 < op2$.

op1	<	op2
;, |>		|
+		|,[>,|>
[>		|,|>

Further, let TR be the set of temporal relations and let T be the set of action trees.

refine: $PTR \times PTR \times TR \times T \to (TR \times PTR)$

is a partial function taking a set of explicit and a set of implicit temporal relations, a single temporal relation, and the appropriate action tree and supplies the resulting sets of explicit and implicit temporal relations if soundness holds.

$$refine(TR^{expl}, TR^{impl}, tr, AH) = \begin{cases} (TR'^{expl}, TR'^{impl}) & ,if\ (1),(2),(3)\ hold \\ undef & ,otherwise \end{cases}$$

where
$TR'^{expl} = TR^{expl} \cup \{tr\}$, and $TR'^{impl} = (TR^{impl} \setminus_< \{tr\}) \cup_< TR^{AH}_{tr}$

with

$S_1 \cup_< S_2 = \{(A_i\ op\ A_j)\ /\ (A_i\ op\ A_j) \in (S_1 \cup S_2) \wedge (not\ \exists\ (A_i\ op'\ A_j) \in (S_1 \cup S_2): op' < op)\}$,

$S_1 \setminus_< S_2 = \{(A_i\ op\ A_j)\ /\ (A_i\ op\ A_j) \in S_1 \wedge (not\ \exists\ (A_i\ op'\ A_j) \in S_2: op' < op)\}$

and

(1) $\forall (A_i\ op\ Aj) \in (\{tr\} \cup TR^{AH}_{tr}):\ not\ \exists\ (A_i\ op'\ A_j) \in TR^{expl}$ with $op < op'$

(2) Let be $tr = (A_i\ op\ A_j)$. If $\exists\ (A_i\ op'\ A_j) \in TR^{impl}$ then $op < op'$

(3) $\forall (A_i\ op\ A_j) \in (TR'^{expl} \cup TR'^{impl}):\ not\ \exists\ (A_j\ op'\ A_i) \in (TR'^{expl} \cup TR'^{impl})$, except $(op = op' \wedge op \in \{\|,+\})$

Conditions (1) and (2) say that it is not allowed to restrict existing explicit temporal relations but an additional temporal relation has to restrict an existing implicit one. One should rather change *AS* of the simple action model than to rewrite an explicit temporal relation. In (3) it is requested that there are no cyclic dependencies in the new set of temporal relations.

Definition 5. (Sound AAM) *Let $TR^{AS}{}_{add}$ the set of additional explicit temporal rela-tions $tr_1,tr_2,...,tr_n$ imposed by AS_{add}. AAM(A) is sound if*
$$refine(...(refine(refine(TR^{AS},TR^{AS,AH},tr_1,AH),tr_2,AH),...,tr_n,AH)$$
is defined.

4.3   An Animation of Adapted Action Models

In the previous section additional temporal constraints were introduced to allow a more specific description of the sequential character of an action. But whereas the sequential description of a simple action model can be animated immediately this is not possible for an adapted model. To get a constructive specification a combined description of AS and AS_{add} is needed. Let us refer to such a process specification as $Constr^{AAS}$. This section does not show a complete solution to find $Constr^{AAS}$ but some aspects. Initially, $Constr^{AAS}$ consists of AS. To fulfil the constraints specified by AS_{add}, new equations are asserted to $Constr^{AAS}$ and others are changed. It is assumed that $AAM(A)$ is sound. Then, a process specification free of deadlocks can be constructed which obeys $TR^{AAM(A)}$ and does not add further temporal relations.

In this paper, the case is considered   that the equations in AS contain no multiple occurrences of subactions and the relations in $TR^{AS}{}_{add}$ have the form $(A_i ; A_j)$ or $(A_i + A_j)$. Let S be a set of pairs of processes which is for $AAM(A)$ initially $S=\{(A_i,A_i)/ A_i \in sub(A) \vee A_i=A\}$. A'_x, C_x are fresh names in the following. We begin with the treatment of sequential relations.

$Pre_{A_i}=\{A_j / (A_j;A_i) \in TR^{AS}{}_{add}\}$ is the set of subactions defined by additional con-straints which have to be performed before A_i can start.

$Post_{A_i}=\{A_j / (A_i;A_j) \in TR^{AS}{}_{add}\}$ contains all subactions which are enabled after the execution of A_i.

In the following, $s1_x$, $s2_x$, $a1_x$, $a2_x$ refer to events for synchronisation, $\bar{s}$ marks a sending event where s is a receiving event.

(1) Processes $Enabled_{A_i}$ and $Fire_{A_i}$ are constructed for every $A_i \in sub(A)$:[7]

$$Enabled_{A_i} = \begin{cases} (s2_{A_{j_1}A_i} | s2_{A_{j_2}A_i} |...| s2_{A_{j_n}A_i}) & \text{,if } Pr\, e_{A_i} = \{A_{j_1},...,A_{j_n}\} \\ Done & \text{,if } Pr\, e_{A_i} = \varnothing \end{cases}$$

$$Fire_{A_i} = \begin{cases} (\overline{s1}_{A_iA_{j_1}} | \overline{s1}_{A_iA_{j_2}} |...| \overline{s1}_{A_iA_{j_n}}) & \text{,if } Post_{A_i} = \{A_{j_1},...,A_{j_n}\} \\ Done & \text{,if } Post_{A_i} = \varnothing \end{cases}$$

(2) For every A_i with $Enabled_{A_i} \neq \varnothing$ or $Fire_{A_i} \neq \varnothing$ an equation $equ_{A'_i}$ is asserted to $Constr^{AAS}$: $A'_i=Enabled_{A_i} ; A_i ; Fire_{A_i}$.

$(A_i,A_i) \in S$ is replaced by (A_i,A'_i).

---

[7] s abbreviates s.Done

(3) Processes $C_{A_i A_j}$ are added to $Constr^{AAS}$ for every $(A_i ; A_j) \in TR^{AS}_{add}$:

$$C_{A_i A_j} = s1_{A_i A_j} \cdot \overline{s2}_{A_i A_j}$$

(4) For every A with $A=context(A_{i_1}, A_{j_1}),...,A=context(A_{i_k}, A_{j_k})$ an equation

$$A'' = (A' | C_{A_{i_1} A_{j_1}} | ... | C_{A_{i_k} A_{j_k}}) \backslash \{s1_{A_{i_1} A_{j_1}}, s2_{A_{i_1} A_{j_1}}, ..., s2_{A_{i_k} A_{j_k}}\}$$

is asserted with $(A,A') \in S$. $(A,A') \in S$ is replaced by (A,A'').

(5) Let be $A \in procs(rhs(equ_{A_j}))$. Then, A is replaced by A' in equ_{A_j} if $(A,A') \in S$ and $A \neq A'$.

Following these points, the constructive specification of the example of Fig.9 would be:

$$Constr^{AAS} = \{(A' = (A/C)\backslash\{s1,s2\}), \; (C = s1.\overline{s2}), \; (A_1 = A_{11}; A'_{12}),$$

$$(A_2 = A_{21} | A'_{22}), \; (A'_{12} = A_{12}; \overline{s1}), \; (A'_{22} = s2.A_{22})\}$$

In order to manage additional alternative relations we have to note that the relations $(A_i + A_j)$, $(A_j + A_k) \in TR^{AS}_{add}$ also imply $(A_i + A_k)$. $(A_i + A_j)$ and $(A_j + A_k)$ are replaced by $(A_i + A_j + A_k)$ and, more generally, by $(A_{i_1} + A_{i_2} + ... + A_{i_n})$. Hence, every A_k can occur at most in one of such a relation.

For every relation $(A_{i_1} + ... + A_{i_n}) \in TR^{AS}_{add}$ following equations are changed in or asserted to $Constr^{AAS}$:

(1) Every $(A_{i_j}, A_{i_j}) \in S$ is replaced by (A_{i_j}, A'_{i_j}) with

$$A'_{i_j} = a1_{A_{i_1}...A_{i_n}} \cdot (A_{i_1} + A_{i_2} + ... + A_{i_n}) + a2_{A_{i_1}...A_{i_n}} \qquad (j = 1,2,...,n) \qquad (*)$$

(2)
$$C_{A_{i_1}...A_{i_n}} = \overline{a1}_{A_{i_1}...A_{i_n}} . \underbrace{\overline{a2}_{A_{i_1}...A_{i_n}} ..... \overline{a2}_{A_{i_1}...A_{i_n}}}_{(n-1)\times}$$

$$C^j = C_{A_{i_{j_1}}...A_{i_{j_{n_j}}}}, \quad ax^j = ax_{A_{i_{j_1}}...A_{i_{j_{n_j}}}} \qquad (1 \leq j \leq k, x \in \{1,2\})$$

(3) $A'' = (A' / C^1 / ... / C^k) \backslash \{a1^1, a2^1, a1^2, ..., a1^k, a2^k\}$ with:

$$A = context(A_{i_{1_{m_1}}}, ..., context(A_{i_{1_2}}, A_{i_{1_1}})..),.., A = context(A_{i_{k_{m_1}}}, ..., context(A_{i_{k_2}}, A_{i_{k_1}})..)$$

for every A with

and $(A,A') \in S$. $(A,A') \in S$ is replaced by (A,A'').

(4) Let be $A \in procs(rhs(equ_{A_j}))$. Then, A is replaced by A' in equ_{A_j} if $(A,A') \in S$ and $A \neq A'$.

But how works a combination of the two cases above? What to do when a subaction A_i occurs in both a sequential and an alternative relation? If, for example, $(A_i ; A_j)$, $(A_i + A_k) \in TR^{AS}_{add}$ nothing is said about that A_k has to enable Aj. The equation marked by (*) has to be changed in the following way:[8]

---

[8] $P /^F Q$ behaves like P / Q, except that the first reaction which involves P / Q has to contain an action of P.

To give an example let us take the action tree as illustrated in Fig.6 but with *AAS* as to be seen in Fig.10.

$$
\begin{array}{llll}
AS & = \{ & equ_A: & A & = & A_1 \mid A_2, \\
 & & equ_{A_1}: & A_1 & = & A_{11} \mid A_{12}, \\
 & & equ_{A_2}: & A_2 & = & A_{21} \mid A_{22} \quad \} \\
\\
AS_{add} & = \{ & equ_{C_1}: & C_1 & = & A_{11}; A_{21}, \\
 & & equ_{C_2}: & C_2 & = & A_{11} + A_{22} \quad \} \\
\\
Constr^{AAs} & = \{ & equ_1: & A' & = & (A \mid C'_1 \mid C'_2)\backslash\{s1, s2, a1, a2\}, \\
 & & equ_2: & C'_1 & = & s1.\,s2, \\
 & & equ_3: & C'_2 & = & a1.\,a2, \\
 & & equ_4: & A & = & A_1 \mid A_2, \\
 & & equ_5: & A_1 & = & A'_{11} \mid A_{12}, \\
 & & equ_6: & A_2 & = & A'_{21} \mid A'_{22}, \\
 & & equ_7: & A'_{11} & = & a1.((\,A_{11};\overline{s1}\,) + (\,A_{22} \mid^F \overline{s1}\,)) + \\
 & & equ_8: & A'_{21} & = & s2.\,A_{21}, \\
 & & equ_9: & A'_{22} & = & A'_{11} \quad \}
\end{array}
$$

Fig. 10. A constructive specification

4.4   Back to the Second Example - Another Kind of Operator

In the second example of Sect. 4.1, the additional constraint was called 'Steam vegetable' *immediately afterwards* 'Roast meat'. The relation should express that there is no subaction which can be performed in between. This cannot be defined by the operators in use. We can add a temporal relation ('Steam vegetable';'Roast meat') which guarantees that the vegetable is steamed before the meat is roasted. But after steaming the potatoes could be prepared before the meat will be roasted.

A similar problem arises if one wants to specify, for example, that the subaction 'Prepare vegetable' with washing, cutting, and steaming the vegetable has not *to be disturbed* by other subactions.

$$A'_{i_k} = a1_{A_{i_1}...A_{i_n}}.$$

$$(Enabled_{A_{i_1}};((A_{i_1};Fire_{A_{i_1}})\mid^F (Fire_{A_{i_2}} \mid Fire_{A_{i_3}} \mid ... \mid Fire_{A_{i_n}})) + ... +$$

$$Enabled_{A_{i_k}};((A_{i_k};Fire_{A_{i_k}})\mid^F (Fire_{A_{i_2}} \mid ... \mid Fire_{A_{i_{k-1}}} \mid Fire_{A_{i_{k+1}}} \mid ... \mid Fire_{A_{i_n}})) + ... +$$

$$Enabled_{A_{i_n}};((A_{i_n};Fire_{A_{i_n}})\mid^F (Fire_{A_{i_2}} \mid ... \mid Fire_{A_{i_{n-1}}})))$$

$$+a2_{A_{i_1}...A_{i_n}}$$

Though the referred subactions are at the same level the 'immediately afterwards-operator' affects, in general, the whole action tree. If operators of this kind are allowed in action specifications the resulting temporal relations have to be treated like additional ones and an appropriate constructive description has to be derived.

5 Summary

Interactive systems, and especially their UI, should reflect the tasks users want to perform by using these systems. Task models can describe at least a part of the conceptual knowledge a human has in order to fulfil a task. An inclusion of the task knowledge into the specification of an interactive system can be supported by formal and constructive models.

In this paper, a task is regarded as a combination of goals and actions which have to be described separately. It is distinguished between the hierarchical and the sequential character of an action. Existing approaches to model these characteristics were explained. Especially, the description of temporal relationships between subactions was deeper explored. It was worked out that there exists a correspondence between the hierarchical and the sequential decomposition within the approaches. The ConcurTaskTrees ([12],[11]) is to be seen as an exception in a certain sense. Here, cooperation can be described by additional cooperative trees which specify a synchronization between the tasks of different users.

But, the examples of Sect. 4.1 pointed out the restrictions of this kind of modelling and motivated a possible extension of sequential descriptions. The idea of asserting additional temporal constraints to a simple action model is quite simple but can be very useful as illustrated by the examples. The derivation of a constructive specification was sketched in Sect. 4.3. Besides the definition of the adapted action model, conditions were given in Sect. 4.2 which have to be fulfilled to get a sound model and, also very important, to get a feasable model.

This opens space for many opportunities. As mentioned above we think that people rather use more general conceptual models together with adapting mechanisms to actual situations than a single model which considers all possible situations. In the case of the sequential descriptions of actions additional temporal constraints were proposed for adaptation. But, these constraints should not be too complicated. Otherwise, it could be more useful to think about a new simple action model by changing the (simple) sequential description or even the action tree itself. One could ask whether a restructuring of the action tree could work in every case. Then, additional temporal constraints would not be necessary at all. One reason for rejecting this idea is that the hierarchical decomposition of actions is often oriented towards the domain objects which have to be manipulated to achieve the goals as to be seen, for example, in Fig.8.

Other problems worth to think about are a deeper exploration of possible additional constraints. This paper treats only additional temporal relations which restrict the existing implicit ones. Further, the introduction of new behavioural operators could be useful (see Sect. 4.4). As a further interesting point the search for other adapting mechanisms of action models could be mentioned.

We believe that the introduced formalism is helpful to describe tasks because it allows more precise specifications.

6   References

1. Biere, M., Bomsdorf, B., Szwillus, G: The Visual Task Model Builder. In: Vanderdonckt, J., Puerta A. (eds.): Proceedings of CADUI, Louvain-la-Neuve. Kluwer Academic Publishers (1999) 245-256
2. Diaper, D.: Task Analysis for Knowledge Descriptions (TAKD); the method and an example. In: Diaper, D. (ed.): Task Analysis For Human-Computer Interaction. John Wiley & Sons, New York, Chichester (1989)
3. Dörner, D.: Die Logik des Mißlingens - Strategisches Denken in komplexen Situationen. Rowohlt Verlag (1989)
4. Duke, D.J. , Harrison, M.D.: Mapping user requirements to implementations. Software Engineering Journal, Vol. 1 (1995) 13-20
5. Elwert, T., Schlungbaum, E.: Modelling and generation of graphical user interfaces in the tadeus approach. In: Design, Specification, Verification of Interactive Systems '95 (1995)
6. Hacker, W.: Arbeitstätigkeitsanalyse - Analyse und Bewertung psychischer Arbeitsanforderungen. Roland Asanger Verlag Heidelberg (1995)
7. Hartson, H.R., Gray P.: Temporal Aspects of Tasks in the User Action Notation, In: Moran, T.P. (ed.): Human Computer Interaction. Lawrence Erlbaum Associates (1992) 1-45
8. Hoare, C.A.R.: Communicating Sequential Processes. Prentice Hall (1985)
9. Johnson, P., Wilson, S., Markopoulos P.: A framework for task based design (1991)
10. Leont'ev A.N.: Activity, Consciousness, Personality. Englewoods Cliffs, NJ:Prentice-Hall (1978)
11. Paterno, F.: Model-Based Design and Evaluation of Interactive Applcations. Springer-Verlag (2000)
12. Paterno, F., Mancini, C., Meniconi, S.: ConcurTaskTrees: A Diagrammatic Notation for Specifying Task Models. In: Human Computer Interaction - INTERACT'97 (1997) 362-369
13. Puerta, A., Cheng, E., Ou, T., Min, J.: MOBILE: User-Centred Interface Building. In: Proceedings of the ACM Conf. on Human Aspects on Computing Systems CHI'99. ACM Press, New York (1999) 426-433
14. Sebilotte, S.: Hierarchical planning as method for task analysis: The example of office task analysis. Behaviour and Information Technology, Vol. 7 (1988) 275-293
15. Shepherd, A.: Analysis and training in information technology tasks. In: Diaper, D. (ed.): .): Task Analysis For Human-Computer Interaction. John Wiley & Sons, New York, Chichester (1989)
16. Stirewalt, R.E.K.: MDL: A Language for Binding User-Interface Models. In: Vanderdonckt, J., Puerta A. (eds.): Proceedings of CADUI, Louvain-la-Neuve. Kluwer Academic Publishers (1999) 159-170
17. Storrs, G.: The Notion of Tasks in Human-Computer Interaction. In: Kirby, M., Dix, A. (eds.): People and Computers X, Proceedings of HCI'95, Cambridge University Press (1995) 357-365
18. Ulich, E.: Arbeitspsychologie. Verlag der Fachvereine Zürich (1991)
19. Wilson, S., Johnson, P., Kelly, C., Cunningham, J., Markopoulos, P.: Beyond hacking: A model based approach to user interface design. In: Alty, J.L., Diaper, D., Guest, S. (eds.): People and Computers VIII, Proceedings of the HCI'93 Conference (1993) 418-423

Formal Interactive Systems Analysis and Usability Inspection Methods: Two Incompatible Worlds?

Karsten Loer and Michael Harrison

BAE SYSTEMS Dependable Computing Systems Centre
Department of Computer Science, University of York
York, YO10 5DD, UK
{Karsten.Loer, Michael.Harrison}@cs.york.ac.uk

Abstract. We present our view on how a formal technique for the analysis of interactive systems can be used to support 'discount' usability inspection methods. As a demonstration, we present a snapshot of our work on supporting heuristic evaluation and on the analysis of selected usability properties. Our method focuses on the exhaustive analysis of functional properties. We claim that the benefits gained by a formal approach like the one presented here justify its extra costs. Moreover, we believe these costs can be kept comparably low by making the analysis technique flexible enough to support a number of other (informal) analysis techniques throughout the different stages of the design process.

1 Introduction

Usability inspection methods [1] are a class of analytic usability evaluation methods that have in common that they aim (i) to identify potential usability problems and (ii) to be usable at low cost to the project. The quality and coverage of the results as well as the required resources for these methods generally depend on the expertise and the number of evaluators involved [2].

Formal modelling and analysis techniques for interactive systems share goal (i), and aim at producing highly reliable results. However, they are generally expensive to apply. We believe that for some systems, especially (but not exclusively) in domains where dependability is critical, these extra costs can be justified by the benefits that formal modelling can add[9].

In this paper we present a formal technique developed in the context of safety-critical interactive systems analysis, that can be applied as an independent method, but that can also support and improve existing analysis techniques. This approach uses a modelling technique based on statecharts [3] and the application of the SMV model-checking tool [4] to the model. The approach is meant to assist a usability analyst without having to acquire extensive knowledge of formal techniques. It can also help non-human factors engineers to check basic functional usability properties for their designs. Finally, the output of the analysis is based on scenario-traces, which

---

[9] In fact, for some types of safety-critical systems the use of formal design techniques is required by authorities (see, for example, UK MoD Defense Standard 00-56, safety integrity level S4 of systematic failure integrity).

P. Palanque and F. Paternò (Eds.): DSV-IS 2000, LNCS 1946, pp. 169–190, 2001.

can be used as a communication medium between the stakeholders of the design process. Due to the operational nature of a model-based approach, the analysis inevitably will be restricted to usability principles that can be derived from functional properties. However, for these properties we can provide an exhaustive analysis while keeping the additional costs reasonably small.

In the following sections we identify usability issues as used in usability inspection methods like heuristic evaluation. Based on a sample system, we then outline a framework for the modelling and analysis of interactive systems. Finally, we demonstrate how to use this framework for the analysis of functional aspects of usability properties.

2   Usability Principles and Usability Inspection Methods

In order to provide designers with a means for analysing the usability of their designs, a number of usability principles and design rules (i.e., standards and guidelines) have been developed (see, for example [5], pp.162 [6], p.269 [7], International Standards Organisation (ISO) standards 9241 and 13714, UK MoD Defence Standard 00-25). These principles and rules are used more or less strictly by a number of usability inspection methods. Heuristic evaluation, pluralistic walkthroughs, and formal usability inspection, for example, use *heuristics* to guide the analysis process. Standards inspection rigorously checks for interface compliance. In this paper, we concentrate on selected usability issues suggested by Dix *et al.* and a set of heuristics that have been suggested by Nielsen [1] (see Table 1) for the heuristic evaluation method.

Table 1. Nielsen's set of usability heuristics (as stated in[1]).

N-1	*Visibility of system status:* The system should always keep the users informed about what is going on, through appropriate feedback within reasonable time.
N-2	*Match between system and the real world:* The system should speak the users' language, with words, phrases, and concepts familiar to the user, rather then system-oriented terms. Follow real-world conventions, making information appear in a natural and logical order.
N-3	*User control and freedom:* Users often choose system functions by mistake and will need a clearly marked "emergency exit" to leave the unwanted state without having to go through an extended dialogue. Support undo and redo.
N-4	*Consistency and standards:* Users should not have to wonder whether different words, situations, or actions mean the same thing. Follow platform conventions.
N-5	*Error prevention:* Even better than good error messages is a careful design which prevents a problem from occurring in the first place.
N-6	*Recognition rather than recall:* Make objects, actions, and options visible. The user should not have to remember information from one part of the dialogue to another. Instructions for use of the system should be visible or easily retrievable whenever appropriate.

N-7	*Flexibility and efficiency of use:* Accelerators –unseen by the novice user– may often speed up the interaction for the expert user to such an extent that the system can cater to both inexperienced and experienced users. Allow users to tailor frequent actions.
N-8	*Aesthetic and minimalist design:* Dialogues should not contain information which is irrelevant or rarely needed. Every extra unit of information in a dialogue competes with the relevant units of information and diminishes their relative visibility.
N-9	*Help users recognise, diagnose, and recover from errors:* Error messages should be expressed in plain language (no codes), precisely indicate the problem, and constructively suggest a solution.
N-10	*Help and documentation:* Even though it is better if the system can be used without documentation, it may be necessary to provide help and documentation. Any such information should be easy to search, focussed on the user's task, list concrete steps to be carried out, and not be too large.

In heuristic evaluation a group of evaluators are asked to provide independent evaluations of an interface or interface design for its compliance with a set of recognised usability principles [1]. The output from heuristic evaluation is a list of usability problems. The completeness and quality of this list depends on the number of evaluators and their expertise [9]. The more evaluators that are involved, the better the coverage of their analysis will be – at increased costs. "Double experts", i.e. analysts with domain expertise who are also trained for using the heuristic evaluation method, may find more significant problems than "single experts". However, evaluators who are more naïve with respect to the problem domain will probably detect different problems than a domain expert could.

We argue that an automated analysis framework can assist an evaluator by providing an exhaustive analysis of basic system properties. In contrast to the standard informal approach, such an approach increases the completeness of the analysis and can improve the quality, since the analyst can then concentrate on problems that can be pointed to, but are not amenable to the analysis tool. Making the problem domain amenable to automated analysis tools requires extra costs, which can be justified by the benefits of improved completeness and quality, and a better understanding of the design, as we shall demonstrate in section 3 on a sample system.

3   A Framework for Modelling and Analysing Interactive Systems

The framework we introduce here (Fig.1) can be applied in various stages of the design cycle. The system to be analysed is specified by a behavioural statechart model (see next section). Depending on the stage of the design the granularity of this model can vary from a fairly abstract to a detailed system description. With respect to detail, this is similar to the various system representations that have been used in informal usability inspection methods so far, for example, cardboard models in the early stages

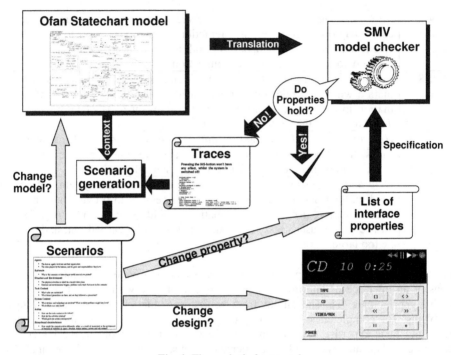

Fig. 1. The analysis framework

and prototypes in the late stages. By restricting ourselves to an operational finite-state system description we lose representational system features, but at the same time we gain the opportunity of exhaustive analysis of properties. This is achieved by a typical model-checking approach, which consists of the following steps: (i) specification of properties to be checked for the model, (ii) checking automatically whether these properties hold for the model, (iii) analysing the traces produced by the model-checking tool if a property does *not* hold. Similar approaches have been used in other work. In the field of dependable systems engineering, a number of authors applied formal verification and validation techniques to mode problems [10-13]. These papers use special-purpose models and leave the question of how to integrate the results obtained from the analysis of these models with less problem-focussed models of the system under development. Other work uses more flexible interface or interaction models and model checking for the analysis of interaction properties. For example, Abowd *et al.* [14] used the SMV model checker of the Carnegie Mellon University to analyse dialogue properties of interactive systems specified as Propositional Production Systems (PPS). Paternò [15] uses model checking and interactor models [16] formulated in Lotos. D'Ausbourg [17] presents a software environment prototype that uses model checking to analyse functional properties of interface representations based on interactor models. In [18] Campos and Harrison combine these approaches. They use (York) interactor models [19] for the analysis of mode problems and selected usability templates with the SMV model-checker.

In contrast to the textual specifications used in these approaches, we work with statecharts because they are more acceptable to system engineers. However, the downside is that the semantics of statecharts is complicated and therefore the ease with which we can make use of the capabilities of existing model checkers is difficult.

Apart from using a familiar notation, we also support designers and human factors specialists by providing formal templates of model-checking properties. Property templates are created in a similar manner, and extend the set of templates presented in [14]. However, we believe our model is sufficiently rich to formulate properties that cover also less system-centered issues. As we demonstrate in this paper, the application of these properties is guided, for example, by approaches like heuristic evaluation.

In some circumstances we can construct the generated traces for counter-examples into scenarios, which might be more readable than the traces. In this context 'scenario' means scenario of work, as suggested in [20], and the scenario representation are templates, as proposed in [21]. This idea is similar to using traces for the creation of test-cases, as presented in [17], but the consistency and completeness properties we are concerned with are different.

The main steps of the framework in Figure 1 will be outlined in the following paragraphs.

3.1   A Sample System

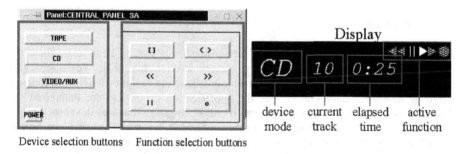

Fig. 2. Input panel and display of Hifi system

The techniques presented in the remainder of this paper, will be demonstrated on a partial model of a commercially available compact HiFi system. We choose this example because it is a dependable system and the domain is widely understood. The system is also complex enough to produce results that can be understood in the context of real-world dependable systems.

The system consists of a tape-deck and a compact disk (CD) player. It also has an audio-input for an external auxiliary device (AUX – a video-recorder or a Mini-Disk player, for example). The system is controlled by a central input-panel for all devices and it provides feedback via a central output panel (see Figure 2). The input panel consists of two sections of push-buttons which are used to activate two types of functions. *Device selection* buttons select the device to be controlled. Depending on the selected device, a number of *functions* can be *select*ed. Table 2 shows a list of basic functions that are available for a device. In addition to these functions the system offers a "*direct play*" function which will switch on the system, select a device, and then invoke the play function when a device selection button is selected while the system is off.

Table 2. Device and function selections of the Hifi system

Button	Function (depending on selected device)		
	TAPE	CD	AUX
•	stop playback		NONE
••	start playback		NONE
•	rewind	skip backward	NONE
••	fast forward	skip forward	NONE
II	pause playback		NONE
•	start tape recording		

Button	Function
TAPE	activate Tape deck
CD	activate CD player
AUX	amplify ext. source
POWER	Hifi system ON/OFF

3.2   Modelling

It has been argued that the process of modelling itself can be beneficial, since the designer is forced to write down design decisions explicitly [22]. We support this argument and we believe that this is especially true if the designer is allowed to use a language he/she already knows. For the specification of the system behaviour we therefore use *statecharts*, a graphical specification language that was developed originally to specify the behaviour of reactive embedded systems [3]. This notation is already used by designers as a standard in the automotive and aviation industry. Beyond these industries, state machines are a widely accepted way to think of a design. Moreover, statecharts are a visual notation that makes it possible for non-experts to identify certain system issues. The statechart notation is also used in Degani's Ofanmodelling technique [23], which we will utilise in this approach. The modelling process is supported by the STATEMATE toolkit [24].

With statecharts a complex system can be specified as a number of potentially hierarchical state machines that describe functional or physical subsystems and run in parallel. A state can contain sub-states that are all active whenever a parent state is active. A global broadcasting mechanism makes it possible to communicate triggering events between these state machines. We have restricted ourselves to a subset of statecharts, called *Safecharts* [25]. For example, we avoid history operators and rather replace them by static data items (cf. the use of the variable ACTMODE in figure 4). Such statechart elements are replaceable `syntactic sugar' and due to their complex semantics can cause problems in the formal analysis [25, 26]. The translation of the statechart model to the model-checker's input language (see [27]) is compliant to the operational STATEMATE semantics of statecharts presented in [28]. For the analysis of interactive systems, it is insufficient to investigate the system separately from the user and the operating environment. This is taken into consideration in the Ofan[10] technique introduced by Degani [23].   An Ofan model describes a system and its environment in five pre-defined categories, which are formulated as orthogonal sub-states:

control elements:	description of the control elements
control mechanism:	model of the system functionality
displays:	description of the output elements
environment:	model of relevant environmental properties
user tasks:	sequence of user actions that are required to accomplish a certain task

The communication between these sub-states works as described in Figure 3.

For our example, the interaction between the system and the environment is irrelevant. In a more complex system, for example an aircraft, we could think of modelling environmental parameters like altitude or heading if they are relevant for the kind of properties one intends to investigate.

To explain how Ofan works we use the model of the HiFi system in Figure 4. It represents a snapshot we used for the analysis and it is supposed to be for demonstration purposes only. The specifications of some elements were left out in order to un-clutter the presentation. In the CONTROL_ELEMENTS sub-chart the specifications of the device's ONOFF_Button through REC_Button are equivalent to the given specification of the PLAY_Button. Similar simplifications were applied to the DISPLAYS elements DEVICE_ID and ACTIVE_FUNCTION. Finally, triggering events generated by CONTROL_MECHANISM and received by DISPLAYS were left out. These work in a similar way to the start_MUSIC event shown in the model.

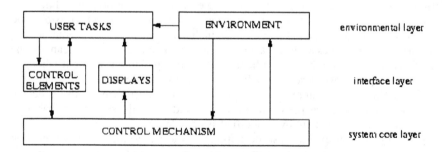

Fig. 3. Information flows in an Ofan model

---

[10]   *Ofan:* Hebrew for a set of perpetuating wheels. Degani emphasises that the concurrent states that describe the components of his model interact like a set of cog-wheels.

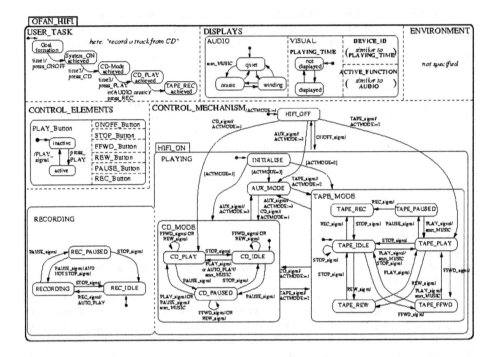

Fig. 4. Ofan model of the Hifi system

As an example of how the statechart works consider a task like "*record a track from CD*". At first one needs to determine the sequence of user-actions that lead to the desired goal. This sequence can be obtained using standard task analysis techniques, like operator function models (OFMs) [29] or hierarchical task analysis (HTA) [30].

Explicit task descriptions constrain the number of possible user-inputs and can be helpful for the analysis of system behaviour in well-defined situations. In addition, we are also interested in the analysis of system behaviour in response to *any* possible, and perhaps unanticipated, user input. Such inputs include, for example, erroneous actions by a trained user as well as arbitrary actions by an inexperienced user. We can use the model-checker to explore the system behaviour for *any* possible user input when we leave out an explicit task description. If a combination of inputs can be found that leads to a failure of a required system property, an analyst then needs to decide whether these inputs are feasible within the anticipated use of the system, and whether they might need to be ruled out by a modified system design.

If we *do* include an explicit task description in the Ofan model, every transition that leads from one sub-task to the next generates one or more triggers that are broadcast from the USER_TASK sub-chart and picked up by the CONTROL_ELEMENTS sub-chart (see Table 3 for a sequence of the transitions within this task). Note that "displays" can address all kinds of modalities rather than just vision.

The system description we used here is quite detailed and will usually not be available in early design stages. An advantage of methods like heuristic evaluation is that they do a lot without an implementation of the system. However, even if no implementation is required, the designer still needs to have a clear idea of what the system is supposed to do. We believe that Ofan models in the early stages need not necessarily be more complex than a pencil-and-paper description of system behaviour. Similar to the standard evolutionary design process one can start with a fairly abstract system description and then refine the system successively. Furthermore, systems will rarely be developed from scratch but be a refinement of predecessor designs, since the design and verification process is often iterative [31]. Therefore, an elaborated system model, as a starting point for Ofan modelling, might be available in early stages. With respect to evolutionary design the modular description of the components in an Ofan model makes it possible to concentrate on the refinement of a certain module per step and leave the remaining modules unchanged. In addition, most systems are likely to use standard input elements (push-buttons, switches, levers, etc.) that can be specified and stored as re-usable generic libraries in STATEMATE. Therefore, most effort will usually be applied to the refinement and analysis of the CONTROL_MECHANISM, ENVIRONMENT, and DISPLAYS modules that are more likely to vary between different systems.

Table 3. A sample trace of triggering events in the Ofan model.

Step	Event in sub-chart			
	USER TASK	CONTROL ELEMENTS	CONTROL MECHANISM	DISPLAYS
...				
N	press_PLAY			
N+1		> PLAY_signal		
N+2			> start_MUSIC	
N+3				> in(AUDIO.music)
N+4	press_REC	<- <- <-	<- <- <-	<- <- <-
...				

3.3 Formalisation of Properties of Interactive Systems

Apart from an adequate representation of the design in the form of the model, the model-checking tool is supplied with a set of properties that should hold. In the context of this paper these properties will be formal specifications of some of the usability heuristics of Fig. 1. The model-checking tool then fires all enabled transitions systematically and tries to reach a configuration where the given property does not hold. If such a configuration does *not* exist, it can be inferred that the property holds for all possible inputs at any time.

Our use of the model checker is somewhat different from the standard approach in that our main interest is in the analysis and refinement of behavioural properties of the model, not the correctness proof of the specification. Most often, model-checkers are used by experienced designers who use their detailed knowledge of the (system-centered) model to constrain the search for a set of required properties. Here, we use the model-checker as an agent that supports analysts and designers by an automatic exploration of generic interface and usability properties, based on a model that takes a user's point of view of the system. This technique has also been used in a similar manner in other work [10-13, 18].

In the case of the SMV model-checker, properties need to be formulated in a temporal logic (Computational Tree Logic — CTL, [32]). Although, we are aware of the fact that temporal logics are usually not part of a user interface designer's standard repertoire, we believe that the notations used here can be made intuitive and supported by CTL templates of the kind presented in [14]. The use of templates, or *"property specification patterns"* to assist the formulation of model checking properties has also been suggested in the context of finite-state verification of concurrent systems [33]. We shall see that some of our templates are closely related to the templates proposed in [14], while others enhance this set by templates for Nielsen's usability heuristics.

Take the *reachability* property, as an underlying principle of many other properties [6], for example. The property *"the state CD_PLAY can always be reached"* can be expressed in CTL as "in all possible execution paths (i.e., from any state – operator A) in all possible futures (operator G) there exists a path (operator E) where at some point in the future (operator F) the active sub-state of the PLAYING state will eventually be CD_PLAY".

```
(EF(playing_state=CD_PLAY))
```

The template "AG(EF(*<term>*))" can also be used to formulate the reachability of transitions or configurations of states (where cd_idle2cd_play is an identifier for the transition from CD_IDLE to CD_PLAY):

```
AG(EF(cd_idle2cd_play))
```

```
AG(EF((playing_state=CD_PLAY)&(rec_state=REC_PAUSED)))
```

This template is the universally quantified (prefix AG) version of the *weak task completeness* template suggested by Abowd *et al.* [14]. Rather than simply being reachable, in a dependable system the property is required to hold for all possible paths and in all states.

A specification like this can lead to *"false positive"* traces, i.e. traces that contain actions one usually would not consider to be valid in a given context. For example, we usually would not consider a reset to be a valid solution to bring the system into CD_PLAY mode. In Cadence SMV we can rule out such traces by imposing *assumptions* on the search. To state that the system shall not be switched off within an execution, we write:

```
NeverSwitchedOff :
    assert !F(ctrl_mech_state=HIFI_ON & press_ONOFF)
    assume NeverSwitchedOff
```

Because of the standard structure of the Ofan models, most of the properties presented below can be generated automatically from the model description via a set of standard query-templates, like the reachability template. In the next section we develop more of such standard templates.

4   Formalisation of Usability Properties

Since the model is specified in a behavioural language, the properties that can be checked tend to be restricted to functional aspects, including dialogue aspects. Representational and textual issues are out of the scope of a functional analysis. Therefore, non-functional properties will usually not be checkable by the system and may need to be left to another analyst (for example, see our discussion of consistency and robustness properties below). However, we can extend the range of properties that can be covered by this approach by enhancing the model at a "meta-level". Such additional definitions (e.g. counters) do not change the design itself, but specify characteristics of the system that can be used to check more elaborated properties. We now demonstrate how to formulate more complex usability properties. We will start with elementary formulations of general properties similar to reachability and then gradually enhance our queries to formalise Nielsen's usability heuristics.

4.1   Robustness

Apart from reachability, *robustness* is an important property that forms the basis for usability properties like *recoverability* (see below). Robustness properties are concerned with questions of the type *"Can the effect of a transition be achieved indirectly, i.e. when this transition cannot be fired?"*. This kind of property is important in order to determine whether a system provides fall-back alternatives in the case of a failure or alternatively whether guards for unsafe states are foolproof. From a human error perspective, robustness also includes possibilities for arriving in a desired configuration by an unintended sequence of inputs. The template for such a property is:

AG (((<*source_state*> & !<*triggering_condition or transitionID*>)
                         -> EF<*target_state*>)

If CD_PLAY is considered to be a crucial system function and the user-input press_PLAY fails (e.g. due to a defective PLAY-Button) while the system is in source state CD_IDLE, one might want to make sure that there is another way to reach CD_PLAY. A possible path is searched with the query:

```
AG((playing_state=CD_IDLE)->(playing_state=CD_PLAY))
NeverSwitchedOff : assert !F(PLAY_signal)
assume NeverSwitchedOff
```

Indeed, there is the alternative of an automatic transition to CD_PLAY by generating the REC_signal, with the clearly unwanted side-effect that the recording is started.

4.2   Nielsen's Usability Heuristics

Consistency and standards: Of Nielsen's usability heuristics the first property we will look at is consistency (N-2). We can analyse consistency in terms of user input. For example, *"will* press_PLAY *always lead to either* CD_PLAY *or* TAPE_PLAY *in the next step?"*

```
AG(press_PLAY    ->
AX(playing_state=CD_PLAY|playing_state=TAPE_PLAY))
```
When we apply this type of query to the PAUSE function, we get an unexpected result. The query
```
AG(press_PAUSE ->
EX(playing_state=CD_PAUSED|playing_state=TAPE_PAUSED))
```
produces a counter-example of a scenario where the next state will be CD_PLAY when the system is in state CD_PAUSED and a PAUSE_signal is received. One could argue that the behaviour of *starting the playback* of a device by calling the PAUSE function is somewhat unintuitive. In fact, this behaviour is also inconsistent, since for the PLAYING state it is only valid for the CD_MODE device, as can be seen from the statechart description. (Note that a similar argument is true for the transitions in the RECORDING state.) In this case the possibility is presented to the analyst who then can decide whether this "feature" is acceptable.

Consistency of textual elements needs to be checked by the analyst, since texts are usually not explicitly part of our model.

User control and freedom: A refinement of the robustness property leads to the availability of recovery mechanisms like UNDO and REDO [34], an important issue of Nielsen's usability heuristic N-3. UNDO and REDO, or *recoverability* in general, can be considered to be more sophisticated cases of reachability properties. Our sample system only provides implicit *reverse* actions, a very simple kind of UNDO/REDO control elements. With respect to the PLAY, REC, FFWD, and REW functions the STOP-button always reverts to IDLE states. In such a case where no special UNDO key exists, one can check for every critical state that there exists another single action (or at least a sequence of user actions) that takes the user from this state back to the previous state. In terms of execution paths of a model-checker this means that for each transition a (direct or indirect) path from its target state back to its source state exists. In the case of an inadvertent action, say, pushing STOP when the system is in CD_PLAY mode the query
```
AG((playing_state=CD_PLAY & STOP_signal) ->
EX(EF(playing_state=CD_PLAY)))
```
will produce a trace with the minimal sequence of actions that are required to return to CD_PLAY mode. Note, that the consequent "playing_state=CD_PLAY" would be insufficient to specify this property since the current state belongs to a path that fulfils this property. We *are* already in state CD_PLAY when the STOP_signal occurs. We therefore need to force the model-checker to actually execute a step. This is achieved by stating that the consequent needs to hold for a path in the future of the *next* step (operators EX). This template corresponds to the *reversibility* template proposed in [14].

More complex UNDO/REDO functions based on the history of user inputs require the extension of a model by a data structure that stores a history and state-machines that update and evaluate this data structure.

Visibility of system status: Nielsen's visibility heuristic (N-1) is a special case of reachability, enhanced by the notions of (1) *appropriate* feedback (2) *within reasonable time*. For example, the HiFi system should provide appropriate feedback when the RECORDING function is active. Otherwise the user might inadvertently overwrite a tape or switch off the source device. When RECORDING is active, the display should show a filled circle in the "active function" area. We can check this easily with the query:

```
AG((recording_state!=RECORDING &         ac-
tive_function_display!=RECORDING)
-> AF(recording_state=RECORDING & ac-
tive_function_display=RECORDING))
```

Abowd *et al.* (*op.cit.*) call this property *state inevitability*. However, showing that the *RECORDING* state is always displayed is not sufficient. As mentioned above, the feedback shall be timely and appropriate. We can analyse the timeliness of feedback by adding meta-level descriptions to the model. In our approach, and in the (synchronous) STATEMATE semantics of statecharts, time is represented by a number of execution steps. The formulation *"within reasonable time"* here is equivalent to *"within n steps from the current state"*, where *n* represents what we mean by "reasonable" and needs to be determined from the context. This property can be formulated by the implementation of an event-counter, as follows:[11]

```
init(NmbOfSystemEvents)  := 0;
next(NmbOfSystemEvents)  :=
case{(ONOFF_SIGNAL ⊕ CD_SIGNAL    ⊕ AUX_SIGNAL  ⊕
      TAPE_SIGNAL  ⊕ PLAY_SIGNAL  ⊕ STOP_SIGNAL ⊕
      REC_SIGNAL   ⊕ PAUSE_SIGNAL ⊕ FFWD_SIGNAL ⊕
      REW_SIGNAL   ⊕ REC_DISP_SIGNAL ⊕ ... ) &
   NmbOfSystemEvents<maxNbmEvents : NmbOfSystemEvents+1;
   TRUE                           : NmbOfSystemEvents;
   };

AG((recording_state!=RECORDING &
    active_function_display!=RECORDING)
 -> AF(recording_state=RECORDING &
       active_function_display=RECORDING &
       NmbOfSystemEvents=2));
```

That is, we first define a variable NmbOfSystemEvents that counts the number of events and add a constraint for that variable to the reachability property. Such a counter can be defined generically and can then be customised for a particular application by the designer. Another counter that can be reset will be introduced below.

The analysis whether a timely feedback is also appropriate needs to be left to the analyst, since it involves issues of the representation of the system state, as well as a user's expectations based on the immediate history and experience. We are currently investigating whether a more sophisticated description of the user beyond the level of task description may make it possible to analyse this latter issue of appropriateness.

---

[11] "⊕" here means: "exclusive or". There is a dyadic operator "^" in Cadence SMV which does not work when nested. One therefore needs to specify the expression "A⊕B⊕C" as (A∧¬(B∨C)) ∨ (B∧¬(A∨C)) ∨ (C∧¬(A∨B)). For briefness reasons we here prefer to use "⊕".

Flexibility and efficiency of use: In heuristic N-2 Nielsen suggests the use of accelerators for expert users to increase the efficiency of use. One option to detect accelerators is simply by looking for the shortest paths in the statechart. These paths can be identified visually if they use inter-level transitions, like the 'direct play' function in the sample system where transitions lead straight from the HIFI_OFF state to the lowest level of the control hierarchy (i.e. to CD_PLAY and TAPE_PLAY).

If the statechart is complex and no obvious shortcuts can be found, we can use the model-checker to search for hidden (and perhaps unwanted) shortcuts allowed by the design. In order to do so, we can add a counter to the model and then check whether a target configuration can be reached from a start configuration within less than m steps, as we did in the previous section. However, this time we need to count user actions only. Furthermore, the counter we used previously always starts counting from the initial state. Since we would like to be able to count from an arbitrary start configuration within a trace, we need to implement a possibility to <u>reset</u> the <u>n</u>umber <u>of</u> <u>u</u>ser <u>a</u>ctions (RESET_NOUA). With these modifications we obtain the following description[12]:

```
1  init(RESET_NOUA):= 0;
2  next(RESET_NOUA):=
3    case{RESET_NOUA : RESET_NOUA;};
4  init(UserActionsFromNow) := 0;
5  next(UserActionsFromNow) :=
6    case{ ~RESET_NOUA                       : 0;
7       (press_ONOFF ⊕ press_CD   ⊕ press_AUX   ⊕
8        press_REC  ⊕ press_TAPE ⊕ press_STOP ⊕
9        press_PLAY ⊕ press_PAUSE⊕ press_FFWD ⊕
10       press_REW) &
11       UserActionsFromNow < m: UserActionsFromNow+1;
12       TRUE                  : UserActionsFromNow;
13      };
```

Note that the value of the reset variable cannot be modified by the model checker, since this could lead to unwanted reset-calls. RESET_NOUA can only be set or removed within the CTL query. For example, to check whether state CD_PLAY can be reached from state TAPE_PLAY in less then two user actions, we write:

```
AG((playing_state=TAPE_PLAY & RESET_NOUA) ->
EF(playing_state=CD_PLAY & UserActionsFromNow<2));
```

Actually, for a small number of user actions the counter can be left out and in our example the statement "... -> EX EX EF(playing_state=CD_PLAY & UserActionsFromNow<2)" will do the same job. But for longer sequences the additional expense of a separate counter pays off.

---

[12] Note that in line 11, parameter m denotes the maximum number of user actions one accepts to go from the source configuration to a target configuration. The value of m will depend on the task and the amount of available user actions. It needs to be replaced by an adequate number of actions, since the model-checker can only work on explicit numbers.

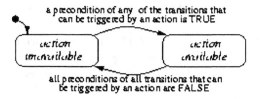

Fig. 5. A template that controls the availability of an action.

Recognition rather than recall: For systems like the HiFi all possible actions are always presented by the push-buttons and users do not need to remember functions (principle N-6). In complex systems with significantly more functions than control elements (e.g. like an electronic flight management system), however, this point becomes crucial. With the functional models we use here it is possible to detect the available functions by extending the DISPLAYS part of the model.

If the availability of an action is announced by, say, the illumination of a button, one could specify availability according to the template given in figure 5 and then make the illumination of the button depend on the state of the resulting availability sub-chart. An action is available when any of the preconditions are true that allow a transition to be fired that is triggered by that action. The PAUSE_signal, for example, is only available if the playing_state is either TAPE_PLAY, CD_IDLE, CD_PAUSED, or CD_PLAY, or if the recording_state is any state but REC_IDLE (cf. Figure 5).

If availability is a representational issue, for example the appearance of a function name in a list of *n* most important functions, then an analysis of this property is out of the scope of this approach and we need to forward this task to an analyst.

The remaining usability properties: There are a number of usability properties that are more abstract and can hardly be considered in a functional model. Generally, all design principles that deal with representational issues and wording are out of scope of our technique. In terms of Nielsen's heuristic the principles *"Aesthetic and minimalist design"* (N-8) and *"Help users recognise, diagnose, and recover from errors"* (N-9) clearly need to be analysed by a human expert.

The *"Help and documentation"* principle (N-10) is also out of scope as far as the help texts are concerned. However, in order to analyse the context-dependency of the help system, one can implement a "watcher" state-machine that logs the user's actions. The help system can be made dependent to some degree on the state of the watcher. With a similar "meta-level" concept it could be possible to check whether information that might appear during the model execution, does appear in a natural and logical order. Therefore one can address some issues of the principle *"Match between system and the real world"* (N-2). These ideas have not been investigated any further, yet, and will be the subject of further research.

Table 4. Summary of presented queries and their CTL templates

Property	CTL template for property
Reachability	AG EF (*<target_configuration>*)
Mutual exclusion	AG !EF (*<configuration1>* & *<configuration2>*)
Robustness	AG ((*<starting_configuration>* & ! *<triggering_condition or transitionID>*) -> EF (*<target_configuration>*))
Visibility (N-1) (appropriateness) (timeliness)	AG ((*<starting_configuration>*) -> AF (*<display_configuration>*)) AG ((*<starting_configuration>* & *<input_signal>*) -> AF (*<target_configuration>* & *event_counter=n*))
Recoverability (N-3)	AG ((*<starting_configuration>* & *<input_signal>*) -> EX EF (*<starting_configuration>*))
Consistency (N-4)	AG ((*<input_signal>*) -> AX (*<intended_target_configurations>*))
Flexibility (N-7)	AG ((*<starting_configuration>* & *<reset_counter>*) -> EF (*<target_configuration>* & *<input_counter = m>*))

Table 5. Summary of usability heuristics covered in the current stage of this approach

N-1	N-2	N-3	N-4	N-5	N-6	N-7	N-8	N-9	N-10
(+)	-	+	+	+	(+)	+	-	-	-

"+" covered, "(+)" partially covered, "-" not covered

4.3   Analysing Execution Traces

Once the model and a set of properties have been formulated in a way that can be processed by the model-checker, we can start the system and check the output. If a property holds, the result will simply be TRUE. If a configuration is found where the property does *not* hold, the model-checker will produce a trace of events that leads to such a configuration (see Figure 6). These traces can be interpreted as abstract representations of scenarios. They contain all relevant information on the user(s), (sub-)systems, interface elements, and environmental factors that are involved in a counter-example. This information can be associated with the relevant fields of the scenario template of [21], possibly leading to a more understandable representation of model-checking traces. The analysis of traces and/or such scenarios may point out a number of possible results:

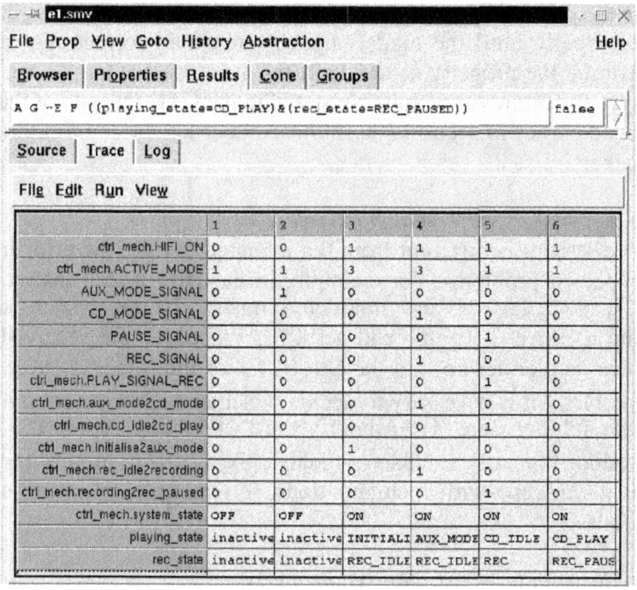

	1	2	3	4	5	6
ctrl_mech.HIFI_ON	0	0	1	1	1	1
ctrl_mech.ACTIVE_MODE	1	1	3	3	1	1
AUX_MODE_SIGNAL	0	1	0	0	0	0
CD_MODE_SIGNAL	0	0	0	1	0	0
PAUSE_SIGNAL	0	0	0	0	1	0
REC_SIGNAL	0	0	0	1	0	0
ctrl_mech.PLAY_SIGNAL_REC	0	0	0	0	1	0
ctrl_mech.aux_mode2cd_mode	0	0	0	1	0	0
ctrl_mech.cd_idle2cd_play	0	0	0	0	1	0
ctrl_mech.initialise2aux_mode	0	0	1	0	0	0
ctrl_mech.rec_idle2recording	0	0	0	1	0	0
ctrl_mech.recording2rec_paused	0	0	0	0	1	0
ctrl_mech.system_state	OFF	OFF	ON	ON	ON	ON
playing_state	inactive	inactive	INITIALI	AUX_MODE	CD_IDLE	CD_PLAY
rec_state	inactive	inactive	REC_IDLE	REC_IDLE	REC	REC_PAUS

Fig. 6. Screen-shot of the model-checking tool with an error-trace: In the initial state the system is switched off and the ACTMODE is initialised to the value '1' (i.e. CD mode was the last active mode before the system had been switched off). In the second step the AUX button is pressed, which leads to the activation of the direct play function. As a result, in the third step, the ACTMODE is set to '3' (i.e. AUX-mode) and the system is initialised. Then the user presses the CD_MODE button and activates the REC function. The system switches to CD_MODE. In addition, the effect of activating the REC functions in the previous step is that the system automatically triggers the PLAY function (cf. transition label from REC_IDLE to RECORDING in Figure 4). At the same time the user activates the PAUSE function (step 5). This leads the system to a configuration where the recording device is in state REC_PAUSED while the playing device is still in state CD_PLAY, because the internal trigger has overwritten the user input. We obviously need to decide whether this behaviour is wanted.

1. The property was not formulated properly

If the CTL property does not match the intended property, for example because the `EX` operator was left out in a recoverability-query, the error-trace will produce unexpected results. The formulation of the property needs to be refined.

2. *The formulated property is incomplete*

Many of the CTL templates presented above cover basic usability properties. It is possible that they need to be refined and customised for a certain model. We do not consider this to be problematic but rather see it as an opportunity to learn about system features. For example, if we check the timeliness of system feedback (N-1), the counter might not work properly if more than one of the specified events occurs during a step. This is a system property the analyst might not have thought about before. The query, and perhaps also the meta-definition of the counter, then needs to be modified in order to account for such system behaviour. By the refinement of queries up to a point where the model-checking result is consistent, the analysts can collect a lot of knowledge about system features that may not have been obvious prior to the analysis. Therefore we do not see this step as "property hacking", i.e. changing the formulation of the property until the model-checking result is correct. We rather see the *process* of refining the property as the main result of this technique, since in the end all relevant system features are explicitly stated in the CTL formula of the property.

As mentioned earlier in section 3.3, in this respect we differ from the standard use of model-checkers.

3. *The model does not properly match the intended design*
If the modelled system is different from the intended design, the error-trace will also describe unexpected problems. For example, in the HiFi model many sub-charts of the CONTROL_MECHANISM are non-deterministic. If the system state is, say, CD_IDLE and a PLAY_signal and a PAUSE_signal are received at the same time, the system can either go into the CD_PLAY or into the CD_PAUSED state. To resolve this problem, it is necessary to decide, whether such a situation is supposed to occur. Possible solutions are (i) to modify the CONTROL_ELEMENTS sub-chart so that it can produce mutually exclusive signals only, or (ii) to modify the system core in a way that it can cope with such situations, for example, by prioritising mutually exclusive signals.

4. *The design does not have the required property*
In this case the design needs to be modified. The error-trace often drives out the critical parts that need to be changed.

The first type of these result classes is highly dependent on the user's experience. However, we believe the templates presented here can help to minimise problems of this kind.

The other types of results often drive out valuable information about (perhaps unwanted) system features that the design team might not have recognised.

5   Tool Support

So far we have only used the STATEMATE toolkit for the development of the models and the Cadence SMV model-checker for the validation. All translation steps and the specification of properties are done manually. Future work will focus on the development of a *safecharts2smv* compiler and a query specification support tool that makes use of the templates presented here. Ideally from a practitioner's point of view these tools should integrate with the STATEMATE toolkit and utilise the SMV system. Figure 7 outlines the current architecture and possible extensions under consideration.

6   Conclusions

We presented a formal framework that is intended to support an analyst with limited formal methods knowledge in the automated analysis of functional properties of interactive systems. We demonstrated how the framework can interface with informal techniques like usability inspection. As with all formal techniques this framework requires extra costs. The detailed design insights one obtains by modelling the system under development justify some of these costs. In addition, the costs for the formal analysis will be reduced once the process is automated. The use of templates developed in this and other work (e.g. [14, 15]) as well as the standardised Ofan model support this goal.

The use of model-checking leads to a more complete overage of system properties than a human analyst might be able to provide. The analyst can therefore concentrate on representational and textual properties that are less amenable to model-checking. The method can be used to drive out potential design and usability problems on more abstract design description in early design stages, as well as more elaborated models in later stages. Since the queries for the model-checker are generated systematically by means of templates from the model, repeatability and traceability are ensured.

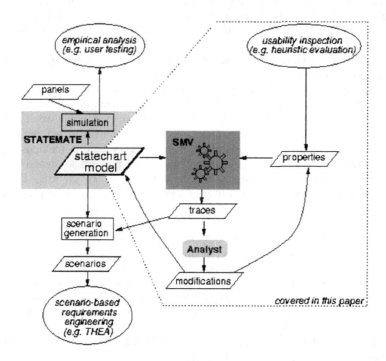

Fig. 7. Possible combination of formal and informal analysis techniques with the approach demonstrated here.

As a side-effect, if the model is used as a central description of the intended design and as information source for other techniques our approach interfaces with, as indicated in Figure 7, we can also ensure some level of consistency, since all the analysis techniques would work on the same version of the design. This issue is subject to current research.

As far as *scalability* of the suggested approach is concerned, we have already performed the analysis on bigger systems than the one used here. Currently a case-study on a real-world system in an aircraft is being conducted. There are two main results so far:

First, the functional decomposition of the system into user, inputs, system, outputs, and environment is helpful to understand the information flows and triggering mechanisms in an interactive system, as has already been shown by Degani. In a bigger system the description of the whole system in one statechart is not feasible. We therefore decided to split up the model into separate statecharts which are combined by a top-level activity chart (i.e. in this context, a super-state that controls the information flows between its concurrent activities).

Secondly, the size of the model that can be handled by the model-checker is a critical point, since the space of reachable states grows exponentially with the number of variables used in the model. Our use of the SMV system in an unusual way (probably never anticipated by its creators) might lead to an increased need for model-checking resources. However, most of our queries concern only relatively small subsets of the model and we have not discovered major problems with excessive use of resources and non-termination of the model-checker, so far. (The biggest model we have used so far has nearly 2^{70} possible states.)

Future work will concentrate on the enhancement and strengthening of the theory as well as tool support.

As mentioned above, for the analysis of some properties a task description as used here is insufficient. We therefore need to investigate options of implementing user models that contain information beyond task descriptions. A possible way to go here may be syndetic modelling (see [35]). Moreover we plan to investigate more potential applications of the approach to support other usability evaluation methods. In particular we are interested in representational and other properties beyond dialogue aspects. Finally, we will explore connections to empirical analysis. Here, the STATEMATE toolkit could be used to generate 'prototypes' based on panels of the kind shown in figure 2, which can be connected to the animated statechart model.

Acknowledgements. The Cadence SMV model-checking tool is provided by the Cadence Berkeley Laboratories and can be obtained from
http://www-cad.eecs.berkeley.edu/~kenmcmil/smv/.
It is an evolution from, and compatible with, the SMV model-checker developed at Carnegie Mellon University by Ken McMillan and that now is maintained by Sergey Berezin (http://www.cs.cmu.edu/~modelcheck/modck.html). We thank both authors for their immediate response to our inquiries.
We also thank Peter Wright and the referees of DSVIS 2000 for their constructive comments on previous versions of this paper.

7   References

1.   J. Nielsen and R.L. Mack, Usability Inspection Methods, John Wiley & Sons, Inc. 1994
2.   Virzi, R.A., Usability Inspection Methods, in Handbook of Human-Computer Interaction, K. Helander, Landauer T.K., and Prabhu P., Editors. 1997, chapter 29, Elsevier Science B.V.
3.   Harel, D., Statecharts: A visual formalism for complex systems. Science of Computer Programming, 1987: p. 231-274.

4.   McMillan, K.L., Symbolic model checking. 1993: Kluwer.
5.   Norman, D.A., Design Principles for Human-Computer Interaction, in Proceedings of CHI'83. 1983, ACM. p. 1-10.
6.   Dix, A., J. Finlay, G. Abowd, and R. Beale, Human Computer Interaction (2nd edition). 1998: Prentice Hall Europe.
7.   Shneiderman, B., Designing the user interface: strategies for effective human-computer-interaction. 1998: Addison Wesley.
8.   Nielsen, J., Enhancing the explanatory power of usability heuristics, in Proceedings of the CHI'94 Conf. 1994, ACM: Boston, MA. p. 152-158.
9.   Nielsen, J. Finding usability problems through heuristic evaluation. in Proc. of ACM CHI'92 Conference on Human Factors in Computing Systems. pp249-256. New York, 1992, ACM.
10. Lüttgen, G. and V. Carreño, Analyzing Mode Confusion via Model Checking. 1999, Technical Report, ICASE.
11. Rushby, J., Using Model Checking to Help Discover Mode Confusions and Other Automation Surprises, in (Pre-) Proceedings of the Workshop on Human Error, Safety, and System Development (HESSD). chapter 13, 1999.
12. Palmer, E. Murphi busts an Altitude: A Murphi Analysis of an Automation Surprise. in Proceedings of the 18th Digital Avionics Systems Conference (DASC). 1999: IEEE Press.
13. Butler, R.W., S.P. Miller, J.N. Potts, and V.A. Carreño. A Formal Methods Approach to the Analysis of Mode Confusion. in Proceedings of the 17th Digital Avionics Systems Conference. 1998. Bellevue, Washington.
14. Abowd, G., H. Wang, and A. Monk, A formal technique for automated dialogue development, in Proceedings of the First Symposium on Designing Interactive Systems, DIS'95. 1995, ACM Press. p. 212-226.
15. Paternò, F.D., A Method for Formal Specification and Verification of Interactive Systems. DPhil Thesis, Department of Computer Science, University of York, UK, 1996.
16. Faconti, G. and F. Paternò. An approach to the formal presentation of the components of an interaction. in Eurographics `90. 1990. Montreaux: North-Holland.
17. d'Ausbourg, B. Using Model Checking for the Automatic Validation of User Interfaces Systems. in P. Markopoulos and P. Johnson, eds., Design, Specification and Verification of Interactive Systems '98. 1998: Eurographics, Springer Verlag.
18. Campos, J.C., Automated Deduction and Usability Reasoning. DPhil Thesis, Department of Computer Science, University of York, UK, 2000.
19. Duke, D.J. and M.D. Harrison, Abstract Interaction Objects. Computer Graphics Forum, 1993. 12(3): p. 25-36.
20. Kyng, M., Creating Contexts for Design, in Scenario Based Design:Envisioning Work and Technology in System Development, J. M. Carroll, Editor. chapter 4, John Wiley & Sons, 1994.
21. Fields, B., M.D. Harrison, and P. Wright, THEA: Human Error Analysis for Requirements Definition. 1997, Technical Report YCS294, Department of Computer Science, University of York.
22. Clarke, E.M., J.M. Wing et al., Formal Methods: State of the Art and Future Directions. ACM Computing Surveys, 1996. 28(4): p. 626-643.
23. Degani, A., On Modes, Error, and Patterns of Interaction, PhD Thesis, Georgia Institute of Technology, 1996.
24. Harel, D., H. Loachover, A. Naamad, A. Pnueli, M. Politi, R. Sherman, A. Shtull-Trauring, and M. Trakhtenbrot, STATEMATE: A Working Environment for the Development od Complex Reactive Systems. IEEE Transactions on Software Engineering, 1990. 16(4): p. 403-413.
25. Armstrong, J.M., Industrial Integration of Graphical and Formal Specifications. Journal of Systems & Software Special Issue on Formal Methods Technology Transfer, 1998. 40: p. 211-225.

26. von der Beeck, M., A Comparison of Statecharts Variants, in Formal Techniques in Real-Time and Fault-Tolerant Systems, H. Langmaack, W.-P. de Roever, and J. Vytopil, Editors. 1994, Springer-Verlag. p. 128-148.
27. Harel, D. and A. Namaad, The STATEMATE Semantics of Statecharts. ACM Transactions on Software Engineering and Methodology, 1996. 5(4): p. 293-333.
28. Loer, K. and Harrison, M., Model-checking statechart interface descriptions. 2000, in preparation.
29. Mitchell, C.M., Operator Models, Model-Based Displays and Intelligent Aiding, in Human/Technology in Complex Systems. 1996, JAI Press Inc. p. 67-172.
30. Kirwan, B., A Guide to Practical Human Reliability Assessment. 1994: Taylor & Francis.
31. Campos, J.C. and M.D. Harrison. The role of verification in interactive system design. in P. Markopoulos and P. Johnson, eds., Design, Specification and Verification of Interactive Systems '98. 1998: Eurographics, Springer Verlag. p. 155-170.
32. Clarke, E.M., E.A. Emerson, and A.P. Sistla, Automatic verification of finite-state concurrent systems using temporal logic specifications. ACM Transactions on Programming Languages and Systems, 1986. 8(2): p. 244-263.
33. Dwyer, M.B., G.S. Avrunin, and J.C. Corbett. Property Specification Patterns for Finite-State Verification. in M. Ardis, ed., 2nd Workshop on Formal Methods in Software Practice. 1998. p. 7-15.
34. Dix, A., R. Mancini, and S. Levaldi, The cube - extending systems for undo, in Proceedings on the 4th Eurographics Workshop on Design, Specification and Verification of Interactive Systems (DSVIS), M.D. Harrison and J.C. Torres, Editors. 1997, Springer-Verlag. p. 119-134.
35. Butterworth, R., A. Blandford, and D. Duke. The role of formal proof in modelling interactive behaviour. in P. Markopoulos and P. Johnson, eds., Design, Specification and Verification of Interactive Systems '98. 1998: Eurographics, Springer Verlag p. 87-101.

Wisdom – A UML Based Architecture for Interactive Systems

Nuno Jardim Nunes[1]and João Falcão e Cunha[2]

[1] Universidade da Madeira, Unidade de Ciências da Computação, Dep. de Matemática,
9000 Funchal, Portugal
njn@math.uma.pt
[2] Universidade do Porto, GEIN, Faculdade de Engenharia,
4099 Porto CODEX, Portugal
jfcunha@fe.up.pt

Abstract. The UML is recognized to be the dominant diagrammatic modeling language in the software industry. However, it's support for building interactive systems is still acknowledged to be insufficient. In this paper we discuss and identify the major problems using the UML framework for interactive system development, specifically, in what concerns the architectural issues. Here we present a conceptual architectural model that expands the analysis framework of the Unified Process and the UML profile for software development processes. Our proposal leverages on user-interface domain knowledge, fostering co-evolutionary development of interactive systems and enabling artifact change between software engineering and human-computer interaction, under the common notation and semantics of the UML.

1 Introduction

Until recently both research and practice didn't focus on the overall organization and coordination of the different processes, models, artifacts and presentation aspects of interactive systems. In fact, it is even difficult to find a clear definition of user interface architecture in the literature.

Artim describes a user interface architecture as "an approach to development processes, organization and artifacts that enables both good UI practices and better coordination with the rest of development activities" [1]. This highly conceptual description focuses mainly the process of building an interactive system and the need for collaboration and coordination between HCI and SE practice. Paternò gives a more traditional (in the software engineering sense) definition "the architectural model of an interactive application is a description of what the basic components of its implementation are, and how they are connected in order to support the required functionality and interactions with the user" [2]. However, this definition, still lacks some key aspects of software architectures, like reuse and pattern composition. Kovacevic adds reuse concerns and some key aspects of model based approaches observing that such an architecture

P. Palanque and F. Paternò (Eds.): DSV-IS 2000, LNCS 1946, pp. 191-205, 2001.

should "maximize leverage of UI domain knowledge and reuse (…) providing design assistance (evaluation, exploration) and run time services (e.g., UI management and context-sensitive help)" [3].

In this paper we claim that an architecture for interactive systems involves the description of the elements from which those systems are built, the overall structure and organizations of the user interface, patterns that guide their composition and how they are connected in order to support the interactions with the users in their tasks.

In the following sections we discuss different contributions for a clear definition of interactive system architecture and present a new UML based architecture. In section 2 we discuss the conceptual and implementation models devised to support interactive system development and address the major concerns in this architectural evolution process. In section 3 we describe the Unified Process [4] analysis framework, discuss how it relates to the user interface conceptual architectures and describe efforts for bridging the gap between both worlds. In section 4 we present a new UML based architecture for interactive systems and provide examples of its expressiveness using the appropriate UML extensions. Finally section 5 presents our conclusions and further work.

2   Software Architecture Models for Interactive Systems

Work on user interface architecture initially started with concerns about conceptual architectural models for user-interface objects (or entities). Examples of conceptual architectural models, depicted in Fig. 1, are MVC [5], PAC [6] and the Lisboa Model [7]. Those models introduced the concepts of abstraction and concurrency to the user interface domain, through a set of collaboration agents (MVC and PAC) or objects (Lisboa). For a discussion and classification framework of conceptual architectural models refer to [8].

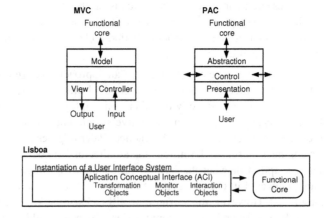

Fig. 1. Conceptual Architectural Models for Interactive Systems

In the late 1980s and early 1990s several approaches of implementation architectural models for interactive systems emerged. Unlike conceptual models, implementation models organize the interactive system as a set of software components and aim at practical software engineering considerations like reusability, maintainability, and performance.

The Seeheim [9] model proposes a simple three-layer model (application, dialogue and presentation) of an interactive system, roughly coupling the semantic, syntactic and lexical functionality's of the user interface. The application component models the domain-specific components, the dialogue component defines the structure of the dialogue between the user and the application and, finally, the presentation component is responsible for the external to internal mapping of basic symbols. The Seeheim model is considered a correct and useful model for specification of interactive systems. However, its support for distribution, concurrency, resource management and performance is recognized to be insufficient [8].

The Arch model [10] is a revision of the Seeheim model aimed at providing a framework for understanding of the engineering tradeoffs, specifically, in what concerns evaluating candidate run-time architectures. The Arch model proposes a five-layer approach balanced around the dialogue component. The components of the Arch model are:

- The interaction toolkit component implements the physical interaction with the end-user;
- The presentation component provides a set of toolkit independent objects;
- The dialogue component is responsible task-level sequencing, providing multiple interaction space consistency, and mapping the between domain specific and user interface specific formalisms;
- The domain adapter component implements domain related tasks required but not available in the domain specific component;
- The domain specific component controls, manipulates and retrieves domain data and performs other domain related functions.

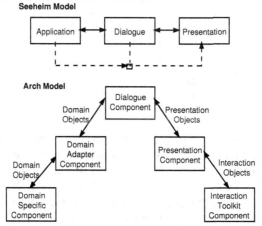

Fig. 2. Reference implementation models for interactive systems: The Seeheim and Arch models

The Arch model provides developers with guidance to tackle the difficult engineering compromises that affect the development process of interactive systems and the quality of the end product. On the one hand the user and the functional core play a symmetric role driving the dialogue component, hence, at high levels of abstraction there is no *a priori* imposition on the control of the interaction. On the other hand, both the domain adapter and interaction toolkit components serve as buffers for the functional core and the user, therefore, isolating and absorbing the effects of change in its direct neighbors [8].

3   The Unified Process Analysis Framework

3.1.   The Original OOSE Analysis Framework

In their initial proposal for the object-oriented software engineering (OOSE) approach, Jacobson and colleagues introduced the concept of use-cases and defined the entity, interface and control analysis framework [11].

The information space for this analysis framework defines three dimensions (depicted in Fig. 3):
- The information dimension specifies the information held in the system in both short and long term – the state of the system;
- The behavior dimension specifies the behavior the system will adopt – when and how the system's state changes;
- The interface dimension specifies the details for presenting the system to the outside world.

OOSE Analysis Framework

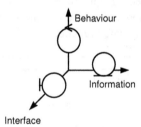

Fig. 3. The dimension space of the OOSE analysis framework

The reason behind this partitioning of analysis classes into information, behavior and interface is to promote a structure more adaptable to changes. Assuming that all systems change, stability will occur in the sense that changes affect (preferably) only one object in the system, i.e., they are local [4]. Therefore, the OOSE analysis framework aims at concentrating changes to the interface and related functionality in interface objects; changes to (passive) information and related functionality in entity objects; and changes to complex functionality (e.g., involving multiple objects) in control objects.

This approach is conceptually similar, although at a different granularity level, to the PAC model presented in the previous section. In fact, the PAC distinction between presentation, abstraction (application) and control relate, conceptually, to the interface, entity and control objects.

3.2. The Unified Process Analysis Framework

With the advent of the UML, unifying the major object-oriented methods and notations, the OOSE framework was adopted by the Rational Approach leading to the Rational Unified Process (RUP) [12] and later to what is known as the Unified Process [4]. The influence of this approach can also be found in the UML standard, in the form of an extension profile for software development processes [13]. In this evolutionary process subtle conceptual and notational changes occurred. The original interface dimension and the interface object are known in the Unified Process as, respectively, presentation dimensions and boundary class stereotype.

The authors of the Unified Process claim that this process is use-case driven, architecture centric and iterative and incremental [4]. Despite the importance of the iterative and incremental nature of the process for adequate interactive system development – as suggested in the ISO standard for user-centered design – it is not our aim here to discuss process related issues. For a discussion of process issues refer to [14] [15].

The same concerns apply, at a different level, to the use-case driven aspect of the unified process. However, since use-cases drive the architecture, and the architecture drives the selection of use-cases, we believe that some of the architectural problems lie within the intrinsic definition of what is a user (and a use-case) in the unified approach. Jacobson and colleagues claim that "the term user refers not only to human users but to other systems (...) someone or something that interacts with the system being developed" [4]. It is our belief that such definition is, in part, responsible for the system-centric nature of use-cases and, as a consequence, conditions a system-centric architecture. In a proposal for essential use-cases Constantine also argued about the imprecise definition and system-centric nature of use-cases [16]. The essential use-case extension enabled the connection between the structure of use and the structure of the user interface, providing a way to connect the design of the user interface back to the essential purpose of the system and the work it supports. However, such concerns about the system-centric nature of use-cases were not considered in the unified process.

The architecture-centric nature of the unified process is responsible for the focus on the early development and base-lining of a software architecture, used as a primary artifact for conceptualizing, constructing, managing and evolving the system under development [4]. Such architecture is responsible for the form that, together with the function captured in the use-case model, shapes the evolution of the software system. The architecture is expressed in the unified process in terms of different UML artifacts (subsystems, nodes, active classes, interfaces, etc.) and grouped in different views.

Although the Unified Process and the UML notation provide a multitude of architectural representations, in the remainder of this paper we concentrate in the analysis framework defined in the analysis model of the Unified Process. We consider the analysis framework an architectural description because the elements that establish the analysis model (boundary, entity and control), and the corresponding relationships amongst them, organize the system defining how the different elements (classes) participate in the realization of the functional requirements captured in the use-case model. We refer to the Unified Process Analysis framework as the Unified Process Analysis Architecture (UPA architecture for short), meaning the overall organization of analysis classes supporting the conceptualization, construction, management and evolution of the system.

3.3   Bridging the Gap

Between 1997 and 1999, several workshops held at major HCI and OO conferences (CHI and ECOOP), discussed the role of object models and task/process analysis in user interface design [17] [18] [15]. All this work, emerging both from industry and academia, stressed the importance, and the opportunity, of using object-technology to bridge the gap between software engineering and human-computer interaction practice. Although the workshops addressed many different issues, a general framework devised at the CHI'97 workshop [17] was consistently used to illustrate an object-oriented conceptual architecture for interactive systems. Fig. 4 illustrates the Wisdom'99 [15] revised version of the original CHI'97 framework.

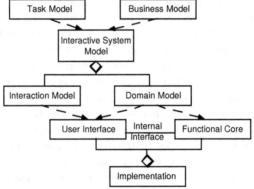

Fig. 4. The Wisdom'99 version of the CHI'97 framework

This conceptual model architecture clearly (logically, not necessarily physically) separates the functional core from the user interface. Note that, while the user interface depends on both the domain and interaction models, the functional core only depends on the domain model. This conceptual model also supports the separation of the presentation (in the user interface) from the conceptual specification of the dialogue (the interaction model) [15] [3].

4 The Wisdom Architecture

In the previous sections we discussed different approaches and contributions to define adequate interactive system architectures. We also discussed the existing Unified Process analysis architecture and argued about its system-centric nature. In this section we start from the unified process analysis architecture (UPA architecture) and expand this approach to accommodate the dialogue and presentation components, present, in the MVC and PAC conceptual models.

4.1 The Dimensions of the Wisdom Architecture

In the previous section we discussed the system-centric nature of the use-case model, and it's impact in the corresponding analysis architecture model. Our proposal for a new architecture for interactive systems introduces a user-centered perspective at the analysis level. Despite all the requirements for interactive system architecture, while devising the new architecture model, we complied with the following criteria:

– the architecture model should build on user interface design knowledge capturing the essence of existing successful and tested architectural models;

– the architecture model should seamlessly integrate the existing unified analysis model, while leveraging cooperation, artifact change and ensuring traceability between human-computer interaction and software engineering models;

– the architecture model should foster separation of concerns between internal functionality and the user interface, not only in its intrinsic structure, but also enabling the co-evolution of the internal and interface architectures;

– the architecture model should conform to the UML standard both at the semantical and notational levels, i.e., the artifacts required to express the architecture should be consistent with the UML and its built-in mechanism;

The information space for the Wisdom UML based architecture is depicted in Fig. 5. The new information space, contrasts the information space of the OOSE and UPA (see Fig. 3), introducing two new dimensions for the dialogue and presentation components. Additionally the UPA presentation dimension is restricted to non-human interface. Note that the information dimension is shared between the two information spaces, leading to a total of five dimensions if we consider both information spaces as a whole.

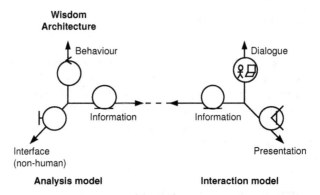

Fig. 5. The Arch model and the Wisdom architecture

The Wisdom architecture proposes a new UML interaction model to accommodate the two new dimensions, plus the shared information dimension. Therefore, the interaction model encompasses the information, dialogue and presentation dimensions, clearly mapping the conceptual architectural models for interactive systems. Accordingly, the analysis model accommodates the existing UPA architecture dimensions, also including the shared information dimensions. Note that the presentation dimension in the UPA architecture is reduced to capture the interface (not the presentation) to external systems. This way we are able to create two information spaces, sharing a common dimension (information) that ties the internal and interface architectures, leveraging the separation of concerns. Moreover, the two information spaces accommodate the domain knowledge of both the OOSE and HCI (or user interface) communities.

The Wisdom architecture - like the MVC, PAC and UPA analysis architectures - is a conceptual architecture. Therefore it should not take into consideration design or implementation criteria, like the Seeheim and Arch models do. However, the Wisdom architecture is at a higher granularity level of the MVC and PAC models, hence, it will eventually suffer subsequent reification at design and implementation. Therefore the Wisdom architecture should support such reification, maintaining qualities like robustness, reuse and location of change; while leveraging the mediating nature of the domain adapter and interaction toolkit components of the Arch model (Fig. 2). This process is typically achieved through precise allocation of information objects (entity classes) to domain adapter and domain specific components at design or implementation time. Such allocation enables semantic enhancement (dividing or joining objects in the domain adapter component) and semantic delegation (enhancing performance by preventing long chains of data transfer to objects in the domain specific component). The same applies to the interaction toolkit component, at this level with presentation objects (interaction space classes).

4.2 Elements of the Analysis Model

In the Wisdom architecture the analysis model concerns the internal architecture of the system. This model structures the functional requirements in terms of analysis classes, postponing the handling of non-functional requirements to subsequent design and implementation models.

The elements of the analysis model are analysis classes, standardized in the UML as class stereotypes [13]. The three stereotypes are [4]:

- Boundary class – the boundary class is used, in the Wisdom architecture, to model interaction between the system and external systems (non-human actors). The interaction involves receiving (not presenting) information to and from external systems. Boundary classes clarify and isolate requirements in the system's boundaries, thus isolating change in the communication interface (not human-interface). Boundary classes often represent external systems, for example, communication interfaces, sensors, actuators, printer interfaces, APIs, etc.
- Control class – the control class represents coordination, sequencing, transactions and control of other objects. Control classes often encapsulate complex derivations and calculations (such as business logic) that cannot be related to specific entity classes. Thereby, control classes isolate changes to control, sequencing, transactions and business logic that involve several other objects.
- Entity class – the entity class is used to model perdurable information (often persistent). Entity classes structure domain (or business) classes and associate behavior, often, representing a logical data structure. As a result, entity classes reflect the information in a way that benefits developers when designing and implementing the system (including support for persistence). Entity objects isolate changes to the information they represent.

4.3 Elements of the Interaction Model

The new interaction model, proposed in the Wisdom architecture, concerns the overall organization of the user interface in an interactive system. This model structures the interaction with users (human actors) in terms of interaction classes, postponing the handling of user interface styles, technologies and other constraints to subsequent design and implementation models.

The elements of the interaction model (Fig. 6) are interaction classes, defined as stereotypes of UML class constructs. The two stereotypes proposed in the Wisdom architecture are:

- Interaction space class[1] – the interaction space class is used to model interaction between the system and the users (human-actors). A interaction space class represents the space within the user interface of a system where the user interacts with all the functions, containers, and information needed for carrying out some par-

---

[1] In previous versions of the Wisdom method the presentation entity was named view class, however we decided to change it's name to interaction space because it reflects more appropriately the notion of a human user interacting with

ticular task or set of interrelated tasks. Interaction space classes are responsible for the physical interaction with the user, including a set of interaction techniques that define the image of the system (output) and the handling of events produced by the user (input). Interaction space classes isolate change in the user interface of the system and often represent abstraction of windows, forms, panes, etc.

– Task class – task classes are used to model the structure of the dialogue between the user and the system. Task classes are responsible for task level sequencing, multiple interaction space consistency and mapping back and forth between entities and interaction space classes. Task classes often encapsulate complex behavior that cannot be related to specific entity classes. Thereby, task classes isolate changes in the dialogue structure of the user interface.

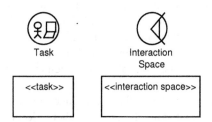

Fig. 6. Alternative representations of the interaction model class stereotypes: task and interaction space.

4.4   An application example of the Wisdom architecture

Figures 7, 8 and 9 illustrate an application example of the Wisdom architecture with different UML artifacts. The example artifacts shown throughout this section are from a simple problem definition based in similar examples worked in the literature [7] [19]. To clarify the scope of the example we cite a definition of this particular problem from [15]:

> "The guest makes a reservation with the Hotel. The Hotel will take as many reservations as it has rooms available. When a guest arrives, he or she is processed by the registration clerk. The clerk will check the details provided by the guest with those that are already recorded. Sometimes guests do not make a reservation before they arrive. Some guests want to stay in non-smoking rooms. When a guest leaves the Hotel, he or she is again processed by the registration clerk. The clerk checks the details of the staying and prints a bill. The guest pays the bill, leaves the Hotel and the room becomes unoccupied."

To the left hand side of Fig. 7 we show a possible use-case structure for the above problem statement. The use-case model illustrates how different interaction and analysis classes collaborate in their realization. For example, the *customer browser* class, the *identify customer* task and the *customer* entity all collaborate in the realization of the three use-cases depicted in Fig. 7. In the middle of the illustration are interaction classes (interaction space and task classes). The task classes accommodate the dialogue of the interactive system, hence, for example, *check avail-*

ability and *identify customer* are high-level tasks belonging to the dialogue structure of this particular architecture. Task objects also guarantee consistency between interaction spaces, one example of such responsibility is visible between the *confirm reservation* task class and the *customer browser* and *customer reservations* interaction spaces. To the right hand side of Fig. 7 is the analysis model. In this example there are no boundary objects to interface external systems.

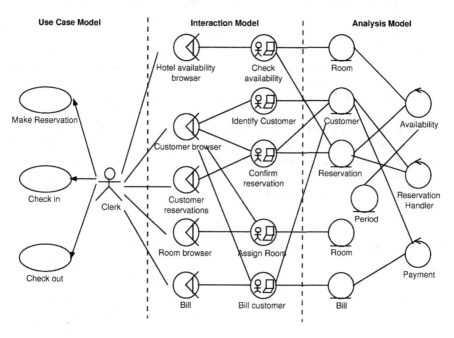

Fig. 7. Example of a use-case model, an user interface architecture and an internal architecture for an simple Hotel Reservation System.

Fig. 8 presents a hypothetical "traditional" solution (i.e., following the existing UML analysis framework). This solution was adapted from the practice illustrated in other examples in the literature (e.g., [4] [20]). Comparing both architectures we can draw some conclusions:

- The usage of boundary classes in traditional approaches, tends to follow the same functional decomposition of use-cases, i.e., there is usually a 1-to-1 mapping between use-cases and boundary classes. Such decomposition is less adaptable to change, compromises the reuse potential of the UI compromising the consistency and coherency of the UI (a major usability factor). The practical consequences of this problem are evident in the example provided. For instance, the *Customer browser* interaction space in the new approach realizes all three use-cases, such responsibility is spread between the three boundary classes in the "traditional" approach. Therefore, there is a greater probability of increased inconsistency in the traditional approach. One can always argue that such considerations should only take place at lower levels of abstraction (e.g. design); but preventing such decisions at design time is the whole purpose of devising the architecture in the first place;

- In "traditional" approaches boundary classes usually presuppose a user-interface technology or style (window, screen, etc.). Although one can argue that this is not explicitly a problem with the architectural framework,, we believe it's closely related to the absence of user interface specific architectural elements (either presentational or dialogue). For instance, the lack of lower level notational extensions supporting the reification of the presentation aspects of the UI is clearly one factor preventing technology free architectural representations;
- Another important problem, visible in both examples, is related to the placement of user interface specific logic. In the "traditional" approach, such logic can only be attributed to control or boundary classes, therefore, UI specific functionality either is bounded to presentational aspects (boundary) or to internal functionality (control). This limitation violates the principle of the separation of concerns. The result is a structure less adaptable to changes and reuse. In addition, there are clearly problems deploying such architectural models into implementation framework, for instance, a 3-tier physical implementation model very common in mainstream client-server applications. Contrasting the two examples provided, there is a clear mapping in the new framework between tasks and client side components and controls and server-side components.

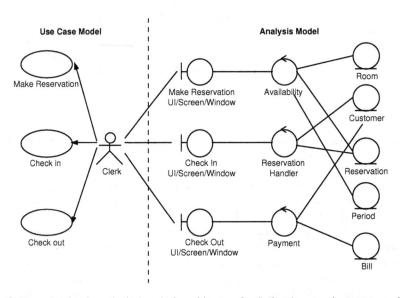

Fig. 8. Example of an hypothetical analysis architecture for the hotel reservation system problem

The following two artifacts (Fig. 9 and 10) illustrate the reification of parts of the architecture in Fig. 7. The artifacts, shown below, typically belong to design level models, in this particular case part of the dialogue model (Fig. 10) and part of the presentation model (Fig. 7). It is not our remit here to present and discuss the notation of dialogue and presentation models, refer to [21]. Alternative notations could be used to realize the analysis model, for example, the task hierarchy in Fig. 9 could be expressed through UML activity diagrams. In Fig. 9 we use an UML based notation similar to the one used by ConcurTaskTrees [2]. This notation expresses temporal dependencies between tasks through UML constraints, task decomposition is accomplished through aggregation relationships. Analogously, Fig. 10 illustrates a possible notation for the presentation model. Containment relationships between interaction spaces are shown as aggregations and navigation between interaction spaces as <<navigates>> relationships (stereotypes of UML associations).

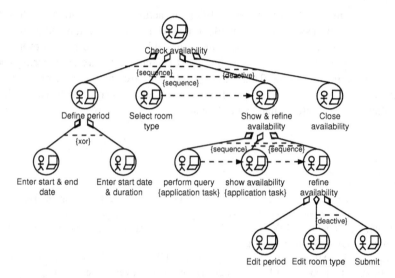

Fig. 9. Example of a Wisdom task model for the check availability top level task.

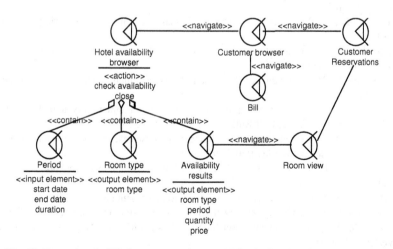

Fig. 10. Example of a Wisdom presentation model for the hotel availability browser

5 Conclusions

In this paper we discussed how the UML could be used to successfully represent conceptual architectures for interactive systems. We presented different successful approaches for conceptual and implementation architectures for interactive systems and discussed the problems with the system-centric nature of the analysis model in the Unified Process approach, also suggested as the UML standard for software development processes.

The Wisdom architecture presented here is actually an evolution of the Unified Process information space to include the dimensions of presentation and dialogue, well known to the interactive system architecture field. Our proposal accomplishes two dimension spaces that leverage both on object-oriented software engineering and user interface design knowledge. That way, the Wisdom architecture is a model that supports co-evolutionary development of models and artifacts from both worlds, leveraging collaboration, artifact change and tool support.

References

1. Artim, J. Integrating User Interface Design and Object-Oriented Development Through Task analysis and Use-cases. in CHI'97 Workshop on Tasks and Objects, 1997.
2. Paternò, F., Model Based Design and Evaluation of Interactive Applications, Applied Computing, London: Springer-Verlag, 1999.
3. Kovacevic, S. UML and User Interface Design. in UML'98, Mulhouse - France, 1998.
4. Jacobson, I., G. Booch, and J. Rumbaugh, The unified software development process, The Addison-Wesley object technology series, Reading, Mass: Addison-Wesley, 1999.
5. M. Goldberg, D.R., Smalltalk-80: The language and its implementation: Addison-Wesley, 1983.
6. Coutaz, J. PAC: An object-oriented model for dialogue design, in INTERACT'87, Elsevier Science Publisher, 1987.
7. D. Duce, D.H., M. Gomes, ed. User Interface Management and Design, Springer Verlag, 1991.
8. Coutaz, J., Software Architecture Modeling for User Interfaces, in Encyclopedia of Software Engineering, Wiley, 1993.
9. Pfaff, G. and P.J.W.t. Haguen, eds. User Interface Management Systems., Springer-Verlag: Berlin, 1985.
10. Bass, L., A metamodel for the runtime architecture of an interactive system: The UIMS developers workshop, SIGCHI Bulletin, 24(1): p. 32-37, 1992.
11. Jacobson, I., Object-oriented software engineering: a use case driven approach, New York: ACM Press - Addison-Wesley Pub, 1992.
12. Kruchten, P., The Rational Unified Process: an Introduction, Object Technology Series: Addison-Wesley, 1998.
13. OMG, Unified Modeling Language 1.3, Object Management Group, 1999.
14. Nunes, N.J. and J.F.e. Cunha, Whitewater Interactive System Development with Object Models, in Object Modeling and User Interface Design, M.v. Harmelen, Editor, Addison-Wesley, to appear.

15. Nunes, N.J., et al., Interactive System Design with Object Models (WISDOM'99), in ECOOP'99 Workshop Reader, A. Moreira, S. Demeyer, Editors, Springer-Verlag, 1999.
16. Constantine, L.L. and L.A.D. Lockwood, Software for use : a practical guide to the models and methods of usage-centered design, Reading, Mass.: Addison Wesley, 1999.
17. Mark van Harmelen, et al., Object Models in User Interface Design. SIGCHI Bulletin, 29(4), 1998.
18. Artim, J., et al., Incorporating work, process and task analysis into industrial object-oriented systems development. SIGCHI Bulletin, 30(4), 1998.
19. Dayton, T., A. McFarland, and J. Kramer, Bridging User Needs to Object Oriented GUI Prototype via Task Object Design, in User Interface Design, L.E. Wood, Editor, CRC Press: Boca Raton - Florida - EUA, 1998.
20. Conallen, J., Building Web Applications with UML. Object Technology Series: Addison-Wesley, 1999.
21. Nuno Jardim Nunes, J.F.e.C. Towards a UML profile for interaction design: the Wisdom approach. in Proc. UML'2000, York - UK: Springer-Verlag LNCS, 2000.

User Interface Declarative Models
and Development Environments: A Survey

Paulo Pinheiro da Silva

Department of Computer Science, University of Manchester
Oxford Road, Manchester M13 9PL, England, UK.
pinheirp@cs.man.ac.uk

Abstract. Model-Based User Interface Development Environments (MB-UIDEs) provide a context within which user interface declarative models can be constructed and related, as part of the user interface design process. This paper provides a review of MB-UIDE technologies. A framework for describing the elements of a MB-UIDE is presented. A representative collection of 14 MB-UIDEs are selected, described in terms of the framework, compared and analysed from the information available in the literature. The framework can be used as an introduction to the MB-UIDE technology since it relates and provides a description for the terms used in MB-UIDE papers.

1 Introduction

The model-based user interface development technology aims to provide an environment where developers can design and implement user interfaces (UIs) in a professional and systematic way, more easily than when using traditional UI development tools. To achieve this aim, UIs are described through the use of declarative models. There are three major advantages that derive from the declarative user interface models (UIMs).

- They can provide a more abstract description of the UI than UI descriptions provided by the other UI development tools [51,35];
- They facilitate the creation of methods to design and implement the UI in a systematic way since they offer capabilities: (1) to model user interfaces using different levels of abstraction; (2) to incrementally refine the models; and (3) to re-use UI specifications.
- They provide the infrastructure required to automate tasks related to the UI design and implementation processes [47].

A major disadvantage of UIMs is the complexity of the models and their notations, which are often hard to learn and use [29,47]. However, it is expected that an appropriate environment should help to overcome the UIM's complexity, providing features such as graphical editors, assistants and design critics to support UI designers. In fact, the development of model-based user interface development environments (MB-UIDEs) is still challenging since some essential problems related to this technology are not completely solved.

P. Palanque and F. Paternò (Eds.): DSV-IS 2000, LNCS 1946, pp. 207–226, 2001.

- It is hard to demonstrate that UIMs describe the relevant aspects of the UI required to generate running user interfaces. In fact, there are few examples of running user interfaces generated from declarative UIMs [50,43].
- The problem of how best to integrate UIs with their underlying applications is introduced in many papers [11,12] but is not entirely addressed for running user interfaces generated by MB-UIDEs.
- There is no consensus as to which set of models is the most suitable set for describing user interfaces. Indeed, there is no consensus as to which aspects of user interfaces should be modelled.

After more than a decade, research into model-based user interface technologies is achieving a level of maturity that can lead to effective development of good quality UIs integrated with applications. Based on the potential benefits these technologies can provide to UI developers, this survey provides a review of these technologies summarising related information available from the literature. Relevant aspects of fourteen MB-UIDEs, as presented in Table 1, are compared and analysed throughout the paper. Details of how specific MB-UIDEs are implemented are not presented here, and nor are specific notations or tools.

Table 1. Surveyed MD-UIDEs.

MB-UIDE	References	Local
ADEPT	[27,23,52]	Queen Mary and Westfield College, UK
AME	[28]	Fachhochschule Augsburg, Germany
FUSE	[38,39,25]	Technische Universität München, Germany
GENIUS	[21]	University of Stuttgart, Germany
HUMANOID	[44,46,26]	University of Southern California, USA
JANUS	[2, 3]	Ruhr-Universität Bochum, Germany
ITS	[50,51]	IBM T. J. Watson Research Center, USA
MASTERMIND	[47,9,43]	University Southern California, Georgia Inst. Tech., USA
MECANO	[32]	Stanford University, USA
MOBI-D	[35,33,34]	Stanford University, USA
TADEUS	[13]	Universität Rostock, Germany
TEALLACH	[16]	U. Manchester, U. Glasgow, U. Napier, UK
TRIDENT	[5,4,6]	Facultés Universitaires Notre-Dame de la Paix, Belgium
UIDE	[24,15,14]	George Washington University, USA

This paper is structured as follows. Section 2 describes MB-UIDE's evolution and presents research efforts. Section 3 introduces a framework for comparing and analysing the architectural components of the UIMs. Section 4 describes the UI development process using a MB-UIDE. Section 5 presents how user interfaces are described through declarative models. Design guidelines are also introduced in this section.

Section 6 describes the design environment through the tools used to model, generate and animate the model-based user interfaces. Conclusions are presented in Section 7.

2   Background

The literature contains many papers describing MB-UIDEs and their UIMs. The first generation of MB-UIDE appeared as improvements to the earlier user interface management systems (UIMSs) since they sought to execute user interfaces represented in a declarative way. The main aim of the MB-UIDEs of this generation was to provide a proper way to execute a UI from the UIM. Examples of the the first generation of MB-UIDEs are COUSIN [18], HUMANOID [44], MIKE [31], UIDE [24] and UofA* [42]. However, the UIMs of the first generation of MB-UIDEs did not provide a high-level of abstraction for the description of the UI. For instance, user interface aspects like layouts and widget customisation appeared early during the UI design process. Therefore, a new generation of MB-UIDEs appeared providing mechanisms for describing UIs at a higher level of abstraction [52]. Examples of the second generation of   MB-UIDEs   are   ADEPT [27],   AME [28],   DIANE+ [48],   FUSE [25], MASTERMIND [47], MECANO [32], MOBI-D [35], TADEUS [13], Teallach [16] and TRIDENT [5]. With MB-UIDEs of the second generation, developers have been able to specify, generate and execute user interfaces. Further, this second generation of MB-UIDE has a more diverse set of aims than previous one. Some MB-UIDEs are considering the use of computer-aided software engineering (CASE) tools and notations such as OMT [36] in their development environment. Others are aiming to achieve complete UI development.

   Most of the papers describing these MB-UIDEs compare some of their features with other MB-UIDEs, showing the differences among them. However, they are focused more on introducing the new approach than introducing the MB-UIDE technology. There are a few papers that provide overviews of the MB-UIDE technology: Schlungbaum [37], Vanderdonckt [49] and Griffiths [17] provide comparisons among many MB-UIDEs, and Szekely [47] provides an excellent insight into what an MB-UIDE is.

3   User Interface Model Framework

User interfaces convey the output of applications and the input from application users. For this reason, UIs have to cope with the complexity of both the applications and the users. In terms of MB-UIDE's architectures, this problem of conciliating application complexity and user interaction complexity is reflected in parts that MB-UIDEs usually have several models describing different aspects of the UI. These models are referred to in this as *component models* or *models*. Table 2 presents the four models considered in the framework, also presenting which aspects of the user interface are described by each model.

Table 2. Component models of a user interface.

Component Model	Abbrev.	Function
Application model	AM	Describes the properties of the application relevant to the UI.
Task-Dialogue model	TDM	Describes the tasks that users are able to perform using the application, as well as how the tasks are related to each other.
Abstract presentation model	APM	Provides a conceptual description of the structure and behaviour of the visual parts of the user interface. There the UI is described in terms abstract objects.
Concrete presentation model	CPM	Describes in details the visual parts of the user interfaces. There is explained how the UI is composed in terms of widgets.

As the purpose of this framework is to provide a comparison among different UIMs, three points should be considered:

- Task models and dialogue models are classified within a single model called the *Task-dialogue model*. Both, task models and dialogue models describe the possible tasks that users can perform during the interaction with the application, but at different levels of abstraction. The reason for classifying them together is that UIMs often only have one of them. Further, the possible constructors of task and dialogue models may have similar roles.
- User models are supported in some UIMs (i.e. ADEPT, MECANO and TADEUS). Indeed, user models are important for the model-based user interface technologies since they can provide a way to model user interface preferences for specific users or groups of users. However, they are a challenging aspect of the UI not well-addressed in MB-UIDEs, and especially not clearly described in the literature. Moreover, in those UIMs that have a user model it appears that the user model can be replaced by design guidelines. In fact, design guidelines usually contain user preferences that can be considered as a model of a group of users.
- Platform models, or environment models, are not contemplated in the framework for the same reasons that user models are not contemplated.

Models are composed of constructors. Table 3 shows the constructors considered in the framework. The table also shows a possible distribution of these constructors into the component models, a concise description of each constructor, and abbreviations for future reference. The distribution of the constructors into component models, as presented in Table 3, helps to clarify their function in the framework. Definitions of application model constructors are partially extracted from UML [8]. Definitions of task model constructors are partially extracted from Johnson [22]. Definitions of abstract and concrete interaction objects are partially extracted from Bodart and Vanderdonckt [6].

Table 3. User interface model constructors.

Comp. model	Constructor	Abbrev.	Function
AM	class	CLASS	An object type defined in terms of attributes, operations and relationships.
	attribute	ATTR	A property of the thing modelled by the objects of a class.
	operation	OPER	A service provided by the object of a specific class.
	relationship	RELAT	A connection among classes.
TDM	task	TASK	An activity that changes the state of specific objects, leading to the achievement of a goal. Tasks can be defined at different levels of abstraction, which means that a task can be a sub-task of an abstract class.
	goal	GOAL	A state to be achieved by the execution of a task.
	action	ACTION	A behaviour that can be executed. Actions are the most concrete tasks.
	sequencing	SEQ	The temporal order that sub-tasks and actions must respect for carrying out the related high-level tasks.
	task pre-condition	PRE	Conditions in terms of object states that must be respected before the execution of a task or an action.
	task post-condition	POST	Conditions in terms of object states that must be respected after the execution of a task or an action.
APM	view	VIEW	A collection of AIO's logically grouped to deal with the inputs and outputs of a task.
	abstract interaction object	AIO	A user interface object without any graphical representation and independent of any environment.
CPM	window	WINDOW	A visible and manipulable representation of a a view.
	concrete interaction object	CIO	A visible and manipulable user interface object that can be used to input/output information related to user's interactive tasks.
	layout	LAY	An algorithm that provides the placement of CIOs in windows.

One point that should be considered in terms of constructors is that MB-UIDEs do not need to have all constructors presented in the framework. Further, constructors can be distributed in a different manner from that proposed in Table 3.

4   User Interface Development in a MB-UIDE

The UI development process is normally an incremental process in a MB-UIDE. User interface design and implementation can easily be repeated however many times are required to refine the UI specification and code. In reality, some MB-UIDEs are not flexible enough in terms of code refinement. Considering the UI development process, two distinct subprocesses can be identified. The first one is the UI design, that results in the creation of a UIM. The second one is the UI implementation, that results in an executable UI. Section 4.1 presents an overview of how possible UI design processes in a MB-UIDE. Section 4.2 presents how parts of the UI design process can be automated. Section 4.3 presents an overview of the UI implementation process.

4.1   User Interface Design Process

In a MB-UIDE, the UI design is the process of creating and refining the UIM. As stated in Section 3, there is not agreement on which set of models are the best for describing UIs in a declarative manner. In terms of UI design, there is also a lack of agreement as to which is the best method for UI modelling.

According to Figure 1[14] , some modelling tools can be provided by MB-UIDEs for editing the models, and modelling assistants can be provided to support UI developers. These modelling tools usually provide a graphical environment that may facilitate the complex work of constructing UIMs. It is expected that these modelling tools can prevent UI developers for worrying about details of the models and their notation, focusing their attention on the design of the UI. Additionally, some MB-UIDEs have modelling assistants that can perform some functions, such as model checking, that provide feedback to developers about the design process.

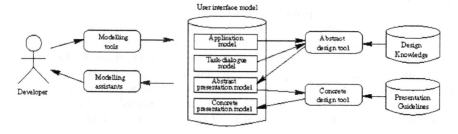

Fig. 1. The user interface design in a MB-UIDE.

MB-UIDEs based on textual UIMs optionally may not require any special editor or assistant. This may be an excellent approach for expert developers that could build and refine models using any text editor. In fact, MB-UIDEs based on textual UIMs that offer model editors and assistants give freedom to developers to use or not the model development environment provided. The problem of MB-UIDEs based on textual models are that they may not offer any special facilities for model manage-

---

[14]Traditional diagram describing the user interface development process in MB-UIDEs, presented in Szekely [45], Schlungbaum [37] and Griffiths *et al.* [16].

ment. In this case, the cost of constructing UIM descriptions might be higher than the benefits provided by such environments, specially for non-expert developers.

There are MB-UIDEs that use existing graphical editors and CASE tools as their model editors. In this case, the problem is that tools could not accept modifications to accommodate specific requirements for editing UIMs.

As UIMs can describe UIs at different levels of abstraction, it is expected that the design process should be incremental. Thus, UIs could initially be described by a very abstract model that can gradually be transformed into a concrete model. Considering this iterative design process, developers can edit the models using the modelling tools, and check the model using the design assistants, until the UIM reaches a point where the relevant details are modelled into the UIM. Further, developers can at any time return to the MB-UIDE to refine the model, even after the implementation of the UI. The problem, in this case, is that the UI should be modified only through the MB-UIDE since modifications not described in the UIM are obviously not regenerated, in the new version of the UI.

4.2   Automated Tasks in User Interface Design Process

Some papers claim that the real advantage of the model-based UI technologies is the support they provide to automate the UI design [30]. Indeed, it is a powerful characteristic of the UIMs that they can describe UIs at different levels of abstraction.

Figure 1 shows how UI design automation fits into the development activity. An *abstract design tool* can generate the abstract presentation model from application models or task-dialogue models, using a design knowledge database to supply information required during the UI design process. Additionally, a *concrete design tool* can generate the concrete presentation model from the abstract presentation model, and using a design guideline database. The design guidelines are not part of the user interface model, but they are part of the MB-UIDE.

Most of the research related with UI development concerns the "look and feel" aspects of the UI. For this reason, there are many well-known guidelines concerning the presentation of the UI [40]. On the other hand, there are some research efforts that analyse how to model tasks during human-computer interaction. However, the guidelines provided by these studies are not established enough to be used as a proper design knowledge database [52]. Therefore, part of the automated UI design process related with the task-dialogue model is affected by this lack of well-established task modelling guidelines.

At the same time such automated design facilitated the work of UI developers, it also creates a new problem: how UI developers can interfere in this automated process to design UIs with different characteristics to those provided by design knowledge design guideline databases [47].

4.3   User Interface Implementation Process

Figure 2 illustrates three approaches to generating and executing a user interface, in the context of a MB-UIDE. In the first approach shown in Figure 2a, the source code of the user interface is generated based on the toolkit class library. In this approach, the MB-UIDE generates the source code of the user interface, and sometimes it generates the skeleton of the application. In the second approach shown in Figure 2b, the UI is executed by the UIMS runtime system linked with the application. A UIMS input-file generator is required, in this case, to convert the UIM into the UIMS input-file format. In the third approach shown in Figure 2c, the application can interpret the UIM directly due to the MB-UIDE runtime system being linked to the application.

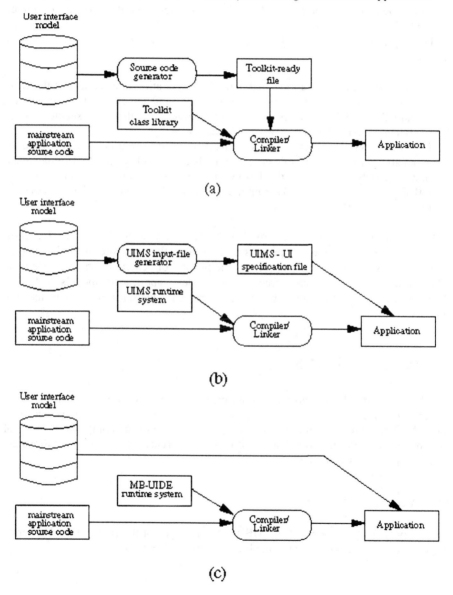

Fig 2. The three approaches for implementing a user interface in MB-UIDE

The UI implemented using the first approach has the advantage that it is entirely coded inside the application, providing a natural integration between the UI and the application. However, the UI produced using the first implementation approach is more static than the UIs produced using the other implementation approaches, which are able to be reconfigured more easily at runtime. The UI implemented using the third implementation approach, however, tends to have a performance worse than the UIs implemented using the first and second approaches since it is expensive to interpret the UIM at runtime.

The implementation tools in Figure 2 can be classified into two categories, defined as follows.

- *UI generators*: These are tools that make the application independent of the UIM. In this case, source code generators (Figure 2a) and UIMS input-file generators (Figure 2b) are UI generators. For instance, MB-UIDEs that can execute a UI directly from the UIM do not have UI generators.
- *UI runtime systems*: They are those tools that execute the user interface when the application is running. In this case, the application itself in the first implementation approach (Figure 2a), the UIMS runtime system (Figure 2b) and the MB-UIDE runtime systems are UI runtime systems. UI runtime systems are essential tools for MB-UIDEs.

One relevant observation concerns MB-UIDE terminology. The term *UI generation* can be used to refer to the process of generating the input-file of the UI runtime system, as described above, or to refer to the process of generating the concrete presentation model from abstract presentation models, application models and task-dialogue models. In this paper, we use the term *UI generation* to refer to the first process.

5   Declarative Models

The UIM is certainly the most important element of a MB-UIDE. In fact, the UI is designed in terms of the UIM, generated from the UIM and sometimes executed from the UIM. Therefore, it is important to understand how UIMs are composed in terms of their models and constructors. Further, it is also important to know what notations are used to represent these models.

5.1   Models

Table 4 presents the models of the MB-UIDEs in terms of the framework. The terms used in the table are those used in the literature to identify the models.

Table 4. MB-UIDE's component models.

MB-UIDE	Application model	Task-Dialogue model
ADEPT	problem domain	task model
AME	application model	OOD
FUSE	problem domain model	task model
HUMANOID	application semantics design	manipulation, sequencing, action side effects
JANUS	problem domain	(none)
ITS	data pool	control specification in dialog
MASTERMIND	application model	task model
MECANO	domain model	user task model/dialogue model
TADEUS	problem domain model	task model/navigation dialogue
TEALLACH	domain model	task model
TRIDENT	application model	task model
ADEPT	abstract user interface model	prototype interface
AME	OOA	prototype
FUSE	logical UI	UI
HUMANOID	presentation	presentation
JANUS	(not surveyed)	(not surveyed)
ITS	frame specification in dialog	style specification
MASTERMIND	(none)	presentation model
MECANO	(none)	presentation model
TADEUS	processing dialogue	processing dialogue
TEALLACH	presentation model	presentation model
TRIDENT	(not surveyed)	presentation model

The application model is present in every user interface model. In fact, the MB-UIDE technology appeared initially as an improvement in the user interface management systems (UIMS), where a clear distinction between the user interface and the mainstream application is required.

The presentation model, like the application model, is always considered in declarative models. However, there are MB-UIDEs that do not have an abstract presentation model such as MASTERMIND and MECANO. In other MB-UIDEs such as HUMANOID, TADEUS and Teallach, it is not clear the distinction between the abstract and concrete presentation models. In this last case, designers normally have the flexibility to gradually refine the presentation description from an abstract model to a concrete model.

Finally, declarative models also consider the use of a task-dialogue model to describe the possible interactions between users and applications using the presentation and application models. Some MB-UIDEs describe these interactions at a dialogue-level such as HUMANOID, MASTERMIND and ITS. Other MB-UIDEs, especially those developed after ADEPT, describe the interactions at a task-level, more abstract than the dialogue-level. However, there are MB-UIDEs such as MECANO and TADEUS that describe the possible interactions at both dialogue and task levels.

5.2   Constructors Having identified the models, we need to identify the model constructors. As we did for models, Table 5presents the model constructors using the terminology available in the literature for the specific proposals. The column *constructor* refers to the abbreviation for constructors introduced in the framework (Table 3). Constructors not present in Table 5 are not used in the specific system, or at least were not identified in the literature.

Table 5. MB-UIDE's constructors.

MB-UIDE	Constructor	Name	MB-UIDE	Constructor	Name
Adept	TASK	task	ITS	CLASS	data table
	GOAL	goal		ATTR	field
	SEQ	ordering operator + sequencing		VIEW	frame
				AIO	dialog object
	AIO	user interface object		EVENT	event
	CIO	UIO		ACT	action
AME	CLASS	OOA class		WINDOW	root unit
	ATTR	slot/OOA attributes		CIO	unit
	OPER	OOA operation		LAY	style attribute
	RELAT	relation type	Mastermind	CLASS	interface
	ACTION	behaviour		ATTR	attribute
	AIO	AIO		OPER	method
	WINDOW	OOD class		TASK	task
	CIO	CIO		GOAL	goal
	LAY	layout-method		SEQU	connection type
Human-oid	CLASS	object type		WINDOW	presentation
	ATTR	slot		CIO	presentation part
	OPER	command		LAY	guides, grids, conditionals
	TASK	data flow constraints			
	GOAL	goal	Teallach	CLASS	class
	ACT	behaviour		ATTR	attribute
	SEQ	guard slots' constraints, Triggers		OPER	operation
				TASK	task
	PRE	sequential pre-condition		SEQ	task temporal relation
	POST	action side-effect			
	AIO	Template		VIEW	free container
	WINDOW	display		AIO	AIO
	CIO	display, interaction Technique		WINDOW	window
				CIO	CIO
	LAY	Layout			
Janus	CLASS	class			
	ATTR	attribute			
	OPER	operation			
	RELAT	association, aggregation			
	CIO	interaction object			
	WINDOW	dialog widow (UIView)			

5.3   Model Notations

While Section 5.1 has indicated what models are present in different proposals, the semantics of the individual models in different contexts has not yet been touched on. Table 6 shows the several different notations used by the models of different proposals.

Table 6. Model notations.

MB-UIDE	Notation	Models
ADEPT	task knowledge structures (TKS) [20]	TDM
	LOTOS [7]	TDM
	Communicating Sequential Process (CSP) [19]	TDM, APM
AME	OOA/OOD [10]	AM
	OMT [36]	AM
FUSE	algebraic specification [53]	AM
	HTA [22]	TDM, UM
	Hierarchic Interaction graph Template (HTI)	APM, CPM
HUMANOID	uses a single notation which was not specified	all models
JANUS	JANUS Definition Language (extended CORBA IDL and ODMG ODL)	AM
ITS	Style rule [50,51]	all models
MASTERMIND	MDL [43] (extended CORBA IDL [41])	all models
MECANO	MIMIC [32] (extended C++)	all models
MOBI-D	MIMIC (see MECANO's notation)	all models
TADEUS	specialised HTA	TDM
	OMT [36]	AM, UM
	Dialogue Graph (specialised Petri net)	TDM
TEALLACH	hierarchical tree with state objects	TDM
	hierarchical tree	AM, APM, CPM
TRIDENT	Entity-Relationship-Attribute (ERA)	AM
	Activity Chaining Graph (ACG)	TDM, APM, CPM

We notice in Table 6 that there are UIs entirely described by models using a single notation. In general, these notations have been developed specifically for the MB-UIDE. They can be completely new as in ITS's Style rules [50,51], or they can be extensions of other notations, as in MASTERMIND's MDL that is an extension of CORBA IDL [41]. The use of a single notation can be useful to describe how the models collaborate with each other. However, specially due to the requirement of graphical notations, UI models tend to use different notations. For example, JANUS, TADEUS, TRIDENT, Teallach, and Adept models use more than one notation. It is not feasible to provide a categorisation of these UIMs in terms of their notations here because they tend to be specific to each MB-UIDE. For instance, there are many MB-UIDEs that use a hierarchical task notation to model their task-dialogue models, however, the notation may not be precisely formalised, as in Teallach.

The use of standard notations appears to be an aim. For instance, MASTERMIND's notation is based on CORBA IDL, and AME and TADEUS apply OMT [36] in some of their component models, since these are notations available for describing other parts of the application. In fact, OMT can be used during the analysis and design of the mainstream application, and CORBA IDL can be used during the implementation of the mainstream application.

A comprehensive explanation of the semantics of these notations is outside of the scope of this survey. The references required to find out more about these notations are also provided in Table 6 .

5.4   Model Integration

Models are integrated, although it is not unusual for the literature to be unclear on the precise nature of such integration. Indeed, Puerta and Eisenstein [34] said that there is a lack of understanding of UIM integration, denoting this problem as *the mapping problem.*

One strategy to finding out how these models are integrated is through the compilation of the relationships of constructors in different component models. Table 7 shows some of those inter-model relationships, relating the relationship constructors with their multiplicity. The multiplicity between brackets is described in UML notation [8]. Additionally, the figure in Table 7 shows graphically how the models are related to each other in the MB-UIDEs.

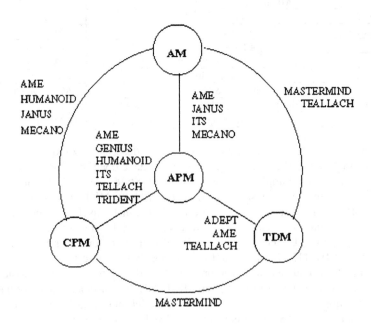

Table 7. Discrete and graphical representation of the inter-model relationships.

MB-UIDE	Inter-model relationship	
	Constructor	Constructor
ADEPT	ACTION (1)	AIO (*)
AME	CLASS (1)	AIO (1..*)
	CLASS (1)	WINDOW (0..1)
	ATTR (1)	AIO (1)
	WINDOW (1)	AIO (1..*)
	ACTION (1)	AIO (1)
GENIUS	VIEW (1)	WINDOW (1)
	AIO (1)	CIO (1)
HUMANOID	CLASS (1)	CIO (1)
	AIO (1)	CIO (1)
JANUS	WINDOW (1)	CLASS (*)
	AIO (1)	ATTR (1)
ITS	VIEW (1)	ATTR (*)
	CLASS (1)	AIO (*)
	AIO (1)	CIO (1..*)
MASTERMIND	TASK (1)	OPER (0..1)
	TASK (1)	CIO (0..1)
	root TASK (1)	WINDOW (1)
MECANO	WINDOW (1)	CLASS (1)
	AIO (1)	ATTR (1)
TEALLACH	TASK (1)	CLASS (0..*)
	TASK (1)	AIO (0..*)
	TASK (1)	VIEW (0..1)
	WINDOW (1)	AIO (0..*)
	AIO (1)	CIO (1..*)
TRIDENT	WINDOW (1..*)	VIEW (1)
	AIO (1)	CIO (0..*)

The presentation model can be considered as a set composed of the APM, the CPM, and the relationships between the APM and CPM. Our strategy to analyse the figure in Table 7is based on the identification of how AMs relate to presentation models. There are two approaches to relating AMs and presentation models. The first and most frequent approach is creating direct relationships between the two models, such as in HUMANOID, JANUS, ITS and MECANO. The second approach is using the TDM. In this case, there are relationships between the AM and the TDM, and between the TDM and the presentation model, such as in MASTERMIND and Teallach.

In AME and ADEPT, for instance, there are relationships between the APM and the TDM, but these relationships do not provide a link with the AM that is directly linked with the APM. In this case, the link is more between the AM and the TDM than between the AM and the presentation model.

6   Environments

MB-UIDEs are composed of tools where users can perform the tasks required to design and generate a user interface, as described in Section 4. Thus, a MB-UIDE architecture can be explained in terms of its tools. In fact, some development environments provide a monolithic tool with which developers perform their tasks. Other environments provide distinct tools where developers perform specific tasks, leading to a complete development of the UI. There is a third kind of environment where developers perform part of their tasks in tools not especially developed for the MB-UIDE, such as CASE tools, and the other part of their tasks in tools especially developed for the MB-UIDE. This section analyses MB-UIDE architectures through a comparison of their tools.

6.1   Design Environment

UI models are generally complex, leading to the modelling process also being a complex task. Thus, modelling tools are usually provided to help the designer to model the user interface. Table 8 produces a classification of environment tools according to our tool classification. It is important to observe that some MB-UIDEs are composed of tools that are responsible for more than one function, then they are classified in more than one category.

Table 8. Design environment tools.

MB-UIDE	Modelling Editors	Modelling Assistant
ADEPT	Task model editor AUI editor	Interface generator object browser
AME	OODevelopTool ODE-editor	code generator layout generator
FUSE	FIRE	FLUID
GENIUS	Model Editing Tool	Model Refinement Tool
HUMANOID	(none)	(none)
JANUS	Paradigm Plus (OO CASE tool) Together C++ (OO CASE tool)	(not surveyed)
ITS	not specified	(none)
MASTERMIND	Application Modeling Suite Task Modeling Suite Presentation Modeling Suite	Dialog Critics
TADEUS	Tadeus	Tadeus
TEALLACH	Teallach	code generator

6.2   Implementation Environment

UI implementation is a key activity in the use of a MB-UIDE. To generate the UI, however, the MB-UIDE depends not only on the UIM, but also on the environment that is being considered. As discussed in Section 4, a MB-UIDE can implement a runtime interpreter for the UIM, generate code for an existing UIMS, or generate code that uses a specific toolkit. Therefore, there are basically three alternatives that can be considered for generating the user interface.

Table 9 summarises the user interface generation tools of the MB-UIDEs. There we see that some MB-UIDEs are based on a UIMS (e.g. TADEUS). Other MB-UIDEs generate code for specific toolkits (e.g. AME, FUSE and MASTERMIND generate code for C++, and Teallach generates code for Java). The others, however, implement the whole environment (e.g. ITS's dialog manager, FUSE's BOSS). One interesting approach is that used by AME and MASTERMIND that provide UI prototyping using UIMSs, but that generate code for C++. That way, these MB-UIDEs can offer to their users the benefits of alternative approaches to generating a user interface.

Table 9. Implementation environment tools.

MB-UIDE	UI Generator	UI Runtime System
ADEPT	interface builder	interpreter
AME	AME/C++ code generator	application code
	Open Interface code generator	Open Interface (UIMS)
	not specified	KAPPA-PC runtime system
FUSE	BOSS[38,39]	(not surveyed)
GENIUS	(not surveyed)	runtime system
HUMANOID	(none)	Humanoid runtime system
JANUS	C++ code generator	application code
ITS	(none)	UI executed from the UIM
MASTERMIND	Mastermind Prototyping Support C++ code generator	AMULET [30] (UIMS) application code
TADEUS	not specified	ISA Dialog Manager (UIMS)
TEALLACH	Java code generator	application code (Swing Toolkit)

The implementation environment can also be composed of *advisors* and *documentation generators*. However, these tools are not discussed in this survey.

7   Conclusions

MB-UIDEs seek to provide a setting within which a collection of complementary declarative models that can be used as a description of UI functionalities. This survey has compared the models and tools provided by 14 MB-UIDEs. Declarative models, model constructors and model notations were presented using a comparative framework. Design and implementation tools were identified.

The MB-UIDE technology is just now becoming stable enough to be commercialised as products e.g. Systemator [1]. Indeed, this is the result of practical experiences with this technology, e.g. ITS was used by IBM to produce the UI of the visitor information system of EXPO'92 [51,50], and FUSE has been used by Siemens to simulate an ISDN telephone.

However, there are many aspects of MB-UIDE technology that must be studied in order to increase the acceptance of MB-UIDEs at the level of other specialised UI development tools [29].

- *Mapping between models.* The aspects of UIs that it is relevant to model in UIMs are well-understood. In fact, most of the surveyed MB-UIDEs provide in some way a similar set of UI aspects that they can describe, as observed in Table 4. However, it is unclear how best to model the relationships between the constructors of the models used to describe UIs, as observed in Table 7.
- *UIM post-editing problem.* Automated generated drafts of UI designs may be manually refined in order to generate final designs. However, manual refinements to generated designs are lost when developers regenerate other draft designs. Therefore, it is still a problem how best to cope with post-editing refinements.
- *Standard notations for UIMs.* The use of a standard notation may be useful in order to describe different UIMs using a common set of constructors. In fact, these constructors may facilitate the comparison and the reuse of UIMs and their MB-UIDEs. For instance, the reuse of UIMs may be difficult these days since they are based on several notations, as presented in Table 6. Further, the reuse of UIMs can be essential for make MB-UIDEs scalable for real applications.

8   Acknowledgements

The author would like to thank Norman W. Paton and the anonymous reviewers of this paper for their valuable comments. The author is sponsored by Conselho Nacional de Desenvolvimento Cientfico e Tecnológico - CNPq (Brazil) – Grant 200153/98-6.

9   Reference

1.   Genera AS. Systemator. http://www.genera.no.
2.   H. Balzert. From OOA to GUI – The JANUS-System. In *Proceedings of INTERACT'95*, pages 319–324, London, UK, June 1995. Chapman & Hall.
3.   H. Balzert, F. Hofmann, V. Kruschinski, and C. Niemann. The JANUS Application Development Environment — Generating More than the User Interface. In *Computer-Aided Design of User Interfaces*, pages 183–206, Namur, Belgium, 1996. Namur University Press.
4.   F. Bodart, A. Hennebert, J. Leheureux, I. Provot, B. Sacre, and J. Vanderdonckt. Towards a Systematic Building of Software Architectures: the TRIDENT Methodological Guide. In *Design, Specification and Verification of Interactive Systems*, pages 262–278, Vienna, 1995. Springer.
5.   F. Bodart, A. Hennebert, J. Leheureux, I. Provot, and J. Vanderdonckt. A Model-Based Approach to Presentation: A Continuum from Task Analysis to Prototype. In *Proceedings of DSV-IS'94*, pages 25–39, Bocca di Magra, June 1994.
6.   F. Bodart and J. Vanderdonckt. Widget Standardisation Through Abstract Interaction Objects. In *Advances in Applied Ergonomics*, pages 300–305, Istanbul - West Lafayette, May 1996. USA Publishing.
7.   T. Bolognesi and E. Brinksma. Introduction to the ISO specification language LOTOS. *Computer Network ISDN Systems*, 14(1), 1987.

8.   G. Booch, J. Rumbaugh, and I. Jacobson. *The Unified Modeling Language User Guide*. Addison-Wesley, Reading, MA, 1999.

9.   T. Browne, D. Dávila, S. Rugaber, and K. Stirewalt. *Formal Methods in Human-Computer Interaction*, chapter Using Declarative Descriptions to Model User Interfaces with MASTERMIND. Springer-Verlag, 1997.

10. P. Coad and E. Yourdon. *Object-Oriented Design*. Prentice-Hall, 1991.

11. J. Coutaz and R. Taylor. Introduction to the Workshop on Software Engineering and Human-Computer Interaction: Joint Research Issues. In *Proceedings of the Software Engineering and Human-Computer Interaction'94*, volume 896 of *Lecture Notes In Computer Science*, pages 1–3, Berlin, May 1995. Springer-Verlag.

12. B. Curtis and B. Hefley. A WIMP No More – The Maturing of User Interface Engineering. *ACM Interactions*, 1(1):22–34, 1994.

13. T. Elwert and E. Schlungbaum. Modelling and Generation of Graphical User Interfaces in the TADEUS Approach. In *Designing, Specification and Verification of Interactive Systems*, pages 193–208, Vienna, 1995. Springer.

14. J. Foley. History, Results and Bibliography of the User Interface Design Environment (UIDE), an Early Model-based Systems for User Interface Design and Implementation. In *Proceedings of DSV-IS'94*, pages 3–14, Vienna, 1995. Springer-Verlag.

15. J. Foley, W. Kim, S. Kovacevic, and K. Murray. UIDE – An Intelligent User Interface Design Environment. In *Intelligent User Interfaces*, pages 339–384. Addison-Wesley, ACM Press, 1991.

16. T. Griffiths, P. Barclay, J. McKirdy, N. Paton, P. Gray, J. Kennedy, R. Cooper, C. Goble, A. West, and M. Smyth. Teallach: A Model-Based User Interface Development Environment for Object Databases. In *Proceedings of UIDIS'99*, pages 86–96, Edinburgh, UK, September 1999. IEEE Press.

17. T. Griffiths, J. McKirdy, G. Forrester, N. Paton, J. Kennedy, P. Barclay, R. Cooper, C. Goble, and P. Gray. Exploiting Model-Based Techniques for User Interfaces to Database. In *Proceedings of Visual Database Systems (VDB) 4*, pages 21–46, Italy, May 1998. Chapman & Hall.

18. P. Hayes, P. Szekely, and R. Lerner. Design Alternatives for User Interface Management Systems Based on Experience with COUSIN. In *Proceedings of SIGCHI'85*, pages 169–175. Addison-Wesley, April 1985.

19. C. Hoare. *Communicating Sequential Processes*. Prentice-Hall, 1985.

20. R. Jacob. A Specification Language for Direct Manipulation User Interfaces. *ACM Transactions on Graphics*, 5(4):283–317, October 1986.

21. C. Janssen, A. Weisbecker, and J. Ziegler. Generating User Interfaces from Data Models and Dialogue Net Specifications. In *Proceedings of InterCHI'93*, pages 418–423, New York, NY, 1993. ACM Press.

22. P. Johnson. *Human Computer Interaction: Psychology, Task Analysis and Software Engineering*. McGraw-Hill, Maidenhead, UK, 1992.

23. P. Johnson, H. Johnson, and S. Wilson. Rapid Prototyping of User Interfaces Driven by Task Models. In *Scenario-Based Design*, pages 209–246, London, UK, 1995. John Wiley.

24. W. Kim and J. Foley. DON: User Interface Presentation Design Assistant. In *Proceedings of UIST'90*, pages 10–20. ACM Press, October 1990.

25. F. Lonczewski and S. Schreiber. The FUSE-System: an Integrated User Interface Desgin Environment. In *Computer-Aided Design of User Interfaces*, pages 37–56, Namur, Belgium, 1996. Namur University Press.

26. P. Luo, P. Szekely, and R. Neches. Management of interface design in HUMANOID. In *Proceedings of InterCHI'93*, pages 107–114, April 1993.

27. P. Markopoulos, J. Pycock, S. Wilson, and P. Johnson. Adept – A task based design environment. In *Proceedings of the 25th Hawaii International Conference on System Sciences*, pages 587–596. IEEE Computer Society Press, 1992.

28. C. Märtin. Software Life Cycle Automation for Interactive Applications: The AME Design Environment. In *Computer-Aided Design of User Interfaces*, pages 57–74, Namur, Belgium, 1996. Namur University Press.

29. B. Myers. User Interface Software Tools. *ACM Transactions on Computer-Human Interaction*, 2(1):64–103, March 1995.

30. B. Myers, R. McDaniel, R. Miller, A. Ferrency, A. Faulring, B. Kyle, A. Mickish, A. Klimovitsky, and P. Doane. The Amulet Environment: New Models for Effective User Interface Software Development. *IEEE Transactions on Software Engineering*, 23(6):346–365, June 1997.

31. D. Olsen. A Programming Language Basis for User Interface Management. In *Proceedings of SIGCHI'89*, pages 171–176, May 1989.

32. Puerta. The Mecano Project: Comprehensive and Integrated Support for Model-Based Interface Development. In *Computer-Aided Design of User Interfaces*, pages 19–36, Namur, Belgium, 1996. Namur University Press.

33. Puerta and J. Eisenstein. Interactively Mapping Task Models to Interfaces in MOBI-D. In *Design, Specification and Verification of Interactive Systems*, pages 261–273, Abingdon, UK, June 1998.

34. Puerta and J. Eisenstein. Towards a General Computational Framework fo Model-Based Interface Development Systems. In *Proceedings of IUI'99*, Los Angeles, CA, January 1999. (to be published).

35. Puerta and D. Maulsby. Management of Interface Design Knowledge with MODI-D. In *Proceedings of IUI'97*, pages 249–252, Orlando, FL, January 1997.

36. J. Rumbaugh, M. Blaha, W. Premerlani, F. Eddy, and W. Lorensen. *Object-Oriented Modeling and Design*. Prentice Hall, Englewood Cliffs, NJ, 1991.

37. E. Schlungbaum. Model-Based User Interface Software Tools - Current State of Declarative Models. Technical Report 96-30, Graphics, Visualization and Usability Center, Georgia Institute of Technology, 1996.

38. S. Schreiber. Specification and Generation od User Interfaces with the BOSS-System. In *Proceedings of EWHCI'94*, volume 876 of *Lecture Notes in Computer Sciences*, pages 107–120, Berlin, 1994. Springer-Verlag.

39. S. Schreiber. The BOSS System: Coupling Visual Programming with Model Based Interface Design. In *Proceedings of DSV-IS'94*, Focus on Computer Graphics, pages 161–179, Berlin, 1995. Springer-Verlag.

40. Shneiderman. *Designing the User Interface: Strategies for Effective Human-Computer Interaction*. Addison-Wesley, Reading, MA, second edition, 1992.

41. J. Siegel. *CORBA: Fundamentals and Programming*. John Wiley, New York, NY, 1996.

42. G. Singh and M. Green. A high-level user interface management system. In *Proceedings of SIGCHI'89*, pages 133–138, May 1989.

43. K. Stirewalt. *Automatic Generation of Interactive Systems from Declarative Models*. PhD thesis, Georgia Institute of Technology, December 1997.

44. P. Szekely. Template-Based Mapping of Application Data to Interactive Displays. In *Proceedings of UIST'90*, pages 1–9. ACM Press, October 1990.

45. P. Szekely. Retrospective and Challenges for Model-Bases Interface Development. In *Computer-Aided Design of User Interfaces*, pages xxi–xliv, Namur, Belgium, 1996. Namur University Press.

46. P. Szekely, P. Luo, and R. Neches. Facilitating the Exploration of Interface Design Alternatives: The HUMANOID Model of Interface Design. In *Proceedings of SIGCHI'92*, pages 507–515, May 1992.

47. P. Szekely, P. Sukaviriya, P. Castells, J. Muthukumarasamy, and E. Salcher. Declarative Interface Models for User Interface Construction Tools: the MASTERMIND Approach. In *Engineering for Human-Computer Interaction*, pages 120–150, London, UK, 1996. Chapman & Hall.

48. J. Tarby and M. Barthet. The DIANE+ Method. In *Computer-Aided Design of User Interfaces*, pages 95–119, Namur, Belgium, 1996. Namur University Press.

49. J. Vanderdonckt. *Conception assistée de la présentation d'une interface homme-machine ergonomique pour une application de gestion hautement interactive.* PhD thesis, Facultés Universitaires Notre-Dame de la Paix, Namur, Belgium, July 1997.

50. Wiecha, W. Bennett, S. Boies, J. Gould, and S. Green. ITS: A Tool for Rapidly Developing Interactive Applications. *ACM Transactions on Information Systems*, 8(3):204–236, July 1990.

51. Wiecha and S. Boies. Generating user interfaces: principles and use of ITS style rules. In *Proceedings of UIST'90*, pages 21–30. ACM Press, October 1990.

52. S. Wilson and P. Johnson. Bridging the Generation Gap: From Work Tasks to User Interface Designs. In *Computer-Aided Design of User Interfaces*, pages 77–94, Namur, Belgium, 1996. Namur University Press.

53. M. Wirsing. Algebraic Specification. In *Handbook of Theoretical Computer Science*, pages 676–788. North Holland, 1990.

The Task-Dialog and Task-Presentation Mapping Problem: Some Preliminary Results

Quentin Limbourg, Jean Vanderdonckt, and Nathalie Souchon

[1] Université catholique de Louvain, Institut d'Administration et de Gestion
Place des Doyens, 1 - B-1348 Louvain-la-Neuve, Belgium
{limbourg,vanderdonckt,amisi}@qant.ucl.ac.be

Abstract. Model-based interface development environments typically involve the manipulation and the organization of multiple component models in order to develop one or many user interfaces corresponding to the models. In this context, the mapping problem poses the challenge of defining the elements of these models and to link them into an appropriate way that reflects design options. The task-dialog and task-presentation mapping problem investigates to what extent a dialog model and a presentation model can be derived from a task model and subsequently linked from it. Some preliminary results for solving this type of mapping problem at a high level of abstraction are provided and exemplified on some particular model representations. A task model for a single-user interactive application is formed with the ConcurTaskTrees notation. From the definition of its operators, a set of systematic rules for simultaneously deriving and linking elements for both dialog and presentation models are presented. These rules are organized into a decision tree presenting designers with design alternatives. To depict the models' elements that can be derived and linked from these rules, the Windows Transition graphical notation is exploited.

1   Introduction

Model-based approaches for user interface development [5,8,14] consist in capturing design knowledge in various models according to a declarative manner that can be further processed by software tools. These models are progressively enriched and exploited to finally obtain a running user interface (UI). Concepts typically abstracted in these models, but not necessarily limited to, are user tasks, domain elements, users, presentation items, and dialog structures [10].

In practice, these modeling activities are rarely achieved one after another because the design activity is intrinsically an open, iterative, and ill-defined problem. This means that designers do not necessarily complete the models that are required to perform the next step in the development life cycle. Rather, they like to early investigate what the other models could look like without waiting that the other one are stabilized, complete, and consistent. Moreover, these models are sometimes built by different persons, at different times, thus potentially leading to independent models that could evolve separately. When such models need to be related one to each other again, several relationships need to be established, updated or even restored, which is a tedious and repetitive task [4]. We hereby define *the mapping problem* [10] as the problem of handling relationships between all involved models so as to support the

P. Palanque and F. Paternò (Eds.): DSV-IS 2000, LNCS 1946, pp. 227–246, 2001.
© Springer-Verlag Berlin Heidelberg 2001

development of a user interface. To keep relationships between these models as they are built when they are evolving, three mechanisms are supplied:

1. *Model derivation*: the elements and the relationships of one or many still unspecified models are derived from the elements and relationships of one or many already specified models according to transformation rules, the parameters of which are controlled by the designer [1,7,12].
2. *Model linking/binding*: the elements and the relationships of one or many already specified models are processed to establish, update or restore previously established relationships (one or many of them) between the models elements [1,3,5].
3. *Model composition*: one or many already specified models are partially or totally assembled either to rebuild the source models (as in reverse engineering) or to build another one [11].

In this paper, we are interested by one type of mapping: to what extent is it possible to solve the mapping problem from a task model onto both a presentation model and a dialog model? The task model is chosen as source model because such a rich model can be effectively exploited to derive elements belonging in other models. Second, presentation and dialog models are chosen as target models because they often work hand in hand and because they are largely intertwined (Fig. 1).

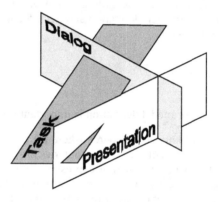

Fig. 1. Intertwining of task, presentation and dialog models.

A *task model* is here understood as a declarative description of an interactive task to be carried out by a user or a population of users through a particular user interface. A task model typically contains two types of internal relationships: *structural relationships* according which a task is recursively decomposed into sub-tasks to end up with actions working on domain objects, and *temporal relationships* that provide constraints for ordering (sub-)tasks according to the task logic.

A *presentation model* is here understood as a declarative description of the external representation of a user interface according to multiple channels of use. A presentation model also involves structural relationships (e.g., how a window container is decomposed into its sub-elements) and arranging relationships (e.g., how two elements are aligned on the users's screen).

A *dialog model* is here understood as a declarative descriptive of how the final user can interact with the presentation through the various interaction devices. It usually contains some specification of the input that the user interface enables and of the output that the system may convey through the user interface.

The *task-presentation mapping* [10] is a type of mapping problem where elements and relationships of a presentation model can be mapped according to those existing in the task model, preferably reflecting how it is organized. Similarly, the *dialog-presentation mapping* [10] is a type of mapping problem where elements and relationships of a dialog model can be mapped according to those existing in the task model, preferably reflecting how it is organized. The goal of this paper is finally to explore how these two types of mapping problems can be addressed in terms of model elements and relationships.

The rest of this paper is structured as follows: Sect. 2 reviews some related work for explaining why starting from the task model is recommended and what kind of strategies have been developed so far for model derivation from a task model. Sect. 3 clarifies the hypotheses assumed in this work and their scope. In particular, notations used for the different models are specified: the ConcurTaskTrees notation [6,9] for task model and the Window Transitions notation for mid-level dialog model. The representation for the presentation model is left open and informal. The different subsections of Sect. 3 explain derivation rules for each ConcurTaskTrees operator and express the results of this derivation according to the Window Transition notation. Sect. 4 provides an example of such derivation and Sect. 5 concludes by reporting on some open issues and future work.

2   Related Work

Starting from a task model for model derivation is important for these reasons:

1. It is a naturally important knowledge source where the task is expressed according to the user words, not in terms of system vocabularies [14].
2. Other models do not contain information expressive enough to derive something significant. The expressiveness power of the derivation can be improved.
3. Other types of models, like data models or domain models are not especially appropriate as they induce a set of particular tasks (e.g., insert, delete, modify, list, check, search, print, transfer), which do not necessarily match the user task. Rather, to carry out another interactive task, which can be any combination of parts or whole of these tasks, the user has to switch from one predefined task to another. This is not user-centered. Exceptions can still occur: for instance, Teallach [1] derives task, presentation and dialog models from a domain model provided by the underlying data base management system. In this case, UIs for data-intensive systems are the target applications, which is a specific domain in information systems.
4. Finally, derivation of other models from a task model is also allowed (e.g., an activity-chaining graph from a task model [13]) to come closer to the designer's world, but there is a potential risk of information loss in the transformation [2].

Tam *et al.* focus on structural relations: by browsing the hierarchical decomposition, the amount of sub-tasks for each level and the amount of levels can be computed to let the designer specify a preference ranging from one window presenting all elements corresponding to all sub-tasks to many windows presenting for example the different levels of sub-tasks, level by level (Fig. 2).

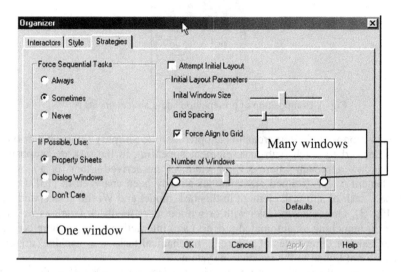

Fig. 2. Derivation of presentation elements from a task model.

SEGUIA [16] also groups presentation elements based on structural relations: a presentation unit is selected for each sub-task of the first level, each presentation unit is consequently decomposed into windows. These can be grouped according to different strategies as long as a threshold for some cognitive load metric is not exceeded.
Paternò et al. have investigated how a presentation model can be derived from a task model [7] specified in the ConcurTaskTrees notation [6]. In this research, a bottom-up approach is exploiting first the structural relationships, and then the temporal relationships to group presentation elements based on the concept of an activation set. Such a set groups the presentation units corresponding to sub-tasks which can be carried out in some related way. An interesting feature of Teallach [2] is its ability to derive new models from existing one and link any pair of models in task, presentation and dialog models.

Zhou [15] developed a planning-based system that infers the presentation of highly interactive graphics according to constraints on presentation elements manipulated through a task model. This inference is based on a form of visual discourse where sequences of temporally ordered actions of a model are parsed to automate the presentation of the elements manipulated by each action.

3   Derivation Rules for Presentation and Dialog Models

Before defining and exploring derivation rules, some hypotheses need to be set up. In the rest of this paper, the ConcurTaskTrees notation [6] is used for representing the task model as it already supports both structural and temporal relations commonly used in task analysis. The Window Transition notation is used for representing the mid-level dialog, which is located at the window interaction level.

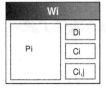

Fig. 3. Composition of presentation and dialog elements for Wi.

First, a mono-window approach is adopted here to simplify the problem: one window is derived for each (sub-)task element appearing in the task decomposition. A multi-window approach where several windows are derived either for a single (sub-)task element or for grouped elements has already been analyzed in [13]. Let Ti denote the ith task or sub-task element in this task model and Wi the corresponding window (Fig. 3). Only system tasks with or without user feedback (such as user confirmation for launching an automated process) and interactive tasks are here considered. No user tasks or other types of task (e.g., mechanical task on a machine) are covered as they are not linked to the interactive system.

Let Pi denote the presentation part which is proprietary to Wi. Pi typically consists of presentation elements like control widgets: edit box, radio button, check box, and list box. Let Di denote the dialog part which is proprietary to Wi. Di typically consists of dialog elements like "Ok", "Cancel", "Close", "Search" push buttons, icons, command gestures, function keys. Let Ci,j denote a dialog widget allowing a transition from Wi to Wj. A *window transition* is defined as any mean to go from one source window (WS) to any target window (WT), where WS and WT are two windows materializing parts or whole of (sub-)tasks. More formally, WS $\xrightarrow{A}$ WS $\Leftrightarrow$ one event generated within source window WS (by user or system) enables a transition of type A to target window WT. A graphical representation of this transition exists (Fig. 4): any window is represented by a window icon, a transition of type A, by an arrow labeled with A, and an arrow marker specifyies that the user can work with WS, while working with WT. If no such marker exists, the user can only work with WT.

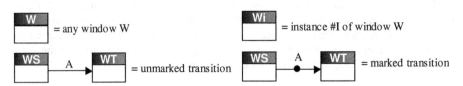

Fig. 4. Graphical notation for a window transition.

A set of basic window transitions is defined in Fig. 5 to specify what are the operations performed on the source and target windows when the window transition is achieved.

Transition icon	Transition name	Transition definition
	maximization	enlarge the window to the maximum possible size to fir the screen boundaries
	titling	reduce the window to its title bar. Note: the window is still active in this position
	minimization	reduce the window to its icon
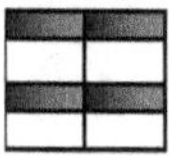	display with tiling technique	arrange the window so that it appears tiled with possibly existing windows.
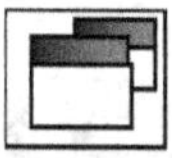	display with normal overlapping technique	arrange the window so that its size and locations allow partial overlapping of windows. When the window has been reduced before, e.g., by a minimization or a titling, then it is restored to its previous size and location.
	display with user-defined overlapping technique	arrange the window so that its size and locations allow a partial overlapping of windows as defined by the user.
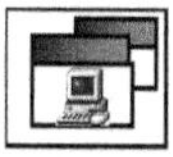	display with system-defined overlapping technique	arrange the window so that its size and locations allow a partial overlapping of windows as defined by the system. When the window has been reduced before, e.g., by a minimization or a titling, then it is restored to its system-defined size and location
	closing	close the window. Note: it can prompts the user to save unsaved documents or information

Fig. 5. Notation for basic window operations.

Third, it is assumed that widget selection is performed independently as follows: each domain element manipulated by the task element Ti gives rise to one or several presentation elements to be included in the presentation model and to be manipulated in the dialog model, e.g. through abstract interaction objects [5,13]. These objects are turned into concrete ones, belonging to Pi.

Fourth, for the simplicity and the concision of this paper, and without any loss of generality, it is assumed that any parent task element (except the root element) is decomposed into two child task elements. From this simplification, a generalization can be easily applied by expanding the derivation rules for any combination of elements.

3.1   The Enabling Operator: T2 >> T3

According to previously stated hypotheses, let us assume that T1 is decomposed into two sub-tasks T2 and T3 which are related by the enabling operator. Fig. 6a depicts the graphical representation of presentation and dialog elements corresponding to this situation: C1,2 allows the transition from the parent window W1 corresponding to T1 to the first child window W2 corresponding to T2 in the sequence. This element can be named accordingly (e.g., with the name of T2). Similarly, C2,1 cancels the current dialog in W2 and returns to W1; C2,3 allows the sequential transition from W2 to W3 and can therefore be labeled "Next" or "Name of T3". C3,2 returns to W2 and can be labeled "Previous" or "Name of T2". C3,1 can be any dialog element for closing W3 to come back to W1 as "Ok", "Close", "Cancel".

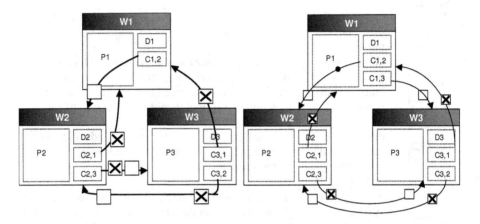

Fig. 6. Alternative specifications for the enabling operator (a,b).

This solution reinforces sequentiality between T2 and T3, but does not visually present T3 accessible from T1. Another solution might be feasible where the above dialog is enriched by presenting the access to T3 (by activating its control C1,3) after T2 is achieved in W2. This solution presented in Fig. 6b emphasizes circularity between elements: C2,1 can be "Ok", "Cancel", C2,3 can be "Next" or "Name of T3", C3,1 can be "Ok" or "Cancel", C3,2 can be "Previous", "Back" or "Name of T2".

3.2 The Enabling Operator with Information Passing: T2 [I]>> T3

This operator is much more rich than the previous one as it allows the presentation of I, the information passed from sub-task T2 to sub-task T3. Let us denote by WI the window materializing I, PI the presentation of this information and by DI the dialog related to this information if needed. For instance, it could be a "Search" push button, a "Validate" icon. In order to explore design alternatives that this operator may engender, we introduce the *visibility* property.

The information passed between task elements is said *visible* if and only if the user is able to access the information in some certain interaction. When no interaction is required, this information is said *observable*. When some interaction is required, this information is said *browsable*. The introduction of this property is motivated by the observation that not all information items should be displayed all together at a time. Critical information should definitely be observable, but unimportant information should not. Rather, the user should be able to access this information, but only on demand. Information browsable can be in this state *internally* or *externally* depending on the information is presented within or outside the scope of the initial window, respectively. In the last case, the dialog can be *modal*, respectively *modeless*, if the externally browsable information should be terminated, respectively not terminated, before returning to the initiating window. Information simultaneously visible in multiple task elements is said *shared*. The designer can specify these parameters either globally for a particular task or locally by redefinition for particular sub-tasks.

Fig. 7 depicts a decision tree resulting from the examination of different configuration cases induced by visibility from sub-tasks T2 and T3. Each configuration ID will be referred to in the text. The A region as graphically defined is repeated for (11), (12, (13), and (14) configurations.

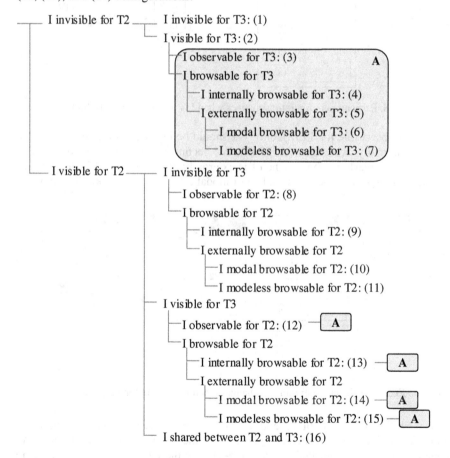

Fig. 7. Decision tree of alternative specifications for the enabling operator with information passing.

Configuration (1) is similar to the simple enabling operator (Fig. 6a). Configuration (2) is similar to that operator too, but W3 is replaced by the window configuration reproduced in Fig. 8a. When I is not observable for T3, it is considered that I should be browsable in some way. When I is internally browsable (4), Fig. 8b reproduces the resulting expanding window with two dedicated dialog elements: CI>> expands the current window to let I appear (e.g., via a "More>>" button) while CI<< reduced the current window to remove I (e.g, via a "Less<<" button). When I is externally browsable (5), two cases between W3 and WI are possible: the dialog could be modal (6) or modeless (7) as represented with the marker on Fig. 8c.

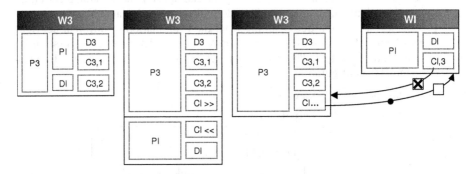

Fig. 8. Particular configuration changes when I is invisible for T2 **(a,b,c)**.

When I is observable for T2 (8), only W2 should be replaced in Fig. 6a by Fig. 9a. When I is internally observable for T2 (9), W2 becomes structured as represented in Fig. 9b. And, similarly to above, when I is externally observable for T2, Fig. 9c provides the change for modeless case (11). For modal case (10), the marker is removed.

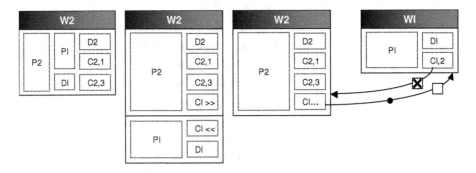

Fig. 9. Particular configuration changes when I is visible for T2 **(a,b,c)**.

The visibility of I for both T2 and T3 raises a potential problem of redundancy and/or consistency. When I is observable for T2, the pattern represented by the "A" rectangle on Fig. 6 is duplicated for each sub-case. In these configurations, there is no risk of redundancy of I presentation and dialog elements since the sequence between T2 and T3 imposes that W2 and W3 cannot be displayed simultaneously. Therefore, I is never displayed two times on the user screen. For instance, Fig. 10a graphically represents the I observability in both T2 and T3, which is a possible configuration in (12). Since opening W3 closes W2 and vice versa, I is only displayed once.

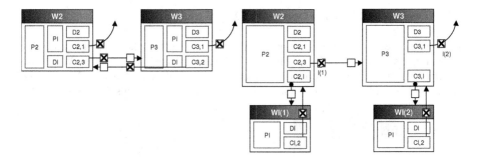

Fig. 10. Particular configuration changes when I is visible for both T2 and T3 **(a,b)**.

This reasoning also holds for subsequent categories (13), (14) and (15) except the case where the two instances of WI are modeless. They should be independent due to the enabling operator between the two sub-tasks: this is why closing W2, respectively W3, also closes the first, respectively the second, instance of WI as shown in Fig. 10b. Fig. 11 graphically depicts the last special configuration (16) where I is shared among W2 and W3. In this case, WI can be created by both W2 and W3, but once. WI should stay visible until T3 is achieved in W3, not before. Therefore, W2 could be created from W2 and destroyed from W3 (i.e. when leaving W3).

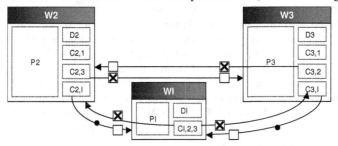

Fig. 11. Particular configuration when I is shared among T2 and T3.

Although theoretically possible configurations are gathered in Fig. 7, it might be desirable to avoid some configurations for usability reasons. Here is an incomplete set of guidelines providing some assistance to the designer this way:

- The invisibility of I from both T2 and T3 (1) should be avoided since no user feedback of I is produced towards the user.
- Modeless browsability of I in T2 and/or T3 should be preferred to modal browsability as the window initiating WI and WI can be used simultaneously, thus not preventing the user to forget information in the initiating window.
- I should be visible in W3 in some way as it will be used to achieve T3.
- WI, as every window, should be controlled by one dialog element at a time, but several dialog elements concurrently. It can be updated according to the results produced in other related windows.
- The presentation and dialog should foster information *persistence*, the faculty of I remaining visible is some way when the transition from W2 to W3 is operated.

3.3   The Suspend/Resume Operator: T2 | > T3

The suspend/resume operator can be specified thanks to the reducing and restoring set of operations defined in [7]. In Fig. 12, W2 reduces itself and restores W3 consequently and vice versa. Of course, it is assumed that W1 initiated both W1 and W2 before with a marked transition. Each window can close itself, thus returning to W1.

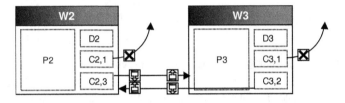

Fig. 12. Specification for the suspend/resume operator.

3.4   The Choice Operator: T2 [ ] T3

Sub-tasks T2 and T3 are considered mutually exclusive in their decomposition with the choice operator. Therefore, this choice can be either *implicit* when the wanted sub-task is initiated from its parent, deactivating the other, or *explicit* when the wanted sub-task is initiated by directly selecting it, automatically reducing the other. In Fig. 13a, the choice between W2 and W3 is made implicit: C1,2 and C1,3 are active at the beginning, but the selection of any of them automatically deactivates the other. For instance, C1,2 is deactivated if C1,3 is cliqued on and vice versa. In Fig. 13b, the choice between W2 and W3 is made explicit: first, W2 and W3 are simultaneously activated, but reduced, from C1,2,3. Closing W2 restores (thus, reactivating) W3 and vice versa. C2,1 and C3,1 are intended to support the achieving of sub-tasks, thus returning to the parent task element.

W2 and W3 are related to each other with a XOR operator. Any other logical operator (AND, OR) and combination of these operators, for example, (W2) XOR (W3 and W4), expressed in first order logic formula should be worth to investigate. AND/OR/XOR graphs provide probably a better notational support in this situation as shown in the Activity Chaining Graph (ACG) of TRIDENT [13].

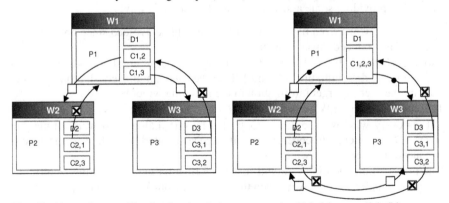

Fig. 13. Alternative specification for the choice operator: implicit (**a**) or explicit (**b**).

3.5   The Disabling Operator: T2 [> T3

The disabling operator mostly relies on the set of reducing operations. The anchor defined in W2 should be responsible for holding the window transition between W2 and W3 (Fig. 14). Another dialog element C3,2 completing the inverse process can be imagined as well.

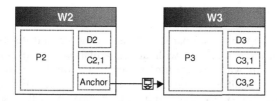

Fig. 14. Specification for the disabling operator.

3.6   The Iteration Operator: T2*

In the iteration operator, the T2 sub-task is repeated n times, where n is unknown. In these circumstances, the creation and access of the multiple instances of T2 can be specified *with* or *without* accumulation, depending on task and user parameters. When multiple instances of T2 are accumulated in many instances of W2 (Fig. 15a), the first W2 instance is created from W1 and subsequent instances ($i = 2,...,n$) from this instance. Each new instance is created from its predecessor, can be closed independently and can return to its predecessor. Multiple instances of W2 could be also created from W1, but it forces the user to switch back to this window to create another one. By creating the successor instance from the current window, there is no change of context of use, thus preserving task continuity. W2 instances are therefore accumulated as overlapping windows (e.g., system defined, or user defined).

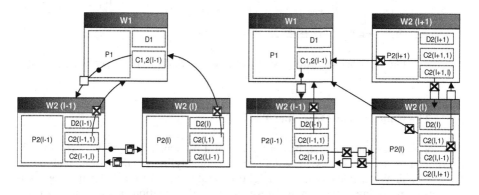

Fig. 15. Alternative specifications for the iteration operator.

Conversely, when multiple instances of W2 are not accumulated (e.g., because having too many instances on the screen could become impossible to manage), there is only one W2 instance at a time, the predecessor being accessible with the CI,I-1 element (e.g., labeled "Previous") and the successor being accessible with the CI,I+1 element (e.g., labeled "Next") with $i = 2,\ldots,n$-1. This situation is represented in Fig. 15b. Each new W2 instance closes its predecessor. Some interconnexion between the multiple instances is here preserved, thus preventing the user to loose task continuity.

3.7   The Finite Iteration Operator: $T2^n$

The finite iteration operator is a particular case of the general iteration operator. As such both specifications with and without accumulation are still applicable for this operator where i is known at design-time rather than at run-time. Therefore, as previously discussed, two additional specifications can be imagined (Fig. 15) provided that the value of n does not exceed the cognitive load capacity of the user. Some studies show for example that most current tasks should not involve more than three windows as carrying out more that three concurrent tasks is usually beyond the users' limit. The left specification in Fig. 16 creates n instances of W2 when the CI dialog element is operated. The multiple instances then reduce themselves to restore the next instance and so forth. In the right specification in Fig. 15, these n instances are considered as completely autonomous as no way switching from one instance to another is provided, except by returning to the parent task. Again, guidelines should be stated here to avoid catastrophic application of this derivation rule.

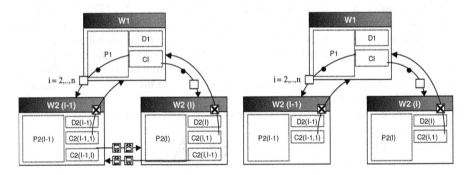

Fig. 16. Other alternative specifications for the finite iteration operator.

3.8   The Concurrency Operator: T2 | | | T3

The concurrency operator can be considered of a particular case of the right specification of Fig. 16. Indeed, as T2 and T3 are completely independent from each other, their W2 and W3 windows can be straightforwardly created from W1 with independent closing returning to the parent. However, these presentations are completely independent. Thus, alternative presentations addressing this condition might be tried as well as tabbed dialog box, switching windows or notebook presentations.

According to the working hypotheses, we focus here on two sub-tasks only. When generalizing this derivation rule to many sub-tasks, it might be important to consider to what extent this rule can be expanded without causing usability problems such as the user getting lost in the work space, the windowitis disease (the user having too many windows to look at simultaneously is becoming ill!), or the user being confused by loosing the focus window. The definition of derivation rules is one aspect to be investigated; the usability of their results is another one that needs validation.

3.9   The Synchronization Operator: T2 |[I]| T3

This operator, as the enabling with information passing operator does, manipulated I, the information passed among sub-tasks. This synchronization operator is rather similar to the enabling with information passing operator, except that no connection should be established between the sub-tasks which are autonomous. Indeed, in the latter operator, the sequence imposes such a relation that the former does not. Therefore, two starting combinations could be imagined:

1. T2 should remain *separate* from T3: in this case, use derivation rules defined in the decision tree of Fig. 6.
2. T2 could be *joined* with T3: in this case, the WI window containing the information passed could be either *independent* (Fig. 17a: WI is controlled from the parent window only) or *dependent* (Fig. 17b: WI is controlled by both parent window W1 and joint window W2+3 containing the merging of T2 and T3).

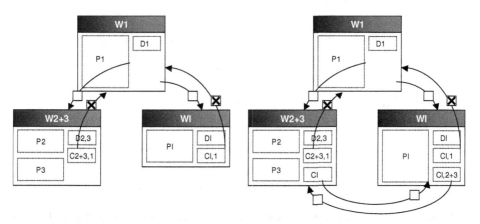

Fig. 17. Other alternative specifications for the synchronization operator (a,b).

4   Example

Fig. 18 depicts the ConcurTaskTrees diagram related to the interactive task "Phone order", one of the tasks belonging to the general application "Product management". The scenario resulting from task analysis is described in [7], section 5. The other tasks of this application are not specified here. Since it consists of three sub-tasks at the first level, only the two first are concurrent: indeed, the user could begin by identifying a customer or depositing an order, but these two sub-tasks are required to perform the final confirmation.

To identify a customer, three alternatives have been identified in the scenario. As only one of them needs to be fulfilled, there is a global choice between them. Only after one of them is the user able to modify the address of the identified person, if needed (optional sub-task). To deposit an order, the user can order several products (hence, the iteration operator).

This task consists of adding a product (whatever the source is), specifying its quantity and computing the line total (by computer). A suspend/resume operator is specified to enable users to switch from any of these views to a list of available products. To confirm an order, the user has to perform sequentially two operations: specifying the payment mode and providing a final confirmation. The "Confirm an order" passes information (i.e., the ordered products and the grand total) so that the user will be able to see the contents of the bag before finally deciding.

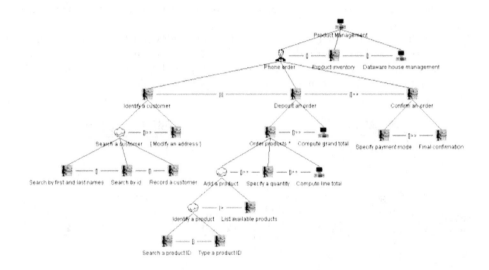

Fig. 18. ConcurTaskTree diagram of the task "Phone order".

Fig. 19 shows a possible use of derivation rules to derive presentation and dialog for the first sub-task of "Phone order". It is assumed here that the names of these three sub-tasks lead to the three items of the "Phone order" sub-menu to reflect this decomposition. Since there is a multiple choice between the leaf nodes of the left sub-tree, an implicit choice (Fig. 13a) has been selected and applied.

The "Record of a customer" leaf node is not presented here to keep the drawing concise, but the dialog is similar. "Modify an address" is conditional to identifying a customer: the "Modify address" push button will therefore be activated after achieving one of them. The optional character of this sub-task makes the separate presentation more appropriate. The ID, which is the information passed here, has been considered important to be observable from both source and target windows (Fig. 18).

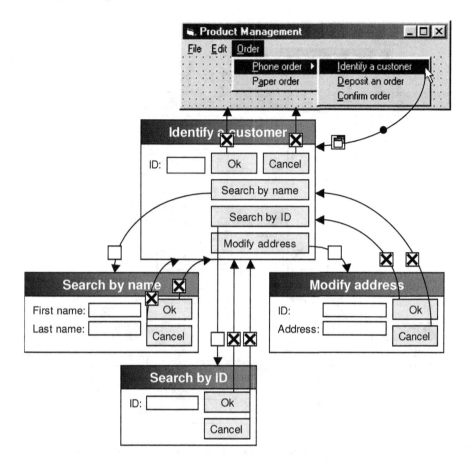

Fig. 19. Derived presentation and dialog for the first sub-task.

Fig. 20 shows a possible use of derivation rules to derive presentation and dialog for the second sub-task "Deposit an order". Due to the concurrency operator between this second sub-task of "Phone order" and the previous one (Fig. 18), derivation rules of Fig. 16a have been applied between them (Fig. 20 upper left). This produces a window entitled "Deposit an order" from which "Add products" children can be repeated due to the repetition attribute on "Order products". The derivation rule for infinite iteration without accumulation (Fig. 13b) has been exploited to produce this window, equipped with "Previous" and "Next" buttons. The "Specify a quantity" and "Compute line total" have been omitted here, but should be part of "Add a product" window as the quantity is an additional information item and the "Compute line total" can be materialized by an appropriate push button to trigger the semantic function (system sub-task). The choice derivation rule that has been applied for "Search a product" and "Type a product" is consistent with the one used in the first sub-task. More interestingly, the suspend/resume operator having "List available products" as right sibling specifies that it should be accessible from both "Search a product ID" and "Type a product ID".

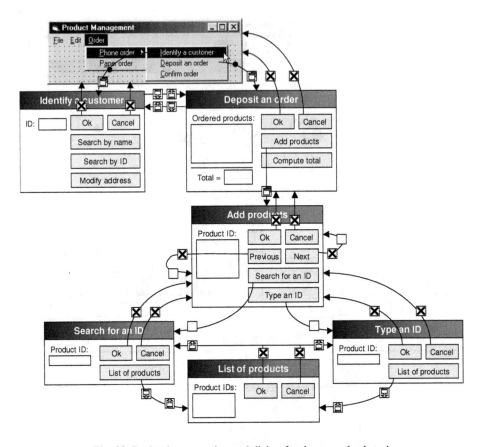

Fig. 20. Derived presentation and dialog for the second sub-task.

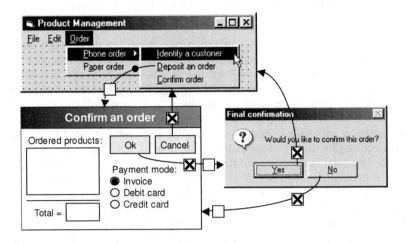

Fig. 21. Derived presentation and dialog for the third sub-task.

Fig. 21 shows a possible use of derivation rules to derive presentation and dialog for the third sub-task "Confirm an order". The information passed between the two children is decided to be observable from "Confirm an order" only. The enabling operator with information passing (Fig. 18) therefore produces two sequential windows, one of them is being here refined as a message dialog box. This is a two-step confirmation: the first being by pushing the "Ok" push button on the first window to complete the order with the payment mode and the second being by pushing the "Yes" push button on the message dialog box.

5   Conclusion and Future Work

Future work can be imagined at least along four dimensions:

1. *Dimension of derivation rules*: under the same working hypotheses that have been assumed here, some other alternative specifications could probably be defined. Nut it is hard to assess the point to which no such new alternatives exist: if one has the sake of completeness, a definition of alternative specifications according to a state space search should be defined to restrict the scope of derivation rules. Generalization of these rules should also be investigated by progressively relaxing the hypotheses that have been assumed one by one. This would permit to verify the ability of each rule to be more general. Finally, only the temporal relations have been used here, not the structural relations (which has been simplified through the hypotheses). Combining both types of relationship should be further analyzed.
2. *Dimension of usability of elements derived*: solving the mapping problem for task-presentation and task-dialog is intended to go beyond the unique goal of automated generation of user interfaces. In this context, the ultimate goal is to automate as much as possible the process of producing a user interface that directly satisfies some usability properties by construction. To prove that such a generated UI is usable, it is required to prove that such properties are intrinsically respected. Bastide & Palanque have argued that only starting with a simple task model might be insufficient to reach these properties [2]. Either the task model does not contain information enough to derive something significant or the task model may lead to any user interface that does not necessarily satisfy such usability properties. In the mapping problem, the ultimate goal is rather to construct model elements and to link them with appropriate relationships that inform the development process. This process should be conducted under the supervisory of the designer.
3. *Dimension of usability assistance on derivation rules*: it is definitely crucial to introduce guidelines to select appropriate use of derivation rules. An important piece of research should implement the different UIs (with their presentation and dialog completed) that can be derived via the derivation rules for a same task and conduct user testing of these different UIs to identify their usability quality, which is not done yet. Only by validating the rules by user testing could guidelines be provided as a confident rule based on experimental validation. Furthermore, as we can more or less predict the quality of any derived UIs, the designer may be better informed about the potential consequences of applying any derivation rule with different values of their parameters. Having a language to describe task, presentation and dialog element would also be important to store the specifications in a

more formal way, thus allowing multiple functions to be executed, such as model checking, verification of properties. We can even imagine that a predictive model such as KLM or a technique like action analysis could be automatically applied on the derived UI to compute their predictive accomplishment complexity and time respectively.

4. *Dimension of tool support for derivation rules*: the definition of derivation rules within a supporting tool have not been examined so far nor the automatic evaluation of guidelines at design time as a critique method. To allow such a tool support, a corresponding formal method is required.

Another direction for future extensive research is the introduction of domain and/or user models along with the task model to derive presentation and dialog models. It could be worthwhile to see how knowledge captured in domain and user models affect the derivation of presentation and dialog models. In particular, the influence of a user model on the presentation model should be very interesting. But this is another story.

6   References

1. Barclay, P.J., Griffiths, T., Mc Kirdy, J., Paton, N.W., Cooper, R., Kennedy, J.: The Teallach Tool: Using Models for Flexible User Interface Design. In: Vanderdonckt, J., Puerta, A. (eds.): Proc. of 3rd Int. Conf. on Computer-Aided Design of User Interfaces CADUI'99 (Louvain-la-Neuve, 21-23 October 1999). Kluwer Academics, Dordrecht (1999) 139–158
2. Bastide, R., Palanque, Ph.: Conformance and Compatibility between Models as Conceptual Tools for a Consistent Design of Interactive Systems. Position paper for the CHI'99 Workshop "Tool Support for Task-Based User Interface Design" (Pittsburgh, May 15-20, 1999).
3. Birnbaum, L., Bareiss, R., Hinrichs, T., Johnson, C.: Interface Design Based on Standardized Task Models. In: Proc. of ACM Int. Conf. on Intelligent User Interfaces IUI'98 (San Francisco, January 1998). ACM Press, New York (1998) 65–72
4. Elnaffar, S.S., Graham, N.T.: Semi-Automated Linking of User Interface Design Artifacts. In: Vanderdonckt, J., Puerta, A. (eds.): Proc. of 3rd Int. Conf. on Computer-Aided Design of User Interfaces CADUI'99 (Louvain-la-Neuve, 21-23 October 1999). Kluwer Academics, Dordrecht (1999) 127–138
5. Johnson, P., Johnson, H., Wilson, S.: Rapid Prototyping of User Interfaces Driven by Task Models. In: Carroll, J.M. (ed.). Scenario-based Design: Envisioning Work and Technology in System Development. John Wiley, New York (1995) 209–246
6. Paternò, F., Mancini, C., Meniconi, S.: ConcurTaskTrees: A Diagrammatic Notation for Specifying Task Models. In: Proc. of IFIP Int. Conf. on Human-Computer Interaction Interact '97 (Sydney, July 1997). Chapman & Hall, London (1997) 362–369
7. Paternò, F., Breedvelt-Shouten, I.M., de Koning, N.M.: Deriving Presentations from Task Models. In: Proc. of IFIP Workshop on Engineering the Human-Computer Interaction EHCI'98 (Creete, September 1998). Kluwer Academics Publisher, Dordrecht (1998)
8. Paternò, F.: Model-Based Design and Evaluation of Interactive Application. Springer Verlag, Berlin (1999)
9. Paternò, F, Mancini, C.: Developing Task Models from Informal Scenarios. In: Proc. of ACM Conf. on Human Aspects in Computing Systems CHI'99 (Pittsburgh, May 1999). ACM Press, New York (1999) 228–229

10. Puerta, A.R., Eisenstein, J.: Towards a General Computational Framework for Model-based Interface Development Systems. In: Proc. of ACM Int. Conf. on Intelligent User Interfaces IUI'99 (Los Angeles, January 1999). ACM Press, New York (1999) 171–178
11. Stirewalt, K.R.E.: MDL: a Language for Binding User Interface Models. In: Vanderdonckt, J., Puerta, A. (eds.): Proc. of 3rd Int. Conf. on Computer-Aided Design of User Interfaces CADUI'99 (Louvain-la-Neuve, 21-23 October 1999). Kluwer Academics, Dordrecht (1999) 159–170
12. Tam, R.C., Maulsby, D., Puerta, A.R.: U-TEL: A Tool for Eliciting User Task Models from Domain Experts. In: Proc. of ACM Int. Conf. on Intelligent User Interfaces IUI'98 (San Francisco, January 1998). ACM Press, New York (1998) 77–80
13. Vanderdonckt, J., Bodart, F.: Encapsulating Knowledge for Intelligent Interaction Objects Selection. In: Proc. of ACM Conf. on Human Aspects in Computing Systems Inter-CHI'93 (Amsterdam, 24-29 April 1993). ACM Press, New York (1993) 424–429
14. Wilson, S., Johnson, P.: Bridging the Generation Gap: From Work Tasks to User Interface Designs. In: Vanderdonckt, J. (ed.): Proc. of the 2nd Int. Workshop on Computer-Aided Design of User Interfaces CADUI'96 (Namur-5-7 June 1996). Presses Universitaires de Namur, Namur (1996) 77–94
15. Zhou, M.: Visual Planning: A Practical Approach to Automated Presentation Design. In Proc. oF IJCAI'99 (Stockholm, August 1999).

Subject Index

Author Index